THE WRITER GOT SCREWED

(but didn't have to)

THE WRITER GOT SCREWED

(but didn't have to)

A GUIDE TO THE LEGAL AND BUSINESS PRACTICES OF WRITING FOR THE ENTERTAINMENT INDUSTRY

Brooke A. Wharton

HarperPerennial
A Division of HarperCollins*Publishers*

First HarperPerennial Edition published 1997.

Designed by Nancy Singer

The Library of Congress has catalogued the hardcover edition as follows:

Wharton, Brooke, 1962–
    The writer got screwed (but didn't have to) : a guide to the legal and business practices of writing for the entertainment industry / Brooke A. Wharton.
        p.   cm.
    ISBN 0-06-270130-4
    1. Motion picture industry—Law and legislation—United States.
    2. Screenwriters—Legal status, laws, etc.—United States. 3. Authors and publishers—United States. I. Title.
KF4302.W48   1996
384'.83'0973—dc20   95-47499

ISBN 0-06-273236-6

97 98 99 00 01 ❖/HC 10 9 8 7 6 5 4 3

To My Mother Edith Wharton—
An Artist in Her Own Right

Contents

Acknowledgments

There are so many people (and one cat) who provided support and encouragement during the creation of this book. Tremendous gratitude to my mother, Edith Wharton, who believed in me and this book long after I had thrown in the towel. Special thanks to my brother, Charles Wharton, for his brilliance, wit, support and excellent jacket photo. My great friend, Kathy Hibbs, was and always has been a constant source of support and "reality testing." Maybe there is another "Midnight Madness" in our future. My friend and colleague, Jonathan Westover, who provided endless resources and laughter and reminded me that someone would like this book. My agent, Susan Golomb, for believing in this project long before anyone else did. My editors, Rick Horgan and Airié Dekidjiev, for climbing on board, even when this book and I became a pain-in-the-ass. My neighbors, Ken and Cathy Garmany, Giovanna Macchia, and Willie Aron, who must have wondered just how crazy I was, were invaluable during "the siege: of '95." All of the wonderful writers, agents, producers, managers, and attorneys who contributed generously to this project—Jane Anderson, Gary Goldstein, Larry Meyers, Steve Kronish, Betsy Snyder, Shonda Rhimes, Bruce Onder, Jeff Sullivan, David Hankin, Phillip Lazebnik—thank you so much for sharing your stories and wisdom. My former mentor in life, John Orders, for always finding the one spot in my 100-page proposal where a comma is missing, and to Onil Chibas for tremendous aid and encouragement. To all of my talented students and colleagues at the University of Southern California School of Cinema-Television for providing the inspiration for this work. . . . And to Houdini, for just being you.

This book is created to help individuals without legal training understand many of the legal and business principles which they will encounter when attempting to work in the entertainment industry.

Nothing in this book should be construed as legal advice, or as a substitute for consulting with an experienced attorney and receiving one-on-one attention regarding the issues in a particular transaction.

Many of the legal concepts are subject to exceptions that may not be explained in this book. In addition, both the statutory and case law is subject to change and may not apply in every state.

Introduction

This book isn't about sex; it's about the New California Gold Rush (NCGR). The NCGR has nothing to do with panning for gold; it's about finding gold in ideas and written expression.

The individuals participating in the NCGR aren't like the pioneer folk who went to California looking for gold in the nineteenth century. Today the stakes are much higher, the industry is more sophisticated, and the participants are much, much more dangerous. (And this gold rush isn't happening only in California; although this is where the activity is most frenetic, prospectors can be found wherever people indulge in celluloid dreams.)

In 1994 the entertainment industry revenue was conservatively estimated at \$5.869 billion per year. Of that \$5.869 billion, Writers Guild of America (WGA) members earned about one-tenth, or \$550 million. This figure promises to soar even higher as Silicon Valley forms ties with Hollywood to create and expand additional entertainment venues in CD ROM, virtual reality, multimedia, and other new technologies.

I mention these numbers to give you, the reader (or should I say the writer?) the proper perspective. Although, as a participant in the entertainment industry (emphasis on "industry"), you're not creating toilets or cars, you're creating a product that, hopefully, will be *exploited* to its maximum potential. The entertainment industry is a business. A big business. One of the biggest in the United States. Like most businesses, it features executives ("the suits," studio and production executives) who buy the product, and workers (writers, directors, producers, actors) who supply it. Sometimes the executives ignore the workers; sometimes the executives pay them big money; and sometimes they screw them.

Art Buchwald was a writer to whom executives paid big money. After all, he was internationally renowned and a Pulitzer Prize winner. When Paramount Pictures bought his treatment and made *Coming to*

America, a movie that was identical to his story, he was ecstatic. His agreement with Paramount guaranteed him "net profit" participation in any movie based on his work. However, when Paramount insisted that the movie was based on Eddie Murphy's story, Buchwald realized that he'd been "screwed."

$2.5 million in legal fees later, Judge Harvey Schneider of the Los Angeles Superior Court found that *Coming to America* was clearly "based upon" Buchwald's story. Based on his "net profit" participation in *Coming to America,* Buchwald and his attorneys expected that he would be awarded his proportionate share of net profits, $6.5 million. However, Buchwald was awarded only $100,000 (and no legal fees), as Paramount successfully asserted that *Coming to America,* a film that grossed over $350 million worldwide, had no "net profits." Unfortunately, Buchwald had not been told a little secret: Within the entertainment industry, "net profits" are referred to as "monkey points" and can have as much value as Orange County municipal bonds.

The irony of this story is not lost on the multitudes of aspiring screenwriters who, unlike Buchwald, have problems getting their work read, much less stolen. Aspiring writers rarely receive legal or business information concerning the entertainment industry until they're sitting in a lawyer's office wondering how their ideas became another person's smash feature film. *Until now.*

This book is written for those of you who:

- are creative souls, right brain people living in a left brain world who'd rather be discussing the French cinema of the 50s than the meaning of "producer's net profits";
- have already worked in the entertainment industry in some capacity but would rather be writing for television or film than blowing up a building in the next hot action-adventure;
- are already working as creative executives, agents, producers, and so forth, and have invented your own definitions for such bothersome legal terms as arbitration, separation of rights, default, and force majeure because no one has ever defined them for you— *even though you encounter them on a daily basis;*
- were creative writing majors in college (and may still have that screenplay tucked away in a desk drawer) but fell prey to the lure

of the practical-wealth-accumulating 80s. You may now find yourself employed as an ad executive, orthopedic surgeon, or lawyer, but occasionally you still wonder if you shouldn't take a stab at writing again.

This book will help you understand what you are encountering when:

- you are given the opportunity to write an entire screenplay with two rewrites and a polish for "deferred compensation" (translation: you'll probably be receiving nothing);
- your screenplay is read by a "hot" producer who wants a *free* option on your work for three years, and promises to give you a portion of his net profits if it's made (translation: kiss your work good-bye. You won't see a dime and it probably won't get made.);
- your agent never calls you or returns your calls: (translation: you probably no longer have an agent);
- you would like to write for interactive but have no idea if you're qualified or what it takes to get started (translation: join the club most people don't).

The goal of this book is to familiarize you with the resources at your disposal and to help you understand some of the basic concepts that must be considered if you plan to write for the entertainment industry. This book is not meant as a replacement for an attorney, agent, or manager, and I definitely don't intend to steer you onto a career path in entertainment law. Rather, this book is meant to serve as a road map to guide you as you begin to write for the entertainment industry. It's also intended, incidentally, to let you know that there are many others like you who don't know what they are doing.

This book is dedicated to writers who have:

- sold a screenplay and subsequently discovered they also sold the rights to write the sequel to their screenplay;
- had an agency "package" their screenplay with some other "elements" in that agency's talent stable, only to find that their hot

screenplay was sold for one-third of what it could have fetched had it not been "packaged";

- taken a writing assignment for next to nothing because a producer promised that there would be "big rewards" in the future—and there weren't.

This book is dedicated to those writers who have been "screwed."

Section 1

PROTECTING IDEAS, YOUR WRITTEN WORK, AND YOURSELF

Until a screenwriter plans to file a lawsuit or has been sued, the education she receives is primarily aesthetic or technical. Rarely does the emerging screenwriter obtain the information necessary to maintain creative control of her work until many critical career mistakes have been made, which inevitably result in a few heart-to-heart chats with an attorney.

The goal of this section is to give you the basic tools to control the exploitation of your scripts and written work, or to at least know when you're being screwed.

Topics raised will be copyright (Chapter 1); libel, right of privacy, and right of publicity (Chapter 2); contracts (Chapter 3); and the Writers Guild of America (WGA)(Chapter 4).

1

Why Do My Ideas Always End Up in Someone Else's Script?

FADE IN:

INTERIOR OF HEALTH CLUB–DAY LATE AFTERNOON

A typical health club. Exercise bikes, stair masters, and free weights litter the carpet-covered room. Men and women clad in shorts and T-shirts furiously pump iron and work their cardiovascular systems. The blare of an aerobics class in progress can be heard in the background. The camera pans to a man and woman who are riding exercise bikes.

MAN

I think I finally came up with a great idea for my screenplay.

Dripping with sweat, the woman, age 27, turns her flushed face to the man as she adds another 30-minute cycle to her workout.

WOMAN

Screenplay? I thought you were an accountant.

The man, thirtyish, strains as he continues pumping his exercise bike.

MAN

Didn't I tell you? I was quite the writer before I got into accounting. And since one of my frat brothers is now a big exec at Universal, I thought, what the hell. So I've been writing . . .

WOMAN

Wait. Let me guess. The Auditor Only Rings Twice*. No. How about . . .* Fatal Subtraction*.*

MAN

Very funny. I'm serious. Imagine Love Boat *meets* Under Siege*: A former nightclub singer is assigned as activities director on the Navy's largest nuclear battleship. She organizes a lavish production of* The Pirates of Penzance *but falls into disfavor with the captain for distracting the troops. Her luck changes when the President of the United States comes aboard for a surprise inspection, and while he's watching the show, she uncovers an elaborate assassination plot . . .*

INTERIOR OF ATTORNEY'S OFFICE–DAY

An ultramodern high-rise office. Lichtenstein prints compete with diplomas for wall space. The accountant sits nervously across from a stylishly dressed woman who takes notes on a yellow legal pad.

ATTORNEY

So you're saying the screenwriter of A Few Good Tenors*, the camp hit of the year, is your workout partner?*

MAN

Well, she was. Now that she has such a big hit on her hands, she has a personal trainer come to her house. And she won't return any of my phone calls; her assistant does that.

ATTORNEY

You think she stole your idea? Did you two have any sort of agreement that while you were sweating off the pounds, you were also working as a team to create this screenplay?

MAN

I didn't need to. The idea was mine, the concept was mine. In fact, when I described it to her, she absolutely hated it and told me that nobody would ever be interested in it because there was no audience for singing sailors on a nuclear battleship.

ATTORNEY

Yeah, well, George Lucas was told that nobody was interested in a story about a bunch of Boy Scouts in space, but he made Star Wars anyway. Did she ever see anything you wrote about these ideas?

MAN

I never wrote anything, I just told her my idea—which she stole and used to create A Few Good Tenors. And now I want you to sue her for copyright infringement because the idea was mine.

ATTORNEY

I don't think you understand. Ideas are not eligible for copyright protection. It is the expression of an idea that is. And since you don't have any agreement with her, there's nothing I can do for you.

MAN

What am I supposed to do?

ATTORNEY

Well, to begin with, why don't you read my script, The Prosecutor. If you like it, would you mind giving it to your frat-buddy friend at Universal?

FADE OUT

I have never met a writer who truly understood copyright. Unfortunately, the above scenario, ludicrous as it may seem, is one that unfolds all too often in my office. The problem is that there is no shortage of misinformation leading writers to think that they understand copyright. Additionally, it's virtually impossible to avoid the quasi-gossip (often disguised as friendly advice) that passes between emerging writers and filmmakers. This advice has produced such popular copyright folklore as:

- "If you put your script in a package and send it to yourself, the postmark proves the date you wrote your script." (Known popularly as "Poorman's Copyright," it's nothing more than a waste of valuable postage.)
- "Registering your script with the Writers Guild of America is the best way for screenwriters to copyright their material."(It's not copyright protection.)

- "You don't have copyright in your screenplay until you send it to the Copyright Office in Washington, D.C." (If you believe this, you've flunked the litmus test for basic knowledge of copyright.)

The reason I stress the need to understand the nature of copyright is that very few writers, especially screenwriters, understand the profession of screenwriting. If you plan to write professionally, you must understand that you are in the business of creating written expression for sale, lease, or rent within the entertainment industry. Your written expression is property—intellectual property—for which you hope to find a buyer. Like all property, your intellectual property may be developed, altered, sold, or leased (that is, "licensed") in sections, or held by you in its pure form for the next generation. Copyright, the international law protecting creative work, is the set of guidelines that enables a writer and his heirs to both exploit and control the writer's intellectual property for the maximum duration of time.

Once you understand that your work is property—which, like any property, you want to protect and control—you must also understand the aspects of your property that can easily be stolen: your ideas. Ideas are the seeds of your intellectual property. Ideas are not protected by copyright, which means that in most circumstances (that is, you are not in a "pitch," a situation we will discuss later) there is nothing to protect your ideas. If you toss your great ideas around in the health club, the laundry, the grocery store, or to your friends, there is nothing to keep another individual from exploiting them. Naturally, if you have an idea that is truly great, you might just as well have given it away; it's like giving away a great piece of property with an ocean view away and throwing in as a bonus the water and mineral rights.

The following answers to important questions will help you avoid finding yourself sitting across from an attorney and wondering how your ideas became someone else's blockbuster movie.

WHAT IS COPYRIGHT AND WHAT DOES IT HAVE TO DO WITH MY WORK?

Copyright is not a magical stamp from an office in Washington, D.C., that keeps unscrupulous people from stealing your work. Literally, copyright is the federal and international law that allows the makers of creative works to have exclusive rights in their creation for a limited period of time.

You should think of copyright as a bundle of rights that protect and allow you and your heirs to make as much money as possible from your work during your life and for a period of time after your death.

WHAT KIND OF WORK IS ELIGIBLE FOR COPYRIGHT PROTECTION?

Copyright protects creative work; it does not protect useful products (which are protected by the area of law known as patent) or identifying marks or symbols (which are protected by the area of law known as trademark). However, not all creative work qualifies: Copyright only protects creative works that are (in legalese) **original works fixed in a tangible medium of expression**. This means that your creative work must have the following characteristics to be eligible for copyright protection:

- **Originality:** Your work should be original, but it's not required to be wholly original for you to have copyright in it. It may contain elements that are similar to other works: It might even contain all the names and listings in your local phone book or closely resemble a play that was written by a well-known author of the classics.

  "Originality" means that your work must contain something new which ensures that you did not simply copy your work from someone else. Thus, if you rearranged the order of the Los Angeles County phone book (The Donnelly Directory) or created a modern-day version of a classic (such as *West Side Story* from *Romeo and Juliet* or *Roxanne* from *Cyrano de Bergerac*), you could claim copyright in the original portion you brought to the work. Using the above examples, your copyright in the rearranged phone book would not be the listings themselves but the manner in which you arranged the listings. Likewise, your copyright in the revamped classic would not be in the story or the plot development but in the dialogue and original manner in which you presented the work.

In case you are still confused by the concept of originality, here is a real-life example: The musical *West Side Story* is clearly taken from *Romeo and Juliet* by William Shakespeare. Although not literally copied, the copyright expert Melville Nimmer has noted that the overall concept and feel of the two works is the same: There are thirteen similarities between the two stories that go beyond the general theme of star-struck lovers amid feuding families. The creators of *West Side Story* cannot claim copyright on the story or plot of their work because it is not their original work. Their copyright is in the original dialogue, music, and lyrics they created.

- **Fixed in a Tangible Medium of Expression:** Your original work must be fixed in a tangible mode of expression to be eligible for copyright status. This means that it must be written down, notated (as in when notations are made to signify which notes comprise a distinct piece or which movements comprise a distinct dance work), or fixed in a solid form that you can show others. Obviously, an idea, improvisation, or choreography that has not been fed into a computer or noted on paper is not eligible for copyright.

Because you can receive copyright only on the original written work that is created when you fix it in a tangible form, you should not throw away your ideas by way of idle discussion until your work is in a tangible form.

WHAT WORKS ARE NOT ELIGIBLE FOR COPYRIGHT PROTECTION?

Copyright does not protect:

- Ideas. Yes, I just said this, but I want to emphasize it. Copyright protects the expression of an idea or a complete work but not an idea.
- Choreographic works that have not been notated or recorded, and improvisational speeches or performances that have not been written or recorded.
- Procedures, methods, systems, processes, concepts, principles, discoveries, or devices, as distinguished from a description, explana-

tion, or illustration. These works tend to be categorized as useful and not creative, and are more likely eligible for patent protection.

- Titles, names, short phrases, and slogans; familiar symbols or designs; mere variations on typographic ornamentation, lettering, or coloring; mere listings of ingredients or contents. Although a title does not qualify for copyright protection, I would avoid calling your screenplay *Jurassic Park* because sometimes titles, phrases, and slogans are protected by other areas of the law.
- Standard calendars, height and weight charts, tape measures and rulers, and lists or tables taken from public documents and other common sources and that contain no original authorship. (These works contain no originality and thus are not eligible for copyright protection.)

If Ideas Are Not Protected by Copyright, How Can I Protect My Ideas When I "Pitch" My Work?

A common way that writers receive employment is through a meeting with the producers, creative executives, or staff writers of a television show, production company, and/or studio where they "pitch," or present, their ideas. If you have read the above section, you should be asking yourself how you can pitch your ideas and yet protect them from being stolen.

Since ideas are not protected by copyright, you should protect the ideas you pitch by ensuring that they're already part of a treatment (a written account of the story line of the film, often no more than one and one-half pages in length) or full-length screenplay, so that the ideas are fixed in a tangible medium of expression.

Prior to your "pitch" meeting, you should register your pitch with the WGA (see below) or give a copy of your treatment to the individuals in the "pitch" meeting after your "pitch" is completed.

WHAT RIGHTS DOES COPYRIGHT GIVE YOU?

When an individual has copyright in a work, the federal and international copyright laws actually grant the writer/creator the following five rights in the work for a limited period of time. These rights represent different methods by which a creator may make money from one individual work.

1. **The right to reproduce copies of the work.** Those of you who have made your own cassette copy of a favorite CD or reproduced an entire book on a photocopy machine probably did not know that you were breaking the law. Most people think that by buying a copy of a book or tape, an individual gains the right to create copies of the item. This is incorrect. When an individual buys a work such as a book or a tape that is protected by copyright, the individual acquires the right to resell only the item that the individual purchased and has no right to create reproductions of the item. Naturally, if you write your own novel, you have the right to make reproductions of it.

   This right is very important if you decide to write a book instead of a screenplay or create a novel from your screenplay. When a writer signs a contract with a publishing company, he is actually selling the right to reproduce multiple copies of the work (one of the rights granted to the writer through copyright) to the publishing company. If another person attempts to reproduce the work without the permission of the publishing company and/or author, the individual can be sued for copyright infringement.

2. **The right to distribute copies of the work.** Along with the popular misconception concerning the right to reproduce work, most people think that when they buy one videotape or book, they also have the right to distribute copies of the work. Again, this is incorrect. When you buy a copy of a book or videotape of a film, the only right you receive is the right to distribute the one copy of the work that you have bought. The creator of the work, or the holder of the license to distribute the work, has the right to distribute the work.

   This right is important for the following reason: As with the right of reproduction, what a writer is selling when signing an agreement with a publishing company is the right to distribute the work (one of the rights granted to the writer through copyright). Like the right of reproduction, if another person attempts to distribute the work without the permission of the publishing company and/or author, the individual can be sued for copyright infringement.

3. **The right to prepare derivative works that are based on the original work.** To a screenwriter and/or novelist, one of the most important rights is the right to prepare derivative works. The concept of a "derivative work" sounds much more confusing than it actually is. A derivative work is nothing more than a work based on another work, described in legalese as a "pre-existing work." For example, a movie or television program that evolves from a screenplay is a derivative work based on the pre-existing screenplay. Likewise, a screenplay that is based on a novel is a derivative work based on the pre-existing novel. Sequels (such as *Lethal Weapon II)*, remakes (such as *The Three Musketeers)*, spin-offs (the movie of *The Beverly Hillbillies)* are also derivative works.

   This right, along with the screenplay itself, is what you sell if you actually sell your work—the right to create a movie or television show based on the screenplay. However, in certain situations, which are explained below, you can retain the right to create other works such as a novel (not novelizations) or live stage productions that are based on the screenplay. Like the previously mentioned rights, if another person attempts to create a derivative work based on your work, the individual may be sued for copyright infringement unless the work is in the public domain (discussed below).

4. **The right to perform the work publicly.** You probably didn't know that every time the Beatles song "Yesterday" is sung in a public performance with a paying audience, the copyright holder of this work receives a royalty. This is because the song is under copyright, and the right to perform the work publicly is being infringed in every situation where the copyright holder is not compensated for the public performance of the work.

   When you sell your work, the right to perform your work in the form of a movie is also sold. Like the previously mentioned rights, if another person attempts to publicly perform your work, the individual may be sued for copyright infringement, unless the work is in the public domain (discussed below).

5. **The right to display the work publicly.** This right is not important for the screenwriter until the motion picture based on the

work is created. At that time the right would be operative when advertising or posters displaying single images from the motion picture are created.

This is yet another right that you sell along with your screenplay.

Conclusion

For a professional writer working within the entertainment industry, the basis of how money is and can be made is represented by the number of the above rights in a single work that a writer can sell or license. For example, Michael Crichton (author of *The Andromeda Strain, Jurassic Park, Rising Sun,* and other works) sold the film rights to his novel *Disclosure* for $3.5 million, seven months before the novel was published! In selling the film rights, Crichton was actually selling a derivative right and a right to perform the work publicly. When *Disclosure* was published, Crichton (who had already received compensation for the sale of the book, the reproduction right, and the distribution right to the work) received more money in the form of royalties for each book sold. If Crichton were to create a television show or live stage play based on the book, he would again exercise the right to create a derivative work based on the novel, for which he could receive compensation.

HOW DO I OBTAIN COPYRIGHT ON MY WORK?

As stated previously, some of the many myths floating through the screenwriting community is that to have copyright in your work you must either: (1) register it with the Copyright Office in Washington, D.C.; (2) register it with the Writers Guild of America (WGA); or (3) put it in a self-addressed envelope and mail it to yourself.

Most screenwriters confuse registering for copyright and having copyright in a work. They do not know that copyright in a work exists at the very moment that an original work of authorship is put in a fixed and tangible form. This means that you have copyright in your work at the moment it is keyed into a computer (that is, in a fixed form) or typed on a piece of paper (again, in a fixed form).

Do I Need to Put a Copyright Symbol on My Work?

The popular wisdom surrounding work protected by copyright is that it must carry a copyright symbol (legally known as "notice of copyright") to ensure protection. The law was changed as of March 1989 so that creative work which is first published (not published as in "published by Random House" but defined in this situation as "put in the marketplace for sale") after March 1989 no longer must carry the notice of copyright to be protected by copyright. This naturally means that works first published *before* March 1989 must carry a copyright symbol.

For the writer working within the entertainment industry, I suggest that anything that is going to be circulated "in the marketplace" (to potential buyers, producers, studios, and so forth) should carry a notice of copyright in order to protect the work. The reason is that for those individuals who do not know that work created after 1989 is protected with or without the symbol, the existence of the symbol acts as a protection against any claim that they "innocently" stole your work because they did not know it was protected by copyright. In addition, the existence of the notice works to (1) assist in ensuring the availability of full damages (money) in actions for infringement brought under U.S. law; (2) provide clear warning that copyright is claimed in the work and is likely to be enforced; and (3) comply with the little-known formalities found in copyright laws of other countries (such as the possibility of your work turning up in Taiwan) that operate under copyright laws that are different from the United States.

What Is "Notice of Copyright," and Where Do I Put It?

If you have listened to the traditional "advice" surrounding copyright, you probably have been told that the copyright symbol ("notice of copyright") is a c in a circle—©—next to your name. This, like all quasi-gossip, is not entirely correct. Notice consists of three items: (1) the word copyright, symbolized by any one of the following three methods: the symbol C enclosed in a circle, the word "Copyright," or the abbreviation "Copr."; (2) the year of first publication (remember: publication is when the work is distributed to the public for sale, not when it is published by a publishing company); and (3) the name of the owner of the copyright in the work. In addition, I recommend including the tag line "All rights reserved" because it offers protection internationally in those countries that do not adhere to the same formalities as the United States.

A proper example of copyright notice is the following: "Copyright Brooke A. Wharton, 1994. All rights reserved." When you sell your work to Universal Pictures and they take copyright in your work as a condition of the sale (as they always do), the copyright notice will read "Copyright Universal Pictures, 1993. All rights reserved." Once you have created the proper notice, put it on the front of your screenplay. If you are worried that the notice will date your work, write the date in Roman numerals rather than Arabic numbers.

Why Register My Work with the Copyright Office if I Already Have Copyright in It?

If you have followed and understood the material in this chapter, the question that should be forming in your mind is why you should bother to register your original work with the Copyright Office if you have copyright in it the moment it is fixed in a tangible medium of expression. There are some very good reasons to register your work:

- Registration is the best public record of your copyright claim;
- You cannot file an action for copyright infringement without having registered your work;
- Registration of your work within five years of publication establishes that your copyright is authentic; if you did not register your work within five years and then register when suing for copyright infringement, it is more difficult to establish that the copyright is legitimate;
- If you register within three months of publication of your work or before infringement of your work has occurred, you can collect, among other things, attorney fees (which can be very high) from your opponent in an action for copyright (naturally, you must win the action).

HOW DO I REGISTER WITH THE COPYRIGHT OFFICE?

Registering with the Copyright Office is fairly simple. You need Copyright Office Form PA (for scripts) or TX (novels or manuscripts of nondramatic literary work), $20.00, and the following:

- One complete copy if the work is unpublished (again, published is defined in this situation as put in the marketplace for sale);
- Two complete copies of the best edition if the work was published in the United States on or after January 1, 1978;
- One complete copy of the work as first published if the work was first published outside of the United States, whenever published.

You are probably wondering where you might get a copy of Form PA or TX. This, too, is very simple. The Copyright Office provides a "hot line"; it is really an answering machine on which you may order the forms you want and leave your address. The phone number of the hot line is (202) 707–9100.

The forms provide detailed instructions on how to fill them out.

HOW LONG DOES COPYRIGHT LAST?

Nothing lasts forever, including copyright. Copyright in a work gives the creator of the work and his heirs the ability to exploit the work as their "property" (an intellectual property) for a specific number of years. Unlike land or other property, one can't own copyright forever because the prevailing thought finds that artistic work should belong "to everyone" after a certain amount of time. How long one can "exploit" the work depends on who the author of the work is, such as:

Sole author: If you wrote your masterpiece after 1978, you and your heirs have copyright in the work for the duration of your life plus fifty years. This means that those lucky folks who inherit your work (and do remember to include copyright to your work in your will!) have fifty years after your death to make as much money as they can from your creative work.

Joint authorship: If you and your partner created a work of art together after 1978 and you both made contributions that are inseparable (you contributed the plot and thematic development, for example, and your partner contributed the dialogue), copyright in the work exists for the life of the longest living partner plus fifty years. (Note: If you and your partner contributed separate elements of the same work, such as one creating the dialogue and the other the music, then the sole authorship rules apply to your situation.)

Work-for-hire: A work created in a work-for-hire situation is generally one that is created in the context of a working situation or job. The classic work-for-hire situation for a writer is one in which he creates a work during the time he is a member of the writing staff on an episodic television show. In another work-for-hire situation, an agreement is signed between the employer and an independent contractor prior to work beginning, and the agreement states that the work is a work for hire. All writing done within the United States entertainment industry becomes a work-for-hire through an agreement, at the time it is sold.

The result of a work-for-hire employment relationship within the context of copyright law is significant: A work created in a work-for-hire context is one in which the employer is considered the "author of the work" and thus is the owner of the copyright and all rights of copyright in the work. Needless to say, it is nearly impossible to sell a script and not have it become a work-for-hire. This is true even if you have sold a spec screenplay (a screenplay that you wrote on your own without being hired or employed to write) in which the work and your original ideas have been yours from start to finish.

The duration of copyright for a work that has been created within a work-for-hire relationship is seventy-five years from publication (defined as "the distribution of copies . . . of a work to the public by sale or other transfer of ownership, or rental, lease, or lending") or one hundred years from creation, whichever is shorter.

Work Created Before January 1, 1978

If you created your screenplay before 1978 and it still has not sold, then you should think about writing something else. (Of course there are examples of screenplays that were in the marketplace for more than twenty years before finally getting made. The screenplay for the movie *Iron Will* was written in 1972!) In any event, if you are concerned about obtaining the rights to work that was created before 1978, the duration of copyright is twenty-eight years from the date of registration with the Copyright Office or from the time it was published (that is, "put in the marketplace for sale"). Unlike works created after January 1, 1978, works created before January 1, 1978, must be renewed during the twenty-eighth year of the first term of copyright. Prior to the change in the Copyright Law in 1976, the second term of copyright was for another twenty-eight years, for a total of fifty-six years. After the revisions to the Copyright Act in 1976, the second term of copyright was extended to forty-seven years, for a total of seventy-five years. Consequently, if a work was renewed in the twenty-eighth year prior to when the Copyright Act took effect (1978), the work was automatically extended to allow a total of seventy-five years of copyright protection. However, if a work was still in its first twenty-eight year copyright term on January 1, 1978, it still must be renewed in the twenty-eighth year. The renewal term will be for forty-seven years, for a total of seventy-five years. If the work in question was created before January 1, 1978, but was neither published nor registered with the Copyright Office, then its term of copyright is for the life of the author plus fifty years.

SEPARATION OF RIGHTS: IF I SELL MY WORK, HAVEN'T I GIVEN ALL OF MY RIGHTS AWAY?

As stated previously, all written work sold within the entertainment industry is bought in a work-for-hire arrangement. This generally means that the writer will lose all rights of copyright to the work. However, if the work is sold to a company that is a member (called "a signatory") to the Writers Guild of America (WGA) and the writer qualifies as a "professional writer" (not necessarily a member of the WGA but someone who has received previous credits in any of the following areas: (1) on the screen as a writer for a television or theatrical motion picture or; (2) for three original stories or one teleplay for a program one-half hour in length or more or; (3) for three radio scripts for dramamtic radio programs one-half hour in length or; (4) for one professionally produced play on the legitimate stage, or one published novel or; (5) received employment for a total of thirteen weeks as a motion picture and/or television writer), then the writer may receive some rights of copyright through "separation of rights." The concept of "separation of rights" is that in the above-stated situations the WGA reserves certain rights, such as literary publishing rights, for the writer who is accorded separated rights for the television or theatrical film. The rights received differ depending on whether you are writing for television or film.

WORK YOU CAN LEGALLY STEAL: WORK IN THE PUBLIC DOMAIN (OR WHAT HAPPENS WHEN COPYRIGHT PROTECTION ENDS)

As stated previously, copyright does not last forever. When copyright protection ends for a creative work, the work is "in the public domain." This means that anyone, including you, may copy this work word for word without fear. There are probably various works in the public domain from which you would like to lift a few phrases. The good news is that you may steal these phrases without obtaining permission or risking a lawsuit for infringement. However, you may never obtain copyright in the work that you have appropriated; your copyright will be in your original contribution to the total work. The bad news is that your original work will also fall someday into the hands of those outside of you and your family for their own commercial exploitation.

REGISTERING YOUR WORK WITH THE WRITERS GUILD OF AMERICA (WGA)

One of the great fallacies floating through the screenwriter's subculture is the fortresslike protection which is accorded work that is "registered with the WGA." Having spoken with, taught, and counseled many writers, I have come to understand that few writers clearly understand the protection that written work is offered when it is "registered" with the Writers Guild of America. As stated in big, bold letters on the registration sheet distributed by the Writers Guild: **Registration does not** confer any statutory protection. It merely provides a record of the writer's claim to authorship of the literary material involved and of the date of its completion.

Added to this is my favorite line, which I believe few writers understand: **REGISTRATION DOES NOT TAKE THE PLACE OF REGISTERING THE COPYRIGHT ON YOUR MATERIAL WITH THE U.S. COPYRIGHT OFFICE.**

What does this mean, and why do so few writers understand it? As stated on the information sheet distributed by the WGA, registration does not confer the advantages of registering with the Copyright Office because:

- You cannot sue for copyright infringement if your work is registered only with the WGA;
- Registration with the WGA within five years of the publication of your work does not validate the copyright in your work;
- You cannot prevent the WGA from registering a work with the identical name and text as your work.

This having been said, what does registration with the WGA provide? It provides a date for the existence and completion of literary property—and, mind you, only literary property written for theatrical motion pictures (movies), television, and radio—for both members and non-members of the WGA. That's it. What is the Writers Guild Registration Service? It is really a depository for work. Once you register your work with the service, you cannot call and ask whether the service received your work, whether your ex-partner has registered your work with the WGA, or whether your work is still in the depository. However, in the event that there is a lawsuit involving your work, you can subpoena the head of the Registration Service (called the custodian of records) to establish that your completed work was registered with the Writers Guild on a specific day. But that's all.

Having written the above, please understand that I do not intend to tarnish the reputation of the Writers Guild of America.

As established in a recent case involving a writer who claimed that Disney stole his ideas for *Honey, I Blew Up the Kid*, the Registration Service can be used to prove the prior existence and completion date of a treatment or screenplay. (In this particular case, the writer had regis-

tered his treatment with the service prior to the time he submitted his
work to Disney; through the use of the service he was able to prove the
prior existence of his work before Disney made the film.)

DESPITE EVERYTHING, CONCEPTS, STORIES, AND IDEAS ARE STILL " STOLEN" EVERY DAY BY WELL-KNOWN PEOPLE IN LEGITIMATE SITUATIONS

It should be clear to you by now that one of the problems in pitching
your ideas to others is that there is no way to protect them. The other
problem is that there are only so many original ideas to go around and
originality can be a subjective concept (defined in certain situations as
"determined to be the already existing idea of the studio executive to
whom you have pitched your idea," but more about this in the section
on release forms). Consequently, it's likely that your "original idea" is
a rehash of already existing ideas.

The difficulty of deciding when an idea is original is shown in the
case of *Murray v. National Broadcasting Company*, a lawsuit involving
"The Cosby Show." In this case, a television executive brought a proposal to NBC in 1980 about a black middle-class family in which the
leading character was a father, a devoted family man, and a compas-
sionate, proud authority figure. The family was to be portrayed in a
nonstereotypical manner. NBC turned down the submission.

"The Cosby Show," a situation comedy series about a black upper-
middle-class family, premiered on NBC. The series centered around the
father, played by Bill Cosby, a physician. The show was a huge commercial success and soared to the top of the Nielsen ratings. In 1985,
Murray sued NBC under various claims, including misappropriation,
breach of implied contract, and fraud. In addition, Murray sought to
be declared the sole owner of all rights in and to the idea, proposal,
and property, known as "Father's Day."

In determining whether Murray was sole owner of the rights, the
court reviewed the trial court's decision that Murray's concept did not
portray sufficient novelty to grant him sole ownership of all rights in
the concept. The court noted that although the portrayal of the black
family was a breakthrough, the breakthrough represented the achieve-

ment of what many black Americans, including Bill Cosby, have recognized for years—the need for a more positive, fair, and realistic portrayal of blacks on television. Consequently, the court concluded that Murray's idea included within "Father's Day" was not novel because it merely represented an "adaptation of existing knowledge" and of "known ingredients" and therefore lacked "genuine novelty and invention." The point of this case is clear: Just because an idea is good does not mean that it is original enough for a court to find it "legally protectible" (that is, worthy of winning a lawsuit).

RELEASE FORMS: WHAT DO THEY DO AND WHAT DO THEY MEAN?

If you are attempting to have your unsolicited script (meaning they didn't ask to read it) read by a producer, production company, and/or studio (collectively referred to as "They") and are not represented by an agent or lawyer, three things will happen:

1. They will refuse to read it and return it to you unopened.
2. They will refuse to read it unless it is submitted by an agent or attorney.
3. They will read it only if you sign a release form.

The reason "They" will refuse to read your work is simple: By accepting your unsolicited work, producers, production companies, and studio executives legally may enter into what is known as an "implied contract." The implied contract is that if a work is produced that is similar to your work and you weren't paid for this work, you may have the basis for a legal action against them. (As discussed in the earlier section on the WGA, this is the basis for the *Honey, I Blew Up the Kid* lawsuit. The writer submitted a treatment to Disney, which Disney didn't want. Later, when *Honey, I Blew Up the Kid* was released, the jury believed the writer's allegation that Disney had used his story without paying him.)

In order to prevent the possibility of a lawsuit, most people in the entertainment business have decided to accept unsolicited work only from agents or lawyers, or after receiving a signed release form from the writer. The following is an example of the typical phrasing found in release forms, an explanation of how the phrases are defined, and a small discussion of their effect. (How to obtain an agent or lawyer will be discussed in the section titled "Representation: Agents, Lawyers, and Managers: What Do They Mean When They Say That They Are Looking for Someone with Passion?")

SAMPLE: TYPICAL RELEASE FORM

Date:
Title of Material Submitted
Big Time Studios
Anywhere, USA

Ladies and Gentlemen:

I *(you, the writer)* acknowledge that the Material *(your script)* that I am submitting to you, *(Big Time Studios)*, was created and written by me without any suggestion or request from you that I write or create the Material. *(Big Time has intentionally stated that sentence was for the following reason: If there is some thought that you were "asked" to write by a Big Time employee, the Writers Guild might argue that you were employed to write and therefore should be paid by Big Time).*

   I. I represent that:
      A. I am the author of the Material and that the Material is original with me. *(This is your promise that there will be no lawsuits by another writer because you have copied his or her work.)*
      B. I have the exclusive rights to submit the Material to you on the terms and conditions set forth in this agreement. *(This is your promise that there will be no lawsuits because you wrote this with a partner and either failed to mention that you had a partner or to obtain your partner's permission to submit the work to Big Time.)*
      C. I have the power and the authority to grant to you all rights in this Material. *(This is your promise that you have not sold any portion of the rights to this work to another company who may sue Big Time.)*
  II. I understand and agree that your use of material containing features and elements similar to or identical with those contained in the Material shall not entitle me to any compensation if you determine that you have an independent

legal right to use such other material, either because such features and elements were not new or novel (*Big Time is reserving the right to steal something from your screenplay if Big Time's attorneys advise them that they can do this without getting sued by you*), were in the public domain (*certain elements of your work were copied from other work that was in the public domain*) or were not originated by me, were independently conceived, or because other persons (including your employees) may have submitted or may hereafter submit material containing similar or identical features and elements. (*Basically, this means that Big Time will make the argument that they were already developing the same ideas or planned to develop the same ideas when you presented them with your work. It is unclear whether Big Time's statement that they were independently creating this would hold up in court. This is said to scare you into thinking that Big Time can get away with anything.*)

III. I agree that, should I bring any action (*a lawsuit*) against you for wrongful appropriation of the Material (*stealing my work*), such action shall be limited to an action at law for damages and in no event shall you be entitled to an injunction or any other equitable relief. (*You can only sue them for money and cannot attempt to close down a movie or production if they are using your work.*) If I am unsuccessful in such action, I agree to pay you all the costs and expenses involved in defending such action. (*If you dare to sue Big Time, and Big Time wins, you will be stuck with Big Time's very expensive attorney fees and costs. What is not said, however, is that if you win this action, Big Time will be stuck with all of your attorney fees and costs.*)

IV. I hereby acknowledge that I have read and understood this Agreement (*you know what you are agreeing to and that Big Time did not confuse you by the meaning of this agreement*) and that no oral representations of any kind have been made. (*There is no agreement between you and Big*

> *Time other than what is on these pages, nor is there any understanding that Big Time will pay you.)*
>
> Signed,
>
> Emerging Writer

Naturally, signing a release form that contains the above elements will make many writers feel as if they are giving their work away. For those writers I suggest attempting to find a friendly lawyer who will pass your work on to the studio.

2

How Can I Write Nasty Things About People I Know and Not Get Sued?

WHAT ABOUT THE FREEDOM OF SPEECH?

Although the First Amendment to the United States Constitution sets forth that "Congress shall make no law. . . abridging the freedom of speech, or of the press. . . ," this basic right does not keep screen and television writers from frequently and regularly being sued by the adoring public for the content of their work. The problem: A writer, like all artists, will occasionally draw upon his personal experience for the basis of his material. Other sources of inspiration for writers are contemporary social and political issues. Generally, using these subjects as a basis for written work is not a problem because these topical areas form the basis of social commentary. It is not a problem, that is, until some individual recognizes himself in the writer's work and either claims that he is portrayed in a manner that could be construed as damaging to his reputation or that potentially subjects him to ridicule, hatred, or contempt, or claims that the writer's work publicly discloses private facts or portrays the individual in an untruthful or "false light." This is when lawyers get involved.

Let me show you how this typically occurs.

Scenario #1: After months of agonizing, you believe that you have the basis for a great screenplay that uses as the main character your quirky ex-girlfriend, the one who brutally dumped you on New Year's Eve. You give the main character all of your girlfriend's idiosyncratic qualities, from the way she sleeps with one foot sticking out to the fact that she has two cats, named Ziegfried and Roy. You decide that, like your girlfriend, the main character should have black hair, blue eyes, a closeted weakness for blueberry Pop-Tarts, a love for running marathons, and a tendency to cry when she hears Edith Piaf recordings. Similar to your ex, the main character has graduated from the Wharton School of Business. However, you break from the prototype of the main character, Stephanie (your ex's name), in one distinct way: You make her a prostitute.

Ah, revenge. What terrific inspiration for the creation of a screenplay. In the above scenario, however, the writer potentially borders on difficulties in the area of the law known as libel.

WHAT IS LIBEL AND HOW DO YOU AVOID IT?

Libel is an area of the law that shields individuals (and corporations) from harmful fabrications. It's a section of the law of defamation which gives rise to legal actions concerning false statements that are *written*; false statements that are *spoken* are covered under the area of defamation known as slander. Libel is defined as a false statement about a person, communicated to at least one other person, that injures the defamed person's reputation or subjects the defamed person to hatred, contempt, or ridicule. To win a legal action for libel, an individual must prove the following:

- The writer wrote fabrications or falsehoods that would qualify as "defamatory language." Roughly translated, "defamatory language" is a written lie that adversely effects an individual's reputation, integrity, sanity, or professional capabilities. Do not think because you are taking "artistic license" or because you phrase something as "your opinion" that you will be exempt from a libel action. Unless you have a truthful and factual basis for "your opinion," you could find yourself facing a legal action if you write a statement that harms an identifiable party's reputation.

- The "defamatory language" was reasonably understood as referring to the party who has filed the legal action. Writing "All Rolling Stones fans are irresponsible party animals" will probably not get you into trouble because it is impossible to identify all Rolling Stones fans. Writing "All members of the Rolling Stones are irresponsible party animals" could get you into trouble because one can identify the members of the Rolling Stones and determine if this statement is true. Be aware that corporations, in addition to individuals, can and have filed legal actions for libel. If you plan to write a nasty statement concerning a corporation, it had better be true.
- The "defamatory language" was communicated to another person. You can write anything about anyone as long as it's not communicated to another person. Once you communicate with another individual concerning your written "defamatory statements," however, you can potentially run into legal problems.
- The party that filed the legal action was injured. Injury is a difficult item to substantiate unless it can be measured in terms of monetary losses, damage to reputation, or mental anguish. Once any of the above items can be proven—that is, that the written "falsehood" caused any of the above-listed damage—then a party may be capable of sustaining an action for libel.

One additional item is added when defamatory statements are expressed in "the media." In an attempt to preserve the Freedom of the Press and the traditions of the First Amendment, the law distinguishes between so-called public personas and private personas regarding the level of intent necessary to establish libel against a member of the mass media. For well-known or public personas (individuals who are celebrities, politicians, or public figures), the individual must establish that the broadcaster or publisher made the "defamatory" statement either knowing it was false or having serious doubts about its truth. Private individuals (individuals who are not celebrities, politicians, or public figures) need only to prove that the publisher or broadcaster acted negligently in failing to ascertain that the statement was false.

With all of this in mind, how, you wonder, is the writer of Scenario #1 potentially guilty of libel? To begin with, the writer modeled the main character with such detail that those who know "Stephanie" (friends, family, and others) could easily recognize her. In addition, the work—and this version of "Stephanie"—has or will be communicated to a third party. Needless to say, the defamatory statement, or falsehood, is that Stephanie is a prostitute. Damages might be difficult to establish unless Stephanie can show that she suffered mental anguish.

A case involving very similar facts actually occurred. In *Springer v. Viking Press*, 457 N.Y.S. 2d 246, *aff'd* 60 N.Y. ed 916, 458 N.E.2d 1256 (1983), the author of the novel *State of Grace* wrote a story involving a very successful hooker named Lisa. During college the author of *State of Grace* dated a woman named Lisa. Unfortunately, the author chose to give the fictional Lisa (the prostitute) the physical characteristics of the real Lisa (the ex-girlfriend). The real Lisa filed a legal action for libel. Although the court found that the similarities between the Lisas were superficial and not enough to establish libel, the point here is that you do not want to find yourself facing this type of legal action.

Scenario #2: Your life has recently been vindicated because you heard that the homecoming queen from your high school, the person who made your high school career a living hell, has turned from the girl-most-likely-to-succeed to the girl-most-likely-to-expand. Currently, she tips the scales at more than three hundred pounds. While you do not usually rejoice in the misery of others, this is too delicious. Your decide to write about her and to title the work "Moo: The Story of a Homecoming Queen Who Became a Cow." This is your chance to get back at her, and you decide to use her real name throughout the story and the intimate details of her life, which you know only too well. You believe that this will make a terrific made-for-TV movie.

Nasty, nasty, nasty. Who would do something like that? As ridiculous as the above scenario may seem, it potentially borders on the area of the law known as invasion of privacy.

INVASION OF PRIVACY

Invasion of privacy covers four distinct areas. These areas or "causes of action," are as follows:

1. **Disclosure of private facts.** This area attempts to protect an individual from the release of harmful but truthful facts concerning an individual that may violate the individual's privacy or could prove embarrassing to him.
2. **False light.** This area seeks to protect the individual from the release of facts that place him in a "false light" or portrays the individual inaccurately.
3. **Commercial appropriation.** This area attempts to shield the individual from the unauthorized use of an individual's likeness or name for the defendant's commercial advantage.
4. **Intrusion.** This area attempts to shield individuals from the intrusion of a defendant upon the plaintiff's seclusion or property.

Unlike libel, which seeks to protect an individual's reputation, invasion of privacy seeks to protect an individual's feelings or sensibilities. Similar to libel actions, individuals other than the complaining party must recognize that the information concerns the complaining party, and enough people must read or be exposed to the information so that it becomes public knowledge.

Since only the first two areas of the right of privacy truly concern writers, only these areas will be discussed.

Disclosure of Public Facts

To win a legal action under the right of privacy area known as disclosure of public facts, an individual must prove that the disclosed facts were "highly offensive" to a person of "ordinary sensibilities" to which the public has no "legitimate concern." Well, given that persons of ordinary sensibilities (you and I, on a good day) are frequently and regularly exposed to information, as members of the public, concerning the sexual conduct of presidents, rock stars, and politicians, it is nearly impossible to find information that would qualify as "highly offensive" or that is not "a legitimate public concern." This is a tough area to establish these days.

False Light

To win a legal action under the area known as false light, an individual must establish that someone has published facts about him that places him in a "false light" in the public eye, that the facts are objectionable to a reasonable person, and that the facts are substantially and materially false. For those of you who have remained awake through this discussion, the obvious question is "How does this differ from libel?" As stated previously, false light seeks to protect an individual's peace of mind or personal feelings. Consequently, to establish a legal action in this area, an individual would have to show that his feelings or sensibilities have been damaged—as opposed to libel where the individual would want to establish that his reputation has been damaged. Similar to libel cases, for a "public figure" or "celebrity" to establish that he has been damaged, he has to establish that the published material was not only false and highly offensive but that it was published with the knowledge that it was false or with reckless disregard for the truth. Referring to the example in Scenario #2, it is clear that the story of a formerly fit cheerleader who has gained a tremendous amount of weight is a "disclosure of private facts" to which there may or may not be "a legitimate public interest." In addition, the jury is out, one might say, as to whether this information is "highly offensive." Clearly, the ex-cheerleader's feelings and sensibilities would be hurt. Whether the ex-cheerleader would win in a trial is a toss-up. It is clear, however, that most individuals about whom this was written would pursue legal action of some nature.

Scenario #3: In a fit of inspiration, you create a multimedia game (computer game) entitled *Who's in Detox Now?* The game is a maze that allows the player to proceed through different levels. At each level the player receives further directions through the maze so the player can correctly identify which celebrity from politics, entertainment, religion, or sports is or has undergone treatment for substance or behavioral abuse. To make your game lively, you use the pictures of numerous hot celebrities from each of these areas: Needless to say, you have not received the permission from any of the celebrities to use their photos. The game is sold in California.

The creator of Scenario #3 has clearly landed on the shores of an area of the law known as the right of publicity. As much fun as it may be to include the image of a well-known celebrity or rock star in one's work, in certain situations this could land an individual in a great deal of trouble. What, you ask, would those situations be?

THE RIGHT OF PUBLICITY

The right of publicity gives an individual a legal claim against the unauthorized use of the individual's name, face, image, or voice for commercial benefit. Nearly half of the states in the United States recognize an individual's right of publicity, including California, New York, and Florida, the states in which most of the United States entertainment industry is located. To establish a legal claim for the right of publicity, an individual must demonstrate the following elements: (1) the use of the person's name, photograph, picture, or likeness; (2) the use was unauthorized; (3) the use was for the purposes of trade or advertising; and (4) the use deprived the person of the commercial value in his or her name or likeness.

The right of publicity does not generally involve a writer's work because the use of an individual's name or likeness in screenplays, books, or articles is usually protected under the First Amendment. In these areas the use of an individual's name or likeness is not generally considered to be "for purposes of trade or advertising" since these items are regarded as "free speech." However, when we turn to the multimedia products, a different result may be reached.

In the example set forth in Scenario #3, the problem we encounter is that the multimedia product, a game, would probably fall into the category of "trade" (as in "for purposes of trade or advertising"). In addition, I tend to think that few politicians or celebrities would authorize the use of their likeness or name in connection with the type of game in Scenario #3. It is possible that an individual could be deprived of commercial value in his or her name or likeness, especially if the individual wanted to associate his or her name with a product line that had a "wholesome" connotation. Needless to say, as much fun as *Who Is in Detox Now* might be to play or create, the potential liability or "exposure" would be enormous.

How Can I Avoid Being Sued?

Obviously, a writer is going to turn to his background for ideas from which to create work. To prevent great work from becoming a living nightmare of legal actions, however, I suggest taking the following steps:

1. **Fictionalize:** Although it is tempting to use the name and exact physical image of the person who destroyed your self-confidence during school, be the bigger person in the situation and keep the person wondering if it's actually him or her when you write your tell-all semiautobiographical tale of teenage angst. In other words, fictionalize your experience. Make that tall brunette cheerleader who destroyed your self-confidence short and blond. Turn that stud captain of the football team who made fun of your creative writing efforts into a klutz who could not jog fifty yards. The girlfriend with a crazy cat who climbed on your chest every night for three years? Make it a parrot named Louie who loved to sing Springsteen's "Born in the USA." The neighbor whose apartment was so messy that you needed a map to get from the door to the living room? Make him a clean freak who unconsciously straightened pencils and small objects. Use your experience as a springboard for your inspiration and create a character who significantly differs from the one about whom you have written.

2. **Release forms:** In the event that you want to write the true story of a living individual and it includes some amazing event that cannot be fictionalized, try to obtain a release of liability from the person. You obtain a release of liability from an individual when the individual signs the release form that you present.

   A release form, such as the one located at the end of the chapter, allows a writer to use a person's name or life story in a written work without fear of liability. A release form also allows the creator of a multimedia product to use an individual's name or image without the threat of litigation.

   Obviously, most individuals are fairly savvy to the value of a great story (for example, note the witnesses and jurors in the

O. J. Simpson trial) and will not give their stories for free. In these situations I recommend using the option agreement for life story rights; it is explained and located at the end of the chapter.

3. **Make Sure the People You Write About Are Dead:** If the individuals you want to write about are dead, you do not have to worry about being sued for libel or invasion of privacy. Dead people cannot defend their reputation (libel actions) and do not have feelings and sensibilities that can be harmed (right of privacy). You must be careful, however, about the reputations and feelings of the dead individual's living relatives; they may sue you if included in your work.

   Please note that in certain states the heirs of dead individuals are allowed to sue for right of publicity after the individual's death. This means that if you plan to use the name or image of a deceased individual in your multimedia extravaganza (product), you should know that you face the possibility of finding yourself at the wrong end of a legal action.

4. **Will the Truth Protect Me from Being Sued?:** You may have heard that in some jurisdictions the truth is an absolute defense to libel. Within these jurisdictions, if you can prove that the utterly outrageous statement that you wrote is true, you will not be guilty of libel or find yourself paying money to the individual about whom you made the statement. This does not mean, however, that you will not be sued for libel.

   As with all defenses, "the truth" must be proven. This means that if you are sued for libel, you will spend time and money to prove that you wrote "the truth." Note that "the truth" is not a defense to a right of privacy or right of publication action. Thus, if you are sued for either of these actions because you wrote "the truth," you may still be found guilty.

5. **A Private Checklist:** In the event that a writer has any doubts regarding the potential liability of the material he has written, I have created a checklist. The following questions may be answered either yes or no. Remember, no cheating: A "maybe" counts as a yes.

   - Am I saying bad things or exposing potentially private information about a living individual?

- Am I using someone's unauthorized name or image in a product?
- Is this person alive?
- Is there any possibility on the face of the earth that this person will recognize him/herself?
- Did I fail to obtain a release form from this person (see below)?
- Did I fail to buy this person off—that is, obtain an option on the life rights of the individual (see below)?
- Did I fail to fictionalize the person or events so that no one would claim to be the individual I have written about?
- Do I love the idea of paying a lawyer so much money that he can put his children through four years of a very expensive private college using my legal fees?

If you have answered any of the above questions with a yes or a maybe, and did not answer questions 5 or 6 with a no, you are potentially facing a serious problem. Review your material. Can't you use that brilliant imagination that stunned all your teachers in high school to create a fictional character that no one but you could recognize?

WHAT IF I CAN'T GET THE RIGHTS OR A RELEASE FORM?

Let's say that you have a burning desire to write the story of the most twisted murder trial that Western civilization has ever seen (the reader is invited to vote for the winner of this category). Can you do this without a release form or the rights to the story?

All statements made by judges, jurors, attorneys, witnesses, and the litigants (plaintiffs or defendants) during an entire judicial proceeding (from start to finish) in the courtroom or in court documents are considered "absolutely privileged." Material which is "absolutely privileged" may contain statements that are defamatory, but the material is liability-free if written or spoken in the context of the "privileged" proceeding. This material may be used by you as a writer without risk of liability for defamation if it is clear that the work was created by you with clear reliance on the courtroom proceedings.

How do you obtain these case documents? Public access to court documents and proceedings is a guaranteed right in the United States. Generally, the court clerk of the location where the trial took place (also usually the location of the documents) will ask you to pay a duplication fee along with your request. That's all. Unless a proceeding is filed "under seal" due to its sensitive nature, one can have access to any document or transcript in the court. In case you are wondering, many works within the entertainment industry have been created from the trial records and transcripts of a specific proceeding.

The absolute privilege mentioned above also applies to the remarks of all legislators when acting in an official capacity and to members of the executive branch. With a proper written request to the correct agency (and an offer to pay for copying), an individual can obtain access to nearly any document in state or federal government that is not filed "under seal" or categorized a matter of "national security," by making the written request under the Freedom of Information Act.

WILL A STUDIO REALLY CARE IF I SAY CONTROVERSIAL THINGS ABOUT LIVING PEOPLE?

Yes. A studio will care so much that the studio will probably make the writer take part in an exercise known as annotations. Annotations require the writer to specify the source of each script element that is not wholly fictional. The "script elements" for which a studio generally has concern include characters, events, settings, and segments of dialogue.

A typical annotations exhibit that is attached to a writer's contract will look similar to the document below.

SAMPLE: ANNOTATIONS

    I. Character List: List all characters, including the following notations:

        A. Whether the character is real, fictional, or composite.

        B. For real characters, whether the actual person is living or dead.

        C. For composite characters, the name(s) on whom the composite character is based and what characteristics can be attributed to such actual person(s).

    II. Scene-by-Scene Notations: Indicate whether the Script Element presents or portrays fact or fiction:

        A. If fact or inference from fact, describe source material for Script Elements, including the following:

            1. For books: title, author, and page(s).

            2. For newspaper or magazine articles: date, page, and column.

            3. For interviews: whether notes or tapes exist and, if so, a page or tape reference, and the participants.

            4. For trial or deposition transcripts: the court or other forum, date, person testifying, and transcript page number.

            5. To the extent possible, multiple sources should be identified for each Script Element.

        B. If partly fact and partly fiction, indicate what parts are fact and what parts fiction. For factual parts, describe source material as specified in Paragraph 2(a) above.

        C. If wholly fictional, notation is not required.

    III. In General:

        A. Copies of all materials referenced in Source Annotations should be retained for no less than five years for review by Producer and cross-indexed by reference to script page and scene numbers.

        B. If marginal annotations are coded to avoid repeated lengthy references, a key to such coding must be separately provided.

Note: The purpose of showing this "annotations" exhibit is to establish that the entertainment industry is very concerned about the potential liability that comes from using the stories of live individuals in written material. Take my advice: Fictionalize. Obtain release forms. Obtain options on life right stories. Use court documents of a trial. Don't make your lawyers rich.

The following is an example of a typical release form that would be used if the owner of the life rights does not ask for money in exchange for a release of liability.

SAMPLE: RELEASE FORM: LIFE STORY RIGHTS

I hereby irrevocably consent and agree that you and your successors, licensees, and assigns in perpetuity and throughout the universe shall have the right to use, fictionalize, and/or exploit in whole or in part my Life Story and my name, likeness, poses, statements, writings, photographs, anecdotes, voices, acts, and appearances. I understand and agree that you may portray me and my Life Story in any manner and by any actor or actors, under my name or any other name. I hereby waive any objection that I may have that your use of such material may be defamatory or constitute an invasion of privacy or otherwise violate any right which I may have in connection with such material. I hereby waive any right to bring and prosecute an action for defamation, invasion of privacy, or right of publicity, or any similar action, whether my Life Story is exploited by you or your successors, licenses, or assigns.

You will have the right to add to, subtract from, arrange, alter, and revise my Life Story and all materials relating thereto in any manner and to combine such materials with materials relating thereto in any manner and hereby waive any rights of "droit moral" that you may have in my Life Story. All rights, licenses, and privileges granted to you shall be cumulative, and you may exercise or use any or all of said rights, licenses, and privileges separately from, simultaneously with, or in connection with any other such rights, licenses, and privileges.

I grant you and your successors, licensees, and assigns in perpetuity and throughout the universe all motion picture rights (including, without limitation, all silent, sound, dialogue, talking, and musical motion picture rights), all television rights, remake and sequel rights, novelization rights, and all allied, ancillary, corollary rights, subsidiary, merchandising rights including, without limitation, videocassette, videodisk, soundtrack interactive, online which may be produced in any and all media, now known or devised in the future in any and all languages, and any and all other rights pertaining thereto, and the right to exploit the aforesaid rights in any manner and by any means, whether now known or hereafter devised.

ACCEPTED AND AGREED:

OPTION AGREEMENT: LIFE STORY RIGHTS CONTRACT

In the event that you are attempting to obtain the rights to a story of a living individual, and the individual in question will not sign a release form because he believes that his story has "value" (that is, he wants money), I suggest that you use an agreement similar to the following option agreement.

This is an option for the life rights to a story. A life rights option is an agreement in which the purchaser takes the rights to the story off the market with the hope that the purchaser can find the financing to create a film or television program from the story. Generally, the purchaser will buy the rights to the story once he has found financing. As with all options, the total purchase price is pre-negotiated at the time that the agreement is signed.

In essence, the option and subsequent purchase of the life rights is something of a paid release form: By buying the rights to the story, the purchaser is buying a release from any potential legal action that may result from creating a film or television project that is based on individuals who are still living.

SAMPLE: OPTION AGREEMENT: LIFE STORY RIGHTS CONTRACT

Big Deal Production Company

Dear Mr. and Mrs. __:

The following will set forth the basic terms of the agreement between you ("Owner") and Big Deal Production Company ("Purchaser") regarding the proposed development and production of a television movie or other production (the "Picture") to be based upon the story of your family and your cat, Fish Breath, including, without limitation, the amazing circumstances surrounding the training, education, search, and rescue of your family that was performed by Fish Breath (the "Property").

I. The Owner hereby grants the Purchaser an exclusive, irrevocable option to acquire all motion picture, television and allied rights in and to the Property, for a period commencing upon the date of execution of this letter agreement and continuing for twelve (12) months. In consideration of such option, the Purchaser shall pay to the Owner the sum of upon execution of this letter agreement. Such option period shall be referred to as the Initial Option Period, and the payment for the Initial Option Period shall apply against the purchase price of the Property. *(The amount that one pays for the option depends on how "hot" the story is and, as stated previously, how savvy the owner of the rights is concerning the market value of the right. You could pay a token sum, such as $50, or you could pay an amount closer to $60,000. Whatever payment is made is deducted from the total purchase price of the rights.)*

II. The Purchaser shall have the right to extend the Initial Option Period for an additional period of twelve (12) months ("the Extended Option Period") commencing on the expiration of the Initial Option Period by payment to the Owner of __ on or before said expiration date. The payment for the Extended Option Period shall also apply against the purchase price of the Property. *(The option periods in this agreement are for twelve months each, for a total of twenty-four months. The parties could agree, however, to make the option periods longer or shorter.)*

III. During the Initial Option Period and/or Extended Option Period, the Purchaser shall have the exclusive right to engage in development, production, and preproduction activities in connection with the project, including, but not limited to, the preparation and submission of treatments, formats, teleplays, and/or screenplays based on the Property. In connection with such activities, the Purchaser shall have the right to fictionalize individuals and/or events in whole or in part. There may be no exploitation by the

Owner or under the Owner's authorization any of the rights in and to the Property granted to the Purchaser hereunder during the Initial Option Period and/or Extended Option Period, or thereafter if the Purchaser exercises the option granted herein. *(The Purchaser of the rights has the prerogative to spice up—that is, fictionalize—the Owner's story if he so chooses without threat of lawsuit from the Owner. In addition, the Owner cannot grant these rights or develop the rights in any manner—that is, exploit them—during the option periods.)*

IV. If the Purchaser exercises its option, the Owner shall receive the applicable sum set forth below as the purchase price of the rights to be acquired in the Property, payable upon exercise of the option or the commencement of principal photography of the first motion picture produced hereunder (the Picture), whichever first occurs:

   A. The sum of ___ (less applicable option payment(s) as set forth above) if the Picture is a 1-hour film; or

   B. The sum of ___ (less the applicable option payment(s) as set forth above) if the Picture is a 2-hour film. *(Generally, a greater sum will be paid if the story is a two-hour rather than a one-hour film.)*

V. If the Purchaser exercises its option, the Purchaser shall own all right, title, and interest in and to the worldwide motion picture, television, allied, and subsidiary rights in the Property, including but not limited to the right to produce theatrical motion picture(s) or television motion picture(s) based on the Property; sequel, remake, television series, and advertising rights; all rights to produce, exploit, distribute, and exhibit any motion picture or other production produced hereunder theatrically, non-theatrically, by means of television cassette, disk or other compact device, and in all media throughout the universe now known or hereafter devised in perpetuity. *(If the Purchaser actually buys the rights to the story, he may create any known entertainment product, now known or created, after this agreement has been signed. Although the agreement states that the Purchaser can create entertainment products which are*

*not in existence at this time with "the rights," the reality is
that the courts have been rather reluctant to support this
language within an agreement. However, you will see this
language in all rights contracts of every kind.)*

VI. The Owner agrees to cooperate with the Purchaser and with
such persons as the Purchaser may designate to the fullest
extent possible and to the best of the Owner's ability in the
preparation or writing of any materials for the Picture and
during the production of any theatrical motion picture or
television production based on the Property, and to provide
the Purchaser with any and all pertinent materials including, but not limited to, court transcripts, documents,
diaries, photographs, letters, etc., in connection with the
Property. *(The sale of "rights" also includes the automatic
submission to the Purchaser of all documentation that the
Owner may have. This may include private diaries, letters,
notebooks, family photographs, and so forth.)*

VII. The Owner agrees to execute the customary depiction
release attached hereto in connection with the Project. The
Owner also agrees to assist the Purchaser in obtaining such
release from any third-party characters as the Purchaser
may deem necessary to enable the Purchaser to exercise its
rights hereunder.

VIII. Except as to matters in the public domain, the Owner
hereby represents and warrants that:

  A. The Owner is the sole owner of all right, title, and
     interest in and to the Property, and the rights granted to
     the Purchaser hereunder are free of all claims, liens, and
     encumbrances by any person, firm, and/or corporation.
     *(The Owner of these rights has not optioned or sold
     these rights to any other party.)*

  B. Neither the Property nor any part thereof in any way
     violates or infringes upon any rights of any nature
     whatsoever of any third party. *(There will not be any
     surprise legal action for libel, invasion of privacy, copy-
     right infringement, right of publicity, or any other pos-
     sible legal claim.)*

  C. All material comprising the Property shall be factually

correct and shall not in any way defame any third party whatsoever. The Owner shall fully and accurately specify all material contained in the Property that is or may be based on any living person or deceased person and/or on actual events. *(Basically, the Purchaser is asking the Owner to annotate the areas of potential liability.)*

D. The rights granted and to be granted to the Purchaser hereunder have not heretofore been granted, licensed, optioned, assigned, encumbered, or hypothecated to any other person, firm, and/or corporation whatsoever; and

IX. The Owner has the right to enter into this agreement and to grant the rights herein granted. *(The Owner may enter into this agreement because the Owner has not granted these rights in any way, shape, or fashion to anyone else.)*

X. The Owner hereby agrees to indemnify, defend, and hold the Purchaser and the Purchaser's assignees and licensees harmless of and from any and all costs and expenses (including, but not limited to, reasonable attorney fees), losses, claims, damages, liabilities, and/or obligations arising out of or in any way connected with the Purchaser's exercise of the rights granted herein, and/or the Owner's breach or alleged breach of any representation, warranty, and/or covenant contained herein. The Purchaser agrees to indemnify, defend, and hold the Owner harmless of and from any and all costs and expenses (including, but not limited to, reasonable attorney fees) losses, claims, damages, liabilities, and/or obligations arising out of any material contained in productions hereunder not contained in the Property. *(Roughly translated, if the Owner does anything to cause the Purchaser to be sued, the Owner will pay for all costs, attorney fees, and damages with which the Purchaser is penalized. The same is true with regard to the Purchaser's responsibilities to the Owner.)*

XI. When executed by both parties, this letter agreement shall be deemed to be the complete, enforceable, and binding agreement between the parties, superseding and merging all prior and contemporaneous agreements and understandings, and embodying the provisions set forth herein and such other terms and conditions as are customary in agreements of this nature, including without limitations the Owner's waiver of equitable and injunctive relief, California governing law, force majeure, and non-modification of this agreement except in a signed writing. *(This document is the final document between the parties and spells out the agreement between the Owner and the Purchaser. Anything which was previously said between the parties that is not included within this agreement no longer counts.)*

If you find the foregoing terms acceptable, please so indicate by signing and dating in the spaces provided below, and return four copies of this letter to me. After I have obtained a countersignature on behalf of Big Deal Production Company, a fully executed copy will be returned to you.

Very truly yours,

Big Deal Production Company

ACCEPTED AND AGREED:

(Owner #1 Signs) (Owner #2 Signs)

3

If Someone Writes an Agreement on a Cocktail Napkin, and I Sign It, Do We Have a Contract?

At some point in your writing career you may be offered some sort of agreement (or, as it's known in legal circles, *contract*) for your writing services. Very few Americans (fewer than 30 percent) know that a valid contract can be *oral* (as in, not in writing).

You may be laboring under the delusion that you do not have a "real" or valid contract unless it is in writing. The individual who "hired" you to perform writing services may be laboring under the delusion that she does not have to pay you because she does not have a "written" contract with you.

Both delusions would be wrong.

As stated previously, most of those involved in the entertainment industry don't know when they have a contract or valid agreement.

Such was the situation in connection with the lawsuit entitled *Main Line Pictures v. Basinger.* As a few of you may remember, Main Line Pictures thought that through a series of conversations, meetings, and letters, they had reached an agreement with Kim Basinger to star in the proposed project *Boxing Helena.* Based on this alleged agreement, Main Line was able to obtain investors in the proposed film.

By contrast, Kim Basinger and her advisers did not believe that a series of conversations, meetings, and letters constituted an agreement. Basinger and her associates made their feeling known. Main Line lost its investors and sued Kim Basinger. Ultimately, the jury found that an agreement had been reached between Basinger and Main Line Pictures. The jury slapped Basinger with a rather large verdict (running to the millions). On appeal, the verdict was reversed, due to a mistake in the jury instructions. (To all attorneys or persons who worked on or followed any aspect of this case, I offer my sincere apologies for my simplistic review of this action.)

Hollywood's reaction was rather interesting. After the verdict was delivered, several actors and actresses quietly decided to do those projects they had previously been "considering."

In the hopes of keeping many of you from experiencing the agony of not knowing when you may or may not have a contract, I present you with an overview of some of the basic concepts concerning contracts.

WHY ARE MOST PEOPLE INTIMIDATED BY CONTRACTS?

Short answer: Because most people are too afraid to read them. The majority of people, throughout life, have been presented with a series of agreements with many pages of fine print attached. Since few bother to read the multiple pages of unintelligible fine print, most become intimidated by signing an agreement *they have not read.*

WHAT IS A CONTRACT?

The classic definition of a contract is "a legally enforceable agreement between two or more parties consisting of reciprocal promises." What does this mean?

Example 1: Anxious Emerging Writer is offered $1,000 to rewrite a screenplay within six weeks by Savvy Producer.

This is a valid contract because the subject matter is legally enforceable (a contract to write a screenplay) between two or more parties (Anxious Emerging Writer and Savvy Producer), which consists of reciprocal promises (Savvy Producer will pay $1,000 to Anxious Emerging Writer [Promise 1] if Anxious Emerging Writer will rewrite a screenplay in six weeks [Reciprocal Promise]). Does it have to be written down to be a valid agreement? No.

That being said, the next question should be: "What is not a valid contract?"

Example 2: Very mad, recently dumped ex-girlfriend offers to sell ex-boyfriend into white slavery for $1.00.

Now this, on the other hand, would not be considered a valid contract because the subject matter of the contract (selling an ex-boyfriend into white slavery), although desirable, is not legal. Thus, a "legally enforceable agreement" could not occur.

Along with the above-stated "classic definition," let me simply state that contracts deal with situations in the future. Contracts provide the standards of behavior for events that have not yet occurred but may occur in the future.

DO ALL CONTRACTS HAVE TO BE IN WRITING TO BE ENFORCEABLE?

As a matter of fact, most contracts do not—repeat: do not—have to be in writing to be valid. This is a great area of misunderstanding for most people. Why do most people put their contracts in writing? It is much easier to show the original intentions of parties when everything is written down. That is, it's much easier for all parties concerned to show what the parties intended in the beginning when all parties are happy than when things fall apart and the parties communicate through attorneys. As stated by one gifted attorney, "A written contract governs the divorce."

A written contract also tends to prevent misunderstandings between parties about the terms of their agreements. Needless to say, for those of you with litigation on the brain (as in: how much can I win if I sue or get sued for this?), a contract that is in writing presents much better evidence if one should go to court.

Example 3: Anxious Emerging (A.E.) Screenwriter believes that he has been offered $1,000 to rewrite a screenplay in six weeks for

Savvy Producer. Savvy Producer believes that he offered Anxious Emerging Screenwriter $1,000 to rewrite his screenplay but is sure that he told A.E. Screenwriter that the $1,000 would come from the net profits (as in, the net profits available from the movie once the movie has been made and released). *(Note: A.E. Screenwriter will never see a dime.)*

Why do you want to write down agreements? So that you don't find yourself in situations like Example 3. Could this agreement be enforceable if it were not written? Absolutely. However, all parties would spend a tremendous amount of time trying to prove what the original agreement stated.

ARE THERE ANY CONTRACTS THAT MUST BE IN WRITING TO BE ENFORCEABLE?

Some contracts must be in writing to be enforceable. By enforceable we mean that a court of law will not enforce the specific type of contract unless the contract is written. Most of these contracts—referred to by an area of the law known as the Statute of Frauds—have nothing to do with the entertainment industry. That is why one commonly hears that all business in the entertainment industry is done with a handshake. (Although a great deal of business takes place within the entertainment industry before a contract is finished, there is always some type of document, whether it is a letter or a memo, that memorializes the deal.) There are, however, some notable exceptions of contracts which *must* be in writing to be valid that do pertain to the entertainment industry.

For better or for worse, the following represents the general group of contracts that must be written to be enforceable. The contracts have been divided into those that clearly apply to the entertainment industry and those that are listed for general knowledge, known as the Statute of Frauds.

Contracts Within the Entertainment Industry That Must Be in Writing to Be Enforceable

WORK-FOR-HIRE

As stated in the chapter on copyright, the "author" of a creative work is the owner of the copyright in the work. In the United States the "work-for-hire" rules find that the employer is considered the "author" of the work if the work is created within the employment context; thus the employer owns the copyright in the work if the employee creates the work within the scope of his employment. An exception exists, however, if the work is created in a context where the employee is an independent contractor. In this situation a *written agreement* (there is a connection to this chapter somewhere) must exist between the parties to consider the creative work a "work-for-hire," or the independent contractor/employee will be considered the owner of the copyright in the work. For example, if Julie hired Larry to write a screenplay based on an idea that Larry pitched to Julie, and Julie and Larry did not sign a *written agreement* that stated the screenplay was a "work-for-hire," Larry would be the "author" of the work and the owner of the copyright in the work because the screenplay was not created in a "work-for-hire" situation.

However, the work-for-hire laws—specifically the ones that apply to independent contractor situations in which the parties must agree that the work is a work-for-hire—do not apply in most countries outside of the United States. In other countries the "author" in the independent contractor situation is always the creator of the work, so that the individual who creates the work will always be the owner of the copyright in the work. In these countries, for another party to become the owner of the copyright, the creator of the work must give the other party *a written contract* for the copyright in the work, known as "an assignment."

ASSIGNMENTS

Another contract that must be in writing is an assignment of copyright. An assignment is a transfer of copyright ownership in a work. The assignment can relate to the entire work or specific aspects of it. For example, the assignment of copyright can be limited by geographical region (the state of Washington only), time (for no longer than twenty years), or specific rights of the work (reproduction rights only). As a practical matter, most written work done within the entertainment industry in independent contractor or employment situations is done with a written agreement that designates the work as a "work-for-hire." But certain work, including interactive or multimedia software, that is created independently may not be a "work-for-hire." For a party other than the creator of the work to obtain copyright of the work, it would have to be done through a written agreement.

For an assignment to be valid, it must be in writing and signed by the owner of the rights conveyed or the owner's authorized agent.

LICENSES

Let's say that you write the most brilliant novel of your generation. A well-known movie producer wants the exclusive right to create a movie from your book and to distribute the movie. Publishers flock to you. You choose one special publisher who will have the exclusive right to publish the work in the United States, and one producer who has a dark vision that is similar to your own. Can you give each of these exclusive rights away?

As stated in the chapter on copyright, a license is the copyright owner's grant of permission to use a copyrighted work in a manner that belongs to the copyright owner. A copyright license can be exclusive (belonging to one person or entity) or non-exclusive (belonging to many). If the license belongs to one—you have granted an exclusive license—then it is considered a transfer of copyright ownership. An exclusive license is not valid unless it is in writing and signed by the copyright owner.

The Statute of Frauds

As stated previously, the items below represent a general area of the contract law that does not have an obvious application to the entertainment industry. These items set forth basic contracts that generally should be in writing, but each area has exceptions.

A CONTRACT FOR THE SALE OF REAL PROPERTY

We all know what real property is. It is a home, land, a valley, farm land. By contrast, real property is not "personal property," which is a car, a book, a couch, and so forth. A contract for the sale of real property generally must be in writing to be "enforceable," but there are a million exceptions to this rule. One exception: If you made a payment on a piece of real property and the payment was accepted by the individuals from whom you were buying the property, a court would generally find that you had entered into a contract.

A CONTRACT FOR THE SALE OF GOODS FOR MORE THAN $500.

The law makes a distinction between goods and services. "Goods" or "a good" is generally a product that has been manufactured. Services do not produce a product. For instance, a lawyer performs services that produce nothing and generally destroy or inhibit the creation of anything. Doctors perform services. Dentists perform services. When a writer is hired for a writing assignment, the writer performs "writing services."

If you buy a manufactured good for more than $500, most state laws require that the transaction be acknowledged by some written document. However, among the numerous exceptions to this rule would be if the goods were specially made or manufactured.

A CONTRACT THAT CANNOT BE PERFORMED WITHIN ONE YEAR OF THE TIME IN WHICH THE CONTRACT IS MADE

What is this, you say? Let's say that you are very, very lucky and because you have written a terrific spec episodic work, you get hired as a staff writer for the hottest show on television. Due to your brilliant wit and "fresh voice," the producers of the show would like you to sign a contract for the next three television seasons. Since this contract would keep you tied up for three years and cannot be performed within one year (you can't perform the work of three seasons in one year because the show wants you around for three designated years), this is a contract that must be in writing.

A CONTRACT TO ANSWER FOR THE DEBT OF ANOTHER

Your business associate (or overburdened parent) tells you that she will pay off all your credit card debt in exchange for your brilliant rewrite of her novel. You agree. To make this particular contract stick, specifically with your debtors (as in MasterCard or Visa), it must be in writing.

AN AGENCY CONTRACT IN WHICH ONE PARTY HAS THE POWER TO SIGN A CONTRACT ON ANOTHER PARTY'S BEHALF

Occasionally, individuals enter into contracts in which they give another person the power to sign a contact on their behalf. An example is a contract with a business manager in which an individual allows the business manager to sign checks on her behalf. Another type is the durable power of attorney in which a sick or incapacitated individual gives another person the power to take care of all his worldly and monetary possessions. Obviously, this kind of contract must and should be in writing because the person entering into this type of arrangement is giving away a great deal of power.

IF A CONTRACT OF AGREEMENT DOES NOT HAVE TO BE IN WRITING TO BE VALID, HOW DO I KNOW IF I HAVE ONE?

Certain features must be present in every contract if the contract is to be valid. These very basic parts must exist in the contract at the time the contract is created. These features or attributes are as follows:

Offer and Acceptance: The basics of contract law find that a contract is formed when one party makes an "offer" that is "accepted" by another party. The offer is an inducement, or proposal, to form an agreement. The "offer" can be as modest as "I will watch your cat over the weekend if you will read my screenplay." An "acceptance," the second party's agreement to the form of the offer, can be as simple as "Okay." Occasionally the acceptance can be shown by conduct. For instance, if the second party in the above cat-watching scenario read the screenplay, this could be construed as an acceptance of the offer.

After an offer has been made, no contract is created until the second party accepts. Thus, if the second party replies, "Let me think about it," the contract has not been accepted. Also, if the accepting party adds additional terms to the offer, such as "Okay, but I won't read your screenplay unless you agree to watch my cat every weekend in the month of June," this is not, I repeat not, an acceptance. What the accepting party has made is a "counteroffer," which starts the whole process over again. At this point the accepting party has become the party making the offer, and the original offering party has become the party accepting the offer.

What if Aspiring Screenwriter finds someone to read his screenplay during the time that Overworked Agent is reviewing Aspiring Screenwriter's offer? Does Aspiring Screenwriter have to keep the offer open forever? The answer is no. If Aspiring Screenwriter revokes his offer before Overworked Agent has accepted the offer, then this is the end of the deal. In addition, Aspiring Screenwriter is free to take his deal to anyone else, including a competitor of Overworked Agent, as long as Overworked Agent has not accepted the deal.

Can Overworked Agent reject Aspiring Screenwriter's offer and then attempt to enter into it again? Overworked Agent could attempt this, but since Overworked Agent has already rejected the offer, a contract will not be formed by Overworked Agent's acceptance unless Aspiring Screenwriter agrees to the deal. However, since Aspiring Screenwriter's offer was no longer open, Overworked Agent cannot form a contract by attempting to accept the offer.

Consideration: Another key feature that must be in every contract is something called "consideration." The legal definition of consideration is "a bargained-for exchange." Literally, "consideration" is what one party will get from the other party for taking part in the contract. For instance, in the above example, the "consideration" that Aspiring Writer will receive is to have his screenplay read. The "consideration" that Overworked Agent will receive is the cat-sitting service. The "consideration" that goes between both parties does not have to be tangible; it can be a promise to do *or* not do something, a release of legal liability, money, or, as in the above example, an exchange of favors.

If both parties to a contract do not receive "consideration" from the "agreement"—for instance, one party makes a promise and the other party offers nothing in exchange—then a situation known as a "gratuitous promise" exists. A "gratuitous promise" is not enforceable as a contract; it is "unenforceable for lack of consideration."

Example: Overworked Agent promises Aspiring Screenwriter that Agent will read Aspiring Screenwriter's screenplay if Agent finds the time. Overworked Agent does not find the time. According to legal doctrine, Overworked Agent's promise is an unenforceable gratuitous promise because Aspiring Screenwriter gave nothing to Overworked Agent in exchange for Agent's promise to read Aspiring Screenwriter's work.

Implied-in-Fact Contracts

This area will be discussed with the greatest of trepidation on my part. Certain factual situations give rise to what the law may designate as an "implied-in-fact contract." In these situations a contract is created by the particular circumstances of the situations. An implied contract may be the result, for example, when a writer pitches an idea to a movie-creating entity such as a production company or studio executive. Let's say that a writer is brought to a meeting to "pitch" an idea for a movie. Implied within the situation is the underlying concept that if the studio decides to use the writer's idea, the writer will be compensated for its use. The offer and acceptance for this situation are considered to be: I offer you my idea. If you accept it, you will pay me.

Naturally, my reason for the trepidation is that everyone believes that a studio has used their idea for the studio's hit movie. (See the chapter on copyright.)

Do I Need a Lawyer to Write a Contract for Me?

Given the above information, it is easy to see that it does not take much to create a contract. Without much effort, an oral (non-written) contract can be created. However, what if you want a written contract?

Obviously, if you want a thirty-five page contract with twenty pages of defining terms, you should seek legal counsel. In addition, if you are presented with a thirty-five page contract with twenty pages of legal terms, you definitely should seek legal counsel.

If you want to create a simple written contract that will include the terms of your agreement, this can be done without an attorney, but there are some things that should be taken into consideration regarding your homemade contract. Your agreement should contain the following elements:

I. It should be a written document. Having said "written" at least twenty times in this chapter, I simply want to make sure that everyone remembers this. When I say "written document," it could be a letter written on simple paper, a memo written on notebook paper, or the basic terms of an agreement written on a cocktail napkin and signed by both parties. (Note, however, that if either one of the parties was drunk when the agreement was written, this would negate the capacity to enter into the agreement.) It does not have to be thirty-five pages long or be on legal letterhead. Within the entertainment industry, many contracts are first notated by having one party send a simple, one-page letter to the other party containing a description of the terms to which both parties have agreed. (See the end of the chapter for a simple letter agreement.) Although, as yet, I have not had an agreement sent to me that was written on a cocktail napkin.

II. It should be written at the time in which you enter into the agreement or as soon as possible thereafter. When you get something in writing at the time in which the agreement has been created, there's a better chance that both parties will remember agreeing to the same terms.

III. It should contain the following elements:
   A. something that identifies the parties by names or by initials;
   B. an adequate description of the subject matter of the agreement; example: "to create one draft of a screenplay based on my outline");
   C. the important terms and conditions, including how much money is involved and when the services are to start and finish;
   D. any other special terms;
   E. the signature of both parties to the agreement.

Your homemade agreement should *not* be written in "legalese" or "like a lawyer." Please. If you want to confuse everyone, put in a few "hereinbefores." There is so little clarity in the world already. Most of us (as in "we attorneys") strive to avoid sounding "like an attorney."

On days when I can't explain something in basic terms, it usually means that I am faking it and falling back on "sounding like an attorney."

You should not use terms that you don't understand or that you've cribbed from a contract you picked up somewhere. Be careful. If you don't understand what your own agreement says, it's highly possible that you won't be getting the things you want from it.

And your homemade contract should not contain obligations that you know you can't meet. Don't agree to something you can't do. This is courting disaster.

For all of you who'd like to create "homemade" contracts, the following is an example of a basic contract, in letter form, that would be a perfectly acceptable written agreement. This is a classic deal memo. Note that both parties would sign the memo.

SAMPLE: WRITER'S DEAL MEMO

Date
Big Time Producer
10100 Main Street
Suite 600
Anytown, USA
re: *"A Stitch in Time"*: *Aspiring Writer*

Dear __:

Pursuant to our discussions, this letter confirms the Agreement between ("Producer") and ("Artist") (SS#) with respect to Artist's writing services in connection with the theatrical motion picture presently entitled "A Stitch in Time" ("Picture").

(a)

Form of Work	Writing Periods	Reading/ Option Periods	Guaranteed Compensation
First Draft	___weeks	___weeks	$_____
Set of Revisions	___weeks	___weeks	$_____
Polish	___weeks	___weeks	$_____

(b) Optional

Form of Work	Writing Periods	Reading/ Option Periods	Guaranteed Compensation
Set of Revisions	___weeks	___weeks	$_____
Polish	___weeks	___weeks	$_____

Compensation: The above Compensation shall be payable one-half ($\frac{1}{2}$) on commencement of services on the applicable form of work and one-half ($\frac{1}{2}$) on delivery of the applicable form of work.

Additional Compensation: If Artist is entitled to sole screenplay credit ("Sole Credit"), Producer shall pay the following: If Artist is entitled to shared screenplay credit ("Shared Credit"), Producer shall pay the following:

Credit: Writing Credit for the Picture shall be determined pursuant to the Writers Guild of America ("WGA") Basic Agreement.

Transportation and Expenses: When Artist's services are required outside the Los Angeles area, Artist shall receive first-class, round-trip air transportation, hotel accommodations, and non-accountable expenses of $____ per week.

Insurance: Artist shall be added as additional insured on Producer's errors and omissions and general liability insurance policies.

Premieres: Artist and companion shall be invited to USA premieres of the Picture.

Videocassette: Artist shall receive one (1) complimentary copy, in format of Artist's choice.

WGA: Producer warrants that it is and shall remain a WGA signatory. Producer shall pay pension, health, and welfare contributions directly to the WGA.

Please confirm the agreement by signing where indicated below. If you do not agree with the terms set forth, please contact me.

Sincerely,

Writer's Representative
cc:

Agreed to and Accepted:

("Producer")

("Artist")

Note: Okay, I tricked you. You may not understand the above deal memo until you read the next chapter. This is, however, an example of an agreement that two parties are capable of creating without the assistance of an attorney. The above writer's deal memo is commonly used to set forth the terms the parties have agreed on when a writer is hired for an assignment. The explanations for these terms are in Chapter 9.

4

Congratulations, You're a Member of the WGA

Maybe your friends have told you that they want to register their work with the "WGA," but they don't know what the WGA is. Maybe you yourself have "registered" some of your work with "the WGA," but you don't know exactly what that means. Maybe you have written something for which you have been paid and were surprised to find that the "WGA" took some money from your check even though you were not a member. Maybe you have never heard of "the WGA" and have wondered throughout the book, who, or what I was talking about.

The following explains what the WGA does and how it can protect you and other writers even if you're not a member. It may also dispel some of the myths concerning the institution. Although this may not be something that you find of interest, you should heed my warning: If you plan to write for the entertainment industry, you will eventually encounter the WGA.

WHAT IS THE WRITERS GUILD OF AMERICA?

The Writers Guild of America (WGA) is a labor union that represents writers working in the fields of motion pictures, television, and radio. The primary purpose of the WGA is to bargain on behalf of writers working in these industries for basic working conditions and minimum payments for writing services. The primary document that guides the entertainment organizations that have agreed to work with the WGA is the WGA Theatrical and Television Minimum Basic Agreement (MBA). This is known as a "collective bargaining agreement" because it has been bargained for on behalf of all writers collectively working within the entertainment industry.

The studios, networks, production companies, and producers that have agreed to abide by the MBA are called "signatories" or "WGA signatories" because these organizations (or individuals) have signed the WGA Minimum Basic Agreement. (Someone who signs the agreement is "a signatory.") If you are unsure as to whether a company is a signatory, you can call the Writers Guild of America and inquire. (WGAwest: [310] 550-1000; WGAeast [212] 767-7800).

The WGA is divided into two areas: WGAeast and WGAwest. WGAeast covers those members living east of the Mississippi and has about two thousand members. WGAwest covers those members living west of the Mississippi and has approximately seventy-five hundred members.

WHAT DOES THE WGA DO?

Minimum Compensation and Working Conditions

As stated previously, the WGA negotiates with those organizations that have become its signatories for minimum compensation for services and basic working conditions through its Minimum Basic Agreement. This is clearly the most important thing the WGA does.

Credit Determination

Ah, yes, the career of the writer. What could be more important to it than credit? Realistically, few things are as important to the writer as the determination of writing credits because a writer's career builds and rises to higher levels according to the credits the writer has accumulated.

The WGA spends a tremendous amount of its resources ensuring that the correct writer has received the proper credit. And not only this, but the WGA "polices" the placement, form, and appearance of credits on screen, in advertising, and in publicity. In addition, in the event of a dispute regarding credit, the WGA has what is known as a "credit arbitration" in which the determination of proper credit on a given project is determined. (This will be discussed in further detail later.)

Legal Disputes

The WGA will pursue certain legal disputes in specific situations. For this the WGA maintains a legal staff that will represent it and its individual members in the following WGA-related matters:

1. Failure to pay a writer for services rendered (not for the sale of work but hired) under the writer's employment contract up to a limit of $300,000 for television and $300,000 for film employment;
2. Failure to abide by the writing credit provisions of the Minimum Basic Agreement;
3. Failure to abide by the MBA in any way, shape, or manner;
4. Misunderstandings between the WGA and any individual signatory or company concerning the interpretation, application, and effect of terms of the MBA.

Registration

If you're at all familiar with the WGA, this is the one area in which you probably know it. The guild has a registration service (which is really a depository) in which all writers (not just members of the WGA) can place, or register, their literary material if it is intended for the entertainment industry. As stated previously, the WGA's registration service is really a depository in which writers may place completed work. The cost is $10.00 for members, and $20.00 for non-members.

The reason for doing this is that the "registration" provides one with proof that a certain work was "registered" with the guild, thus perhaps enabling a writer to establish the date at which a work was finished. In the event of a dispute as to "who-did-what-when" (such as wanting to establish that your work was in existence and that you gave your work to the Big-Time Studio Executive three years before the Big-Time Studio announced the production of a work that sounds remarkably similar to yours), you can have your work subpoenaed from the registration service to show that, indeed, your work did exist. As stated previously, registration does not establish statutory copyright protection and does not take the place of registering your work with the United States Copyright Office. Do note, however, that this service has successfully been used by writers in those "who-did-what-when" lawsuits.

Working Rules and Discipline of the WGA

Like all good unions, the guild has rules that govern the working relationship of members with employers, agents, and others in the entertainment industry. As with all collective groups, one cardinal rule is that to protect the group (the WGA) is to protect the individual.

To ensure that the WGA remains strong and dominant among working writers, the WGA prohibits its members from accepting employment, working for, or selling literary material to any person, firm, or organization that is not a signatory to the MBA. If a worker violates this rule (known as Working Rule 8), the member can be forced to pay the WGA any money received from the deal. Accordingly, a writer must verify that the party for whom he is working is a signatory to the WGA by personally calling the WGA Signatories Department.

Other Ways to Get Your Hand Slapped

Other methods by which members of the WGA may find themselves in hot water include Working Rule 6, which provides that members are prohibited from making any agreement to write for less than minimum compensation. In addition, Working Rule 14 prohibits members from doing "spec" or "speculative" writing, which is writing done on the understanding that the writer will receive compensation for his work only if the producer or hiring party manages to find financing for the project. Also, Working Rule 3 states that all agreements for writing services between a writer and producer will be in writing. It follows that Working Rule 4 should prohibit a writer from working without a contract.

In Addition

The WGA also collects and distributes residuals that writers receive for work previously done. It maintains a pension plan and health fund for its members (which is discussed below) and maintains an agreement with the agencies regarding the treatment and terms between writers and their agents (see the discussion of Rider W in Chapter 5). Also, it distributes unfair lists and strike lists, and provides legislation and judicial participation in legal matters concerning writers.

WHAT DOES THE WGA NOT DO?

The WGA does not find employment or agents for writers. It does not offer writing instruction or advice. In addition, it does not accept literary material for submission to production companies, studios, networks, or producers.

Except for legal issues relating to the Minimum Basic Agreement, the WGA is not in the position to give legal advice to writers. Accordingly, it will not give legal advice in the areas of copyright, copyright infringement, or defamation. In addition, the WGA does not provide representation in the negotiation of individual deals.

HOW DOES ONE BECOME A MEMBER OF THE WGA?

Generally, a person may be admitted to current membership in the WGA if during the three preceding years he has accumulated an aggregate of twenty-four units as defined by the WGA's Schedule of Units of Credit. According to this schedule a writer receives a certain number of units for each completed work. For example, for the drafting of an entire screenplay for a feature-length theatrical motion picture, radio play, or teleplay the writer would earn twenty-four units, or enough units to become a current member of the WGA. A rewrite earns half the number of units allotted to the applicable category of work, and "polishing" earns one-fourth the number of units allotted to the category.

As defined within the Schedule of Units of Credits, the units are based on work that is completed under a contract of employment or on the sale or option of previously unexploited literary material with a company that is a signatory to the WGA's Minimum Basic Agreement. Needless to say, work done for a non–WGA signatory does not obtain membership units for the writer.

The initiation fee for new members is steep: currently it is $2,500. In addition, members must pay an amount equal to 1.5 percent of the gross income from the sale or licensing of unexploited material and earnings from motion picture and television employment. The percentage dues are credited against the basic dues per quarter.

In addition to current membership, the WGA also offers three other classes of membership: In Arrears, Withdrawn, and Emeritus.

DOES THE WGA PROTECT ME IF I AM NOT A MEMBER?

In certain situations you'll receive the benefits and protection of the Minimum Basic Agreement even if you're not a member. If you're hired to write for a WGA signatory and are not a member, you're still "covered" by the Minimum Basic Agreement, which means that you won't be paid less than what's been agreed to in the MBA. Also, you'll be granted the same working conditions as members of the WGA. The sale of work to a signatory company is a different kettle of fish. For whatever reason, if you sell your work to a signatory company of the WGA, you are not "covered" by the MBA unless you are considered a "professional writer."

A "professional writer," as defined by the WGA, is "a person who sells or licenses to the Company the ownership of or rights to use literary material written by such writer which has not been previously published or exploited in any manner or by any medium whatever, and who at such time:

1. "has received employment for a total of 13 weeks as a motion picture and/or television writer, or radio writer for dramatic programs; or
2. "has received credit on the screen as a writer for a television or theatrical motion picture; or

3. "has received credit for 3 original stories or one teleplay for a program ½ hour or more in length in the field of live television; or

4. "has received credit for 3 radio scripts for dramatic radio programs ½ hour in length; or

5. "has received credit for one professionally produced play on the legitimate stage, or one published novel."

If you fall into the above categories, you will receive "professional writer" status with the WGA and thus be accorded the provisions and protection of the Minimum Basic Agreement when your spec screenplay is sold to a WGA signatory company.

WHAT IS WGA CREDIT ARBITRATION?

As stated previously, the award of writing credit carries with it many benefits, including back-end compensation, production bonuses, and future writing assignments. Accordingly, the WGA will be asked to intervene through credit arbitration in the situation in which a writer disputes the credit that is being assigned. The WGA will also automatically do a credit arbitration in any situation in which a director or production executive believes he should be awarded credit on the production.

The credit arbitration takes place in the following manner: The Notice of Tentative Writing Credits is first sent to all concerned parties (that is, who is tentatively awarded screenplay by, written by, and so forth). The writer who is disputing the credit then writes a statement as to how he deserves the credit. All copies of the "work" (original screenplay, rewrites, and working draft) are then sent to three screenwriters. The three screenwriters, working independently of one another, decide who deserves credit. If two out of three make the same decision concerning the award of credit, then the credit is awarded in that manner.

There is no appeal of the decision unless it can be shown that there was dereliction of duty by the writers, violation of WGA policy, or important new material that the writers had not considered.

DOES THE WGA HAVE A HEALTH AND/OR PENSION PLAN?

I'm sure that most of you do not really care about this, but for the far-sighted among you, I will respond: Yes.

To qualify for the WGA Health and Pension fund, a writer must make $15,172 in any four quarters through employment income. This means, once again, that you must be employed to write and cannot make this level through sale of a spec screenplay unless you are hired to write the rewrite of your work.

Section 2

REPRESENTATION: AGENTS, LAWYERS, AND MANAGERS

What Do They Mean When They Say That They Are Looking for Someone with Passion?

In the land of Hollywood there is a myth that a writer can't get work writing in the entertainment industry without an agent. Read this three times: This is not true.

Despite my conviction, I have no doubt that this is the first chapter that you turned to when you picked up this book. If you are newly pursuing a career writing for the entertainment industry, you may believe that once you have an agent, all your worries will be solved and that the next step is to buy a home in Bel Air. Think again.

As a writer, what you need to propel your career forward is a passionate advocate. By passionate advocate, I mean someone who has the ability and desire to have your work read by those members of the entertainment industry who are buying scripts or hiring writers.

Whether this is an agent, a literary manager, a producer, or a friend does not really matter. What's important is that the individual who is your advocate will pound the pavement for you (metaphorically speaking), get your work read, get you invited to meetings with production companies and studios to discuss your ideas, and, it is hoped, sell your work or get you a writing assignment.

Having said all this, the following chapters discuss the distinctions among agents, lawyers, and literary managers. Since most of you—despite anything I write, implore, or insist—are primarily interested in the answer to the question "How Do I Get an Agent?" Chapter 5 begins by discussing those lovable creatures: agents. Chapter 6 is an explanation of lawyers, and then Chapter 7 is an exploration of the emerging role of the literary manager. To keep those of you who don't presently have an agent, lawyer, or literary manager from jumping off a high building, the final chapter of this section, Chapter 8, is a discussion of how writers may advance their careers on their own.

5

Agents: What Do They Mean When They Say That They Are Looking for Someone with Passion?

WHY AN AGENT (OR WHAT IS AN AGENT)?

Many of you are probably shaking your head, thinking that of course you know what an agent is. For those of you who are willing to admit the truth—that you may not know exactly what an agent is or does but you know that everyone seems to have one—please read on.

An agent is usually a person who is licensed to obtain work for individuals who are working within the entertainment industry. If the agent works in California, the agent is within the jurisdiction of the laws of the California Labor Code and is therefore regulated by the State of California. Basically, the provisions of the code provide the following:

1. The Labor Commissioner must approve the agent's contract with the client. If the contract appears unfair to the artist, it will not be approved. (At the bottom of many agency contracts, you will see the notation "This contract has been approved by the

California Labor Commission.")

2. Agents must be licensed by the California Labor Commissioner. What actually happens in practice, however, is that rather than each individual agent having a license, an agency obtains one license and the agents are covered under the umbrella of the agency license.

3. The agent or agency must maintain accurate records of the money or money transactions that the agent handles for the client.

4. The list of fees charged by the agent must be filed with the Labor Commissioner for scrutiny.

5. The agent is prohibited from splitting his fee with an employer of the writer.

The agents and agencies who represent film and television writers have a second set of standards with which to contend: those of the Writers Guild of America. The WGA has negotiated the basic terms and conditions within the contractual relationship of a literary agent and a client who is working in film and television. These standards are set forth in Rider W of the Artists' Managers Basic Agreement negotiated by the Writers Guild of America. (To make life easier on you, and to keep you from having to read the nearly unintelligible Basic Agreement, the basics of Rider W are included at the end of the chapter.)

What's important to know about the WGA and the agencies representing screen and television writers is that the WGA will provide anyone, including those who are not members, with a list of agents and agencies who have agreed to abide by the terms and conditions of Rider W. More to the point, this list contains the agents (representing film and television writers only) who are "approved" by the WGA. This list may be obtained by writing the WGA and sending a check for $2.00 with a self-addressed stamped envelope. WGAwest, Inc., is located at 7000 West 3rd Street, West Hollywood, California 90048; telephone (310) 550-1000. WGAeast, Inc., is at 555 West 57th Street, New York, New York 10019; telephone (212) 767-7800. (A partial list of agencies that are signatories to Rider W of the Artists' Managers Basic Agreement is included at the end of the book.)

HOW DOES SOMEONE BECOME AN AGENT?

The first thing you should know is that agents are not magical beings who sprung from the ground with the wisdom and ability to make any writer the next big-time screenwriter. Most agents have gone through a fairly tortuous process to become an agent, a process that involves a great deal of groveling.

The process of becoming an agent varies throughout the entertainment industry. The large agencies (International Creative Management (ICM), William Morris, Creative Artists Agency (CAA), and United Talent) and some of the mid-sized agencies have what is known as a "training program." Traditionally, the training program has the agents start in what is known as "the mail room," which may actually be the mail room of the agency. Here the trainee gets the opportunity to sort and deliver mail throughout the agency. The trainee may also perform such duties as food service, in which he must arrive at five in the morning to buy and prepare all the food that the agency will require for the day. The trainee may be required to pick up the dry-cleaning of an agent, get the agent's car washed, order the agent's usual "decaf cap, light foam." Needless to say, being a trainee can be hell. Might I add that the hours are grueling, the pay is very low, and the competition for the position in the large agencies is staggering. I personally know many agents who started in "the mail room" after they had finished law school. (In Los Angeles the large agencies are able to pick from a select group of the best and brightest graduates from universities throughout the country.)

After a certain period of time, a trainee who survives the above training may be promoted and become an agent's assistant. This involves taking all calls for the agent and arranging all of his appointments, phone calls, and paperwork. Basically, the agent's assistant handles the agent's desk, a job that is very stressful and involves ensuring that the agent's life runs smoothly. If the agent's assistant survives this rite of passage and the agency has the business or has an opening, the agent's assistant becomes a junior agent, generally in a distinct department such as motion picture lit (that is, representing writers for film) or long-form television (representing writers for miniseries and movies-for-television). This is the process in a large agency.

In a smaller or boutique agency, the road to becoming an agent is much different. An individual can become an agent by starting out in a non-paid internship in the position of the agent's assistant. Once again, if the assistant survives the trial by fire and the agency believes the assistant can bring in business, the assistant may become an agent. However, some individuals become agents because they have worked in a specific industry (such as publishing) for a long time and have the contacts and knowledge of the industry to make deals and get people on the phone. These people generally know from the buying side what the industry is looking for (having previously worked in the position of, for instance, an editor in a publishing house) and thus can understand the market in which they are working.

All of the above is to indicate that agents do not participate in a special course in "how to sell the script of a novice writer" or "how to know from reading someone's work whether the writer will be an extraordinary success." An agent's knowledge of what is "good" and "what will sell" is purely subjective.

HOW DO WRITERS FIND AGENTS WHO WILL READ THEIR WORK?

One way to receive an agent's attention is to obtain a recommendation from someone who knows the agent. As a rule, agents will not look at an emerging writer's work without a recommendation. Generally, the agent will accept a recommendation from someone he believes has good taste.

The recommendation can come from a variety of sources: a producer, a lawyer, a professor at a film school, or even another writer whom the agent represents. In this process the agent is receiving work that he has "solicited." This means the agent has heard about the writer and the writer's work from someone he trusts and has asked to receive a copy of the work from the source advocating the writer. By contrast, work that comes in the mail without an introduction or recommendation from a known source is called "unsolicited" work. Agents rarely accept unsolicited work.

Another way for a writer to receive an agent's attention is to enter contests that are given for emerging screenwriters. These contests are something of a "Star Search" (without Ed McMahon) for screenwriters and are regularly reviewed by agents for potential new clients. (A list of competitions for screenwriters is included in the back of the book.) If you place in one of these contests, it is likely that you will be contacted by a few young and aggressive agents who are anxious to find the next big-deal screenwriter.

The last and the least recommended method is to write a query letter to an agent in an agency that will accept query letters. The short, unsolicited query letter to an agent would describe your work and who you are, but you may not receive a response. The letter may be similar to the following:

Aggressive Young Agent
Aggressive Literary Agency
Anytown, USA

Dear Aggressive Young Agent:

Have you ever thought about what would happen if there was a conspiracy to ruin the film industry by kidnapping all plastic surgeons working in West Los Angeles, Beverly Hills, and Santa Monica, California? I have, and it is set forth in my screenplay entitled *A Stitch in Time*. *A Stitch in Time* is a psychological thriller that is a combination of *Death Becomes Her* and *In the Line of Fire*.

If you are interested in receiving a copy of *A Stitch in Time*, please contact me at the following address and/or telephone number *(insert them here)*.

Sincerely,

Aspiring Writer

If the agent likes the description of the work, he may ask to see your screenplay. A reminder: Not all agencies respond to query letters.

HOW DO I FIND SOMEONE TO RECOMMEND MY WORK TO AN AGENT?

Find someone who knows anyone. The process of finding a person to recommend your work to an agent happens in a million different ways, such as the following:

1. **Find a Producer Who Will Recommend You.** One method is to find a producer and/or production company interested in your work and you as a writer. Production companies, companies led by individuals who are in the business of making movies, are always in a desperate crunch to find new material. In addition, most production companies business in Hollywood are listed in a book called *The Hollywood Creative Directory,* which is published by Hollywood Creative Directory, 3000 Olympic Boulevard, Suite 2413, Santa Monica, California 90404; telephone (310) 315-4815 or, outside California, (800) 815-0503; fax (310) 315-4816.

   Once again, if you do not know anyone who is working in a production company, the query letter approach above, with a description of your work, is one way to go. Many production companies are not as hesitant as agents to accept unsolicited material because they are always on the search for new screenplays. However, if you are not represented by an agent or lawyer, you will probably be expected to sign a release form before they will accept your material.

   If a producer or creative executive likes your work, he will probably contact all of his agent friends as soon as possible with "his new discovery." Before you start thinking that this is done for altruistic purposes (like helping you), think again: These individuals usually do this because if a creative executive helps an agent find a hot young talent (that is, does the agent a "big favor"), the agent will be inclined to do the creative executive a "big favor" and send him a "hot" spec script when it goes on the market.

2. **Internships.** If you're still in the stage of your life in which you do not have to work for a living (full time, at least)—as in, you're still in school—I highly recommend finding an internship with a production company that makes films you like. Yes, it is likely

that the internship is unpaid, but if the internship is decent (that is, it is evenly balanced between the amount of slave labor and abuse required and what you can learn about the industry), the internship will be very worthwhile to your future. At best, internships can provide you with insight into how the entertainment industry works, a possible paid position with the production company when an opening appears (they are more likely to hire you if they know your work and like it), and contacts and referrals to agents and other producers within the industry. By this I mean that if you have been a good worker, the producer or creative executive may be willing to "read your script" and give you comments about your work. In addition, if they like your work, they may be willing to call their friends at other production companies and urge them to read your work or connect you with other agents.

3. **Entertainment attorney.** Generally, attorneys working in the entertainment industry count among their acquaintances agents who are interested in reading material that the attorney sends them. Attorneys regularly send screenplays to agents for the purpose of obtaining representation for a client.

4. **Literary managers.** A literary manager is generally someone with previous experience and extensive contacts within the entertainment industry. Generally, a literary manager can help a client obtain agency representation.

5. **Speak to anyone you know.** Let's say your mother mentioned that her best friend from college has a son who knows someone who dated a woman who worked for an agent. Perfect: Call this woman immediately. Seriously, as maniacal as this may seem, people have received recommendations to agents through crazier methods. If you do not live in a film-producing area, this may be the only method you have to contact an agent.

DO AGENTS EVER CHASE A WRITER?

Agents are like sharks who smell blood: If they hear about something that sounds good, they will go after it with gusto. This is a variation of "the recommendation" because the agent has heard about the writer through the entertainment industry gossip-grapevine. Even if the agent has heard about the "hot" writer through the gossip-grapevine, however, the agent will still want to read the writer's work and make a subjective evaluation of the writer's potential.

WHAT MAKES AN AGENT DECIDE TO TAKE A WRITER AS A CLIENT?

The basic agent line with regard to the type of client he is seeking is "I'm looking for someone with passion." This statement is not untrue: Most agents are looking for someone who strongly believes in his work and who will do anything to create the best work possible. The reality, however, boys and girls, is that this is a business, and agents need to make money to survive. Consequently, although an agent may initially love the independent spirit of your Jim Jarmusch–type work, if he decides to sign you as a client, it is because he has some gut instinct that your work will eventually be very profitable and look more like *Lethal Weapon III* than *Brother from Another Planet*. The bottom line is this: For an agent to take on a client, the agent must feel that the client will eventually, if not in the near future, be a revenue stream for the agency. Generally, this means that the agent will receive a minimum of $15,000 to $20,000 per year in commissions.

One other thing to consider: Television is much more profitable for an agency than film. Television writers receive a weekly paycheck from which the agency receives its weekly percentage (generally, unless special circumstances occur, it is 10 percent). Writers for film may not work as regularly and may take longer to deliver a screenplay from which the agency can take a percentage. If the agency believes that a writer can write for television, it is not unlikely that a client will receive considerable attention from the agency's television department and less attention from the agency's film department (motion picture lit. department). Needless to say, this is not entirely bad if the writer desires to have a career in television. However, if the writer is planning to be the next Quentin Tarantino and the agency is submitting the writer's work for a staff position on a television series, the writer should know that the writer's career may not be heading in the direction which he had intended.

How Does an Agent Determine Whether a Writer Is Marketable?

Dirty Secret #1: Great Work is always marketable. Why is this? Because there is so little of it. Most of the work that is circulating through the entertainment industry is pretty bad. Consequently, if a great script emerges from a fresh voice that is undiscovered, everyone wants to meet that writer and read the writer's work. This does not mean that a screenplay, even a great screenplay, will sell. What it does mean is that the writer will be invited to meetings with creative executives who have assignments and will probably be considered for writing assignments in the future.

Dirty Secret #2: Writers are categorized: comedy, action-adventure, television, and so forth. They also tend to be categorized by race, sex, and age. What does this have to do with marketability? Agents know the type of assignments that are open at the studios and know when they have a writer that can create the type of work the studio is seeking. Consequently, if an agent should find a young, extremely gifted African-American female writer who has a great writing sample, and the agent knows that the writer will be a good "fit" for many of the assignments, the agent will be anxious to sign that writer. This is what it means to be marketable. This is why an agent decides to add a client to his client list.

What Factors Should I Take into Consideration Before I Sign with an Agent?

The first thing to remember is that you will be signing with the agent, not the agency. This is important to remember. Many writers are in awe with the idea that they will be represented by the "Big Deal" agency. But it is important to realize that it is the agent, or team of agents, who will be representing you. Another important consideration along these lines is the number of writers represented by the agency. If the agency represents a large number of writers, this does not mean that you will not be well represented if your agent is ambitious and aggressive on your behalf. You should take into consideration, however, that as an emerging writer in an agency that already represents many established writers, you may get lost.

One factor to consider is whether it is a packaging agency. An agency that packages, such as the larger agencies, puts together the producer, director, writer, and lead actors in a film, or a "package." This package is presented to the studio when attempting to get the studio to buy the project. As a writer, the packaging concept may represent a plus to you because you allegedly have access to all the other talent represented by the agency. It may also represent a tremendous negative, however, because you are the lowest compensated person in "the package." The compensation for your work may not be negotiated as "aggressively" if Mr. Big Star is in the package and he is demanding an outrageous fee.

Another factor is whether the agency is more interested in making money than in creating a career for you. How will you determine this? Ask other emerging writers who are handled by the agency how often they are contacted by the agency and the type of work they are offered. If they are consistently offered work in areas in which they have no interest, receive little or no comments when they turn in their work, and are not sent out on meetings, then you should decide whether you want to be represented in this manner.

WHAT IF I AM NOT COMFORTABLE WITH THE STYLE OF AN AGENT BUT HE IS THE ONLY ONE WHO WILL SIGN ME?

No one says that you must love your agent. No one says that you necessarily have to like your agent. It is important, however, that you like what your agent can and will do for you. Prior to signing, it is crucial that you discuss your career goals with your agent. By contrast, it is important that your agent let you know what he thinks the direction of your career should be. If both of you do not seem to have a meeting of the minds—as in, he thinks you will have a terrific career in TV, and you think you cannot ever write for television—then you may have a problem.

The other thing to look for is what department your agent is in. For instance, if the agent who wants to sign you is considered a TV agent and you are looking to do nothing but film, then this should be taken into consideration. Needless to say, it is highly probable that your career will be pushed in the direction of a TV career.

If this is the only agent who will sign you, and you're not sure you want to be represented by him, then it might make sense to continue looking for representation. Just because this person is the only one who wants to represent you *at this time* does not mean that you won't find someone you're more compatible with in the future.

How Do I Know if My Agent Is Doing a Good Job?

Do you occasionally hear from your agent? He should call you every so often just to find out what you're doing. This type of attention is determined somewhat by the type of person you are and the type of relationship you have with your agent. If you are the kind of person who likes a great deal of contact (hand-holding), then you need to determine if you are receiving the den-mothering you require. Even if you only want to talk with your agent when you have business to discuss, your agent should call you occasionally just to keep in touch with you (*Note:* Some agents call every one of their clients once a week in an effort to stay in contact with them.)

Are you asked to go to meetings by your agent? The job of an agent is to assist you in getting known as a writer in the entertainment community. There are several ways to accomplish this: Your work must be sent out. You must go to or "take" meetings. You should eventually get hired to write something within the entertainment community, or possibly (but not always probably) you might have a spec script that sells. You should also be asked to attend meetings for the *type of work in which you would like to develop a career.*

The purpose in "taking meetings" is to form a relationship with creative executives who are in a position to hire writers. You attend these meetings because you have ideas for new scripts that you would like to pitch or because you have passionate ideas concerning the ideal director and star of your fabulous script or because the production company has a writing assignment for which you are being considered. Sometimes the meetings are simply "general meetings"—that is, the executives were so amazed by your work that they wanted to meet you. Generally, as long as you can carry a semi-linear conversation and are not too impossible (you don't arrive for the meeting two hours late), you are in the position of being considered for future writing assignments.

Does your agent or agent's assistant return your phone calls? Unfortunately, many clients do not have their phone calls returned by agents. This sad but true situation occurs because agents have a great deal of work on their hands and sometimes have too much to do. This is another area, however, that the emerging writer should inquire about before agreeing to sign with an agent. Ask your friends or other writers you know what you can expect in terms of professional courtesy from this agent and/or agency. You might also ask the agent how he likes to work and what you can expect in terms of returned phone calls. If you are represented by an agent who never returns your phone calls, then you might seriously start wondering if the agent is still representing you.

Are you getting work? Despite every sarcastic remark I have made about agents, let me assure you that being an agent is not easy. It takes an incredible amount of effort to obtain writing assignments for unknown writers. Not only must you assure nervous production executives that the writer is capable of delivering work of the necessary caliber, but you must assure everyone that your inexperienced writer is capable of delivering on time. All of this can take time. For those writers who would like to write for a television show, it can take two years or longer (if ever) to get a staff position. For those writers who would like to obtain assignments to write feature films, it can take even longer. But despite all of the above, you should begin to get work no later than the two-year mark if you are represented by an agent. By that time you and your hardworking agent should have had the opportunity to introduce you to the entertainment community.

WHAT ARE THE CLIENT'S OBLIGATIONS TO THE AGENT?

Many people think that the agent-client relationship is a one-way street, that the client has no obligations or responsibilities. But that isn't how it works.

An agent who is performing well works very hard to obtain writing assignments for his client. It is the client's obligation to "make good" on every assignment she is given. It is also the writer's responsibility to prepare thoroughly for any meeting in which she is being considered for a writing assignment. This is not the time to "wing it"—as was done on all those term papers written the night before they were due in school. It just won't work, and you might become known as a sloppy writer with stale ideas.

It is also the writer's responsibility to report any interest she has generated on her own. If, for instance, the writer meets a producer at a dinner party and the producer asks to see the writer's work, it is the responsibility of the writer to immediately relay this information to her agent.

In the same vein (and it should not be necessary to mention this), a writer should never, never consider negotiating her own deal. In the unusual situation that a writing job happens to fall into a writer's lap without the agent's knowledge, it is the writer's obligation to tell the agent.

Finally, a writer has an obligation to herself to produce at least one new spec script per year. This is important because a writer must continue to develop her craft. It is also important for the writer's career because the writer must continue to expand the number of her supporters within the entertainment industry.

AM I READY FOR AN AGENT?

This question really goes to the heart of the matter. The true question is "Are you ready to work with anyone, be it agent, lawyer, or literary manager?" Very few writers would answer "no" to this question. However, not everyone is ready to write for the entertainment industry right after graduation from college. For some it is a slow process that takes many years before they can create a screenplay that demonstrates a distinctive voice. The point at which the writer becomes ready is when he has two or three screenplays and/or episodic works that demonstrate his ability to deliver work at a consistently high level.

By contrast, some writers are ready to work and are working in the

entertainment industry before they graduate from college. This might
happen when a writer has a family member who is working in the
entertainment industry (nepotism), or has an internship in a production
company and stumbles into a writing opportunity, or simply has an
outrageously fortunate stroke of luck. Mind you, it is very, very rare.
For most writers it is a process that takes time.

IS IT POSSIBLE FOR ME TO BE REPRESENTED BY AN AGENT ON A DEAL BUT NOT BE OR BECOME A CLIENT?

Occasionally (or perhaps I should say frequently) an agent finds a
project created by a partnership in which one partner is a client of
the agency and the other is not a client. In other situations the agent
finds a project that he can package with other existing clients of the
agency. For some reason the agent does not want to sign the previously non-represented writer of the project as a client (perhaps the
writer is not marketable enough, or perhaps the agent does not want
the responsibility of "breaking" the writer's career, or possibly the
agent is representing the project only as a favor to the existing client
of the agency). In these arrangements the agent may "hip-pocket" the
project.

Hip-pocketing is the practice of representing an individual on a single project, with no obligation to continue to represent the individual
after the project has ended. I don't like it. Basically, it gives an agent
the opportunity to "cherry-pick" a project (that is to say, to sell a project, collect the money, and move on) and have no responsibility for
aiding the writer in developing a career.

WHAT DOES A CONTRACT WITH AN AGENT LOOK LIKE AND WHAT DOES IT MEAN?

As stated previously, if you receive an offer of representation from an
agent, the agent or agency generally expects you to sign a contract setting forth the basic terms of the agent-client (or agency-client) relationship.

Basically, there are two kinds of contracts that a writer enters into with an agency: a services contract (in which the agency represents the writer in terms of receiving writing assignments) and a materials contract (in which the agency represents the writer with regard to a specific piece of work, such as a spec script).

EXAMPLE OF AN AGENCY CONTRACT

The following is an example of a generic services contract. The meaning of each unintelligible paragraph is given in italics.

SAMPLE: AGENCY CONTRACT

Big Time Talent Agency
(General Services Contract)

Ladies and Gentlemen:

1. I hereby engage you as my sole and exclusive representative and agent throughout the world for a term of two (2) years commencing with the date here of ___ (the "term"). *(I, the writer, retain you to be the only individual[s] whom I have designated to obtain work for me in the fields set forth in paragraph 2. We agree that there are no other individuals who have been retained to obtain work for me in any of the fields set forth in paragraph 2. The length of this initial contract shall be two years. [Note: Although it is stated that the engagement shall last for two years, most contracts should have a provision for terminating the agent-client relationship before the end of two years if specific circumstances occur.])*

2. Your duties hereunder shall be to use all reasonable efforts to procure the engagement of my services as a writer, composer, editor, author, lyricist, musician, artist, performer, designer, consultant, cameraman, technician, director, producer, associate producer, supervisor, executive, and in any other capacity in the entertainment, literary, and related fields, and to advise, counsel, and direct me in the development of my professional career. The aforesaid duties outside of the continental United States may, at your election, be performed by anyone else appointed by you. *(As my agent[s], you are to use "reasonable" efforts, an amount of effort that is clearly open to subjective interpretation, to obtain work in the designated field. As a writer, this will generally include work as a writer, director, or producer within the entertainment industry. In addition, as my agent[s], you are to advise me as to what steps and/or direction I should take in my career. In reality, I would say that the larger the agency, the smaller the amount of advice or counsel you will receive as a client; however, this is not a hard-and-fast rule and may differ according to the style*

of the individual agent whom you have retained. In addition, this paragraph also clearly states that if your work happens to go outside of the United States, the agent retains the right to appoint someone else to act as an agent. Of course, you will be charged for this "extra" service.)

3. You hereby accept this engagement and agree to perform the services specified herein. I understand that you may render other or similar services to other persons, firms, and corporations. I agree not to engage any other person, firm, or corporation to act for me in the capacity in which I have engaged you. I hereby represent and warrant that I am free to enter into this Agreement and that I do not have and will not have any contract or obligation that will conflict herewith. (*I understand that you will not spend all, most, or a great deal of your time on me unless you are making lots of money on me. By signing this agreement, I recognize that you will or hope to have many other clients from whom you will make money. I guarantee that I have not entered into any other agency contract that would keep you from receiving your entire 10 percent from whatever compensation I may receive.)*

4. I agree to pay you ten (10) percent of the gross compensation earned or received by me for, or in connection with, (i) any contracts for, or engagements of, my services collectively and individually (hereinafter sometimes referred to as "employment") now in existence or entered into or negotiated for during the term, including but not limited to all gross compensation therefrom, and payments thereon, that are earned or received by me or become due or payable to me after the expiration of the term , and (ii) for, or in connection with, all modifications, renewals, additions, substitutions, supplements, replacements, or extensions of or to such contracts and engagements, whether negotiated during or after the term. You shall continue to perform your obligations hereunder after the term with respect to all employment to which you are entitled to your commission as provided in the immediately preceding sentence. "Gross compensation" includes all forms of compensation, money, things of value, or other emoluments, including but not limited to salaries, earnings, fees, royalties, bonuses,

gifts, monetary and non-monetary consideration, securities, and shares of profits or gross reception received by me or any person, firm, or corporation, partnership, joint venture, or other entity now or hereafter owned or controlled by me (hereinafter "my firm") or in which I may have any right, title, or interest, on my behalf, from such contracts or engagements and modifications, renewals, additions, substitutions, supplements, replacements, and extensions of or to such contracts or engagements, whether or nor procured by you or by anyone else, as well as from any form of advertising or commercial tie-ups using my name, likeness, or voice. *(I agree to pay you 10 percent of whatever "gross compensation" I make for anything that I enter into during the time you are my agent. Even if you are no longer my agent, I agree to pay you 10 percent of whatever any residual, bonus, addition, renewal, or supplement I receive on any employment within the entertainment industry that I entered, that was in existence, or that was negotiated for during the time you were my agent. Even if I become a corporation, because my accountant might advise me that it is more advantageous to do so, or if I become a production company, because I am so fortunate that I receive this kind of deal with a studio, I will still be obligated to pay you 10 percent of whatever "gross compensation" I receive. The term "gross compensation" can mean money, before taxes and other deductions have been taken out, or any stock or securities, land, or anything I receive in terms of compensation for my employment.)*

5. No breach or failure by you to perform the terms hereof, which breach or failure would otherwise be deemed a material breach of this Agreement, shall be considered as such unless within twenty (20) days after I acquire knowledge of such breach or failure, or of facts sufficient to put me on notice thereof, I serve written notice upon you of such breach or failure and you do not cure said breach or failure within a period of ten (10) days after your receipt of the notice. *(If you happen to do something that would be considered a violation of this contract, such as fail to turn over a check to me that has been paid by someone who has employed me, and I find you doing*

this, even though it could be considered a breach of this agree-
ment, I must give you written notice within twenty days after
the time I discover this "mistake" of yours, and then give you
ten days to correct this mistake. If you do not correct your
mistake within ten days, then I may consider it a breach of
this contract.)

6. Your commissions under this Agreement shall be payable as
and when gross compensation is received by you or me, my
firm, or any other person or entity on my behalf. From all
gross compensation subject to this Agreement that you may
receive you have the right to deduct the amount of any and all
commissions that are due and payable to you hereunder or
under any other representation agreement between you and
me. With respect to gross compensation subject to this
Agreement that is paid directly to me, my firm, or any other
person or entity on my behalf, an amount equal to said commission shall be deemed to be received and held by me or
them in trust for you, and your commission thereon shall be
paid to you promptly after receipt by me or them of such gross
compensation. (*As my agent, you're to be paid immediately*
when I receive any gross compensation. If my personal man-
ager or I receive the money, then your fees of 10 percent are to
be held by me or my representatives in trust for you and are to
be promptly paid to you. If you receive the gross compensa-
tion, then you are allowed to deduct your 10 percent commis-
sion as soon as you receive the money. Note: Don't laugh.
Agents tend to put in a great deal of effort to obtain work for
a client. In the beginning of the agent-client relationship, the
ratio of agent hours to dollars can resemble an inverted pyra-
mid or be something of the relationship of ten to one. If the
agent is allowed to deduct his fee immediately, you should
think of it as the price of doing business.)

7. If I'm not offered employment that is subject to this
Agreement from a responsible employer with respect to my
services covered by this Agreement during any period in excess
of four (4) consecutive months during the term, during all of
which time I am ready, able, and willing to accept employment, either party hereto shall have the right to terminate this

Agreement by a notice in writing sent to the last known address of the other party by registered mail; provided, however, that such right shall be deemed waived by me and any exercise thereof by me shall be ineffective if after the expiration of any such four- (4-) month period and prior to the time of your receipt of the notice I receive an offer for employment by a responsible employer; and provided further that such termination shall not affect your rights or my obligations under Paragraphs 4 and 5 of this Agreement. *(If I, the writer, am not offered employment as a writer, director, or producer in any period of time in excess of four months, and I am capable of doing work during this period of time, then either you or I can end our agency-client relationship. However, to end the relationship one of us must send the other a letter by registered mail. In addition, if prior to the point that I send or receive the registered letter I am offered employment, then this agency-client agreement may not be ended. The point of this paragraph is to provide an "escape clause" that does not bind either party to the contract for two years in the event that the agency-client relationship is not going well. Not going well may mean that the agent and client do not like each other or that one party determines the other party has career plans that are other than were originally stated. For those of you who are entering into contracts in states that do not regulate the agent-client relationships, you should watch for contract terms (as in length of the contract) that do not allow an escape from the contract before the end of its term. Try to negotiate some situations that will allow you to terminate the relationship in under two years, or you may find yourself in an agency-client relationship that is detrimental to your career. This works for the agent also, of course, because he may find that you are a difficult client to obtain work for. This rarely happens as a practical reality because it takes a great deal of time to get a writer's career off the ground, and the writer may go through a dry period where no work is offered. In this situation the writer would be reluctant to break the relationship with the agent because the writer would find it difficult to obtain representation if he is not obtaining employment.)*

Insofar as this Agreement refers to any employment subject to the jurisdiction of the State of California, controversies arising between us under the Labor Code of the State of California and the rules and regulations for the enforcement thereof shall be referred to the Labor Commissioner of the State of California, as provided in Section 1700.44 of said Labor Code, except to the extent that the laws of the State of California now or hereafter in force may permit the reference of any such controversy to any other person or group of persons. (*In any contract in a state that regulates the agency-client relationship, there should be a provision that sets forth the laws that regulate the relationship. This paragraph sets forth the laws (called statutes) that regulate the agency-client relationship within the State of California.*)

8. This document, together with any forms of agency agreement you and I are required to execute by any guild or union having jurisdiction over my services covered by this Agreement, sets forth the entire agreement between us with respect to the fields of endeavor recited in Paragraph 1 of this Agreement. If you become a member of the WGA, then Rider W to the WGA Artists' Managers Agreement will supersede anything that I have written in this agreement. This Agreement shall not become effective until accepted and executed by you. I hereby represent and warrant in executing this Agreement that I have not relied on any statements, promises, representations, or inducements except as specifically set forth herein. This Agreement may not be changed, modified, waived, or discharged in whole or in part except by an instrument in writing signed by you and me; provided further that any substantial changes in this Agreement must first be approved by the California Labor Commissioner unless said changes operate to my advantage. This Agreement shall inure to the benefit of and be binding upon you and myself and your and my respective heirs, distributees, executors, administrators, and assigns, and you shall have the right to assign this Agreement to any successor entity or to any person, corporation, partnership, or other firm pursuant to any reorganization, consolidation, combination, or merger. Should any provision of this

Agreement be void or unenforceable for any reason, such provision shall he deemed omitted, and this Agreement with such provision omitted shall remain in full force and effect. *(The most important provisions in this paragraph are that this agreement is to be superseded by any guild contract, such as a Rider W of the Artists' Managers Basic Agreement [see below] in the situation in which the writer-client is a member of the WGA; that nothing that has been said between the writer and the agent which is not written in this document is to be considered part of the agreement; that the agency-client relationship that is written in this document cannot be changed unless those changes are written and signed by both parties; and that if the agency should merge with another agency or change its structure, the agency has the right to assign [give] your contract to the successor agency.)*

Very truly yours,

Aspiring Writer

Agreed to and Accepted:

This Talent Agency is licensed by the Labor Commissioner of the State of ___. The form of this contract was approved by the State Labor Commissioner on July 1, 1994. *(This agency has taken the time both to be licensed and to have this contract reviewed by the state labor commission. In California and those states in which the labor commissioner controls the agent-client relationship, this means that the labor commissioner has designated that this contract is not oppressive or unfair to the writer-client.)*

IF I AM A MEMBER OF THE WGA, HOW WILL MY AGENCY-CLIENT AGREEMENT CHANGE (OR WHAT IS RIDER W)?

If you're a member of the Writers Guild of America, your agency contract will be superseded by the provisions of Rider W of the Artists' Managers Basic Agreement. So that you may understand Rider W, the following are responses to questions concerning this agreement.

What Is Rider W to the Writers Guild of America's Artists' Managers Basic Agreement?

Rider W is a prenegotiated set of terms that the WGA has negotiated as part of its Artists' Managers Basic Agreement. What is meant by prenegotiated is that the WGA has negotiated the terms of the agency-client contract between WGA members and signatories to the WGA and has set forth certain terms and provisions that must be included in every contract between WGA members and agency signatories. For WGA members signing with signatory agencies, the good news is that the agency-client contract negotiated by the WGA is very advantageous to the writer-client.

If I Am Not a Member of the WGA, Does It Apply to Me?

Rider W protects only WGA members. In addition, it has control over only those agencies that are signatories (that is, have signed or agreed to abide by the stipulations) of the 1976 Artists' Manager Basic Agreement). However, most reputable agencies representing writers in the radio, television, and motion picture areas are signatories. (If you want to know whether an agency is a signatory, the status of a particular agency can be verified by calling the guild. In addition, the WGA will provide anyone with a complete and current list of agents and agencies that have agreed to abide by Rider W and a copy of Rider W. Please note, however, that some very powerful agencies that are signatories have chosen not to be listed on the Rider W list in an effort not to be inundated with scripts. At the end of the book is a partial list of agencies representing writers who have agreed to abide by the terms and conditions of the WGA.)

However, Rider W provides protection only to WGA members who are rendering services in radio, television, and motion picture areas. Writers who are working in book publishing and dramatic stage areas are not covered. For those writers who are working in areas not covered by Rider W, it should be noted that many agency contracts are negotiable; this means if you are not covered by Rider W and do not like the terms of the agreement with your agency, it is possible for you to have portions of Rider W incorporated in your agency contract.

What Is the Length of Agency-Writer Agreements under Rider W?

The maximum term of any writer's agency agreement is two years for either services or materials contracts. At the end of the two years you must sign another agreement for representation. For those of you who read the daily or weekly entertainment newspapers known as "the trades" *(The Hollywood Reporter, Daily Variety, Weekly Variety),* the term "re-upped" (as in Mr. Big-Time Writer re-upped with X agency) means that the individual has agreed to sign with the agency for another term of representation. By contrast, the phrase "ankled" (as in Ms. Big-Star "ankled" the agency) denotes that the individual has chosen not to continue with the agency for representation.

Under Rider W the writer is given a break during the initial period of representation (the first two years): The writer may terminate the agreement for services and/or materials at any time within eighteen months of the inception of the agreement without cause, and the termination is effective at the expiration of the eighteen-month period.

In addition, if an agent or agency is unable to sell the writer's spec screenplay or other episodic work within one year of submission to the agent, the writer or agent may decide not to continue representing the work.

Sixty Ways to Leave Your Agent

In addition to limiting the maximum length of the agent-client or agency-client term, Rider W provides the following methods by which a writer may leave the agency before the end of the agreement's term:

I. Ninety-day clause—termination of services agreement: During any ninety-day period in which the agent is unable to obtain offers or employment for work in which the writer would receive at least $30,344 in fields in which the agent is authorized to represent him, the writer may terminate the agreement. The ninety-day termination also applies to periods in which the writer does not receive a "bona fide and appropriate" offer of employment that guarantees the writer in the aggregate $30,344. "Bona fide and appropriate" is defined by the WGA as a combination of prestige, appropriateness, and position of the writer in the market.

II. The writer may terminate the agency-client relationship at any time if the agent:

A. materially breaches any of his fiduciary obligations to the writer (that is, he fails to hold on to the writer's money, breaches a confidence, and so forth);

B. during a strike, obtains employment or sells any literary material to a producer or any other person with whom the WGA is on strike;

C. represents a writer who has been denied membership in the WGA or who has had his membership revoked due to the writer's performing acts that are prejudicial to the welfare of the WGA;

D. no longer subscribes to the WGA Basic Agreement; that is, he does not agree to Rider W;

E. can only obtain employment for the writer on WGA minimum terms in any six-month period;

F. negotiates or approves on behalf of the writer an employment agreement or contract of sale of materials that violates the WGA Minimum Basic Agreement or a WGA working rule, unless the writer is aware of the violation and insists that the contract be negotiated.

Under Rider W, How Much Does My Agent Get Paid?

As in non–Rider W agency-client contracts, an agent's payment or "commission" is calculated on the writer's gross compensation. This means that an agent will take 10 percent of your money before taxes and other necessary deductions are subtracted. The agent cannot collect a commission on "back-end" payments (such as residuals, passive rights, and supplemental markets) unless the back-end payments are in excess of the WGA minimum, and such commissions cannot reduce the writer's compensation to a sum less than the WGA minimum.

Agency commissions on any one deal may not exceed 10 percent (for domestic) or 15 percent (for foreign) unless the writer failed to disclose the existence of a prior relationship with an agent who may assert a claim against the writer (that is, if the writer fails to tell the agent that he was already represented by someone else) or, after signing agency contracts, the writer incurs an obligation to pay a commission to another without the consent of the agent (such as allowing another agent to obtain work for him and failing to mention to the agent that he is represented by someone else).

Where the agent represents both the writer and the packager (that is, the owner or the producer) of a particular television show, the agent cannot take a packaging fee from the writer for compensation received with respect to the television package program. This is in contrast to non–Rider W agreements, in which the agent may take a commission on packaging.

At the beginning of representation, the writer must designate whether existing deals are commissionable by the agent in the future. At the end of representation, the writer is obligated to pay a commission on contracts of employment procured by his former agent and on any options that have been picked up. However, the former agent will not be entitled to commissions on increased compensation or improvements in the employment agreement negotiated after the termination of the representation agreement. At the conclusion of the agency agreement, the writer may request within thirty days a list of all engagements entered into during the term of the agreement or that are in negotiation at the time of expiration. If the writer objects to the agent's receiving a commission on any such engagement, the writer must make his objection within thirty days.

If I Am Represented by Two Agents from the Same Agency, Who Is Responsible for My Career?

In order to assure that those agents responsible for causing a writer to sign with a particular agency will continue to service the writer, the agency may designate up to two persons who will be active in the operation of the agency and who will be available generally to render services to the writer at the writer's request. If the agency has more than 150 employees, the agency may designate one more person who will be responsible for the client. If all persons designated cease to be active in the agency, the agency must notify the writer, and the writer will have the right to terminate the agency agreement. What generally happens is that larger agencies (those with more than 150 employees) have junior agents who are the point persons, the ones who answer the writers' questions and keep the writers in touch with the agency, while more senior persons are responsible for making the phone calls and submissions that expose the writers to the entertainment community.

What if My Agent Represents Me and the Producer Who Wants to Buy My Material (or What Do We Do if There Is a Clear Conflict of Interest)?

In the world of agency representation, it happens many times that an agent represents not only the writer on a project but also the producer. In many circles this is known as a "conflict of interest." In fact, as stated above under "packaging," many times an agent purposely takes on a writer-client specifically because the agent knows the agent can "package" the client. Under Rider W, however, if the agent represents a producer or other individual who may be the purchaser of the writer's services, the agent must inform the writer of the agent's commission, profit participation, or other financial interest in the production, project, sale, literary material show, package, or services involved prior to making a commitment for the writer. After the writer learns of the agent's interest, he may represent himself or obtain representation by another agent or attorney.

Things That Your Agent May Not Want to Do for You

Occasionally it happens that a studio, executive, or production that has hired the writer or purchased the writer's screenplay does not pay the writer. In these situations some agents may not want to intervene on behalf of the writer because the agent does not want to damage his relationship with the non-paying entity (that is, the studio, the executive, or the individual). Consequently, it may become necessary to hire an attorney in order to convince the non-paying party that it is in his best interests to pay the writer.

If it is necessary for a writer to engage an attorney to collect monies due from an employer or purchaser, Rider W states that the agent's commission will be based on the "net sum" received after deducting the writer's legal expenses. For example, if the writer receives $100,000 for work he has done and the agent's usual commission is 10 percent, or $10,000, the agent's commission in these situations would be based on 10 percent of the writer's fee minus attorney fees (that is, 10 percent of the sum remaining after the attorney fees have been deducted).

Do I Still Have an Agent if My Agent's Agency Dissolves?

Sometimes an agency prospers and becomes a megaforce, such as Creative Artists Agencies (CAA). Sometimes two agencies consolidate and become a powerhouse, such as United Talent Agency (UTA). Sometimes, despite the greatest of agents and the best of clients, an agency closes its doors and dissolves, such as InterTalent.

When an agency is dissolved or sells its assets, one valuable item it may have is its contract with Jane Q. Superstar Writer. In many situations an agencyless agent would be tempted to bring his clients to a new agency and to assign Jane Q. Superstar Writer's contract to the agency. Rider W provides, however, that the agency agreement existing between the agent and the writer may not be assigned without the writer's consent. (Note: The exception to this rule takes place when the original agent incorporates. In this situation an agent is able to assign the contract from himself as an agent to himself as an incorporated entity [as in from J. Q. Agent to J. Q. Agent, Inc.). By contrast, if a writer chooses to follow his agent, agencyless or not, Rider W will not prevent the writer from doing so. To answer the above question: If the agency dissolves, you may still have your agent if that agent plans to stay in business.

How Does My Agent Receive My Money?

As stated previously, the standard commission that an agent receives is 10 percent. The standard position is that an agent is paid first—that is, before the writer. This occurs in the following way: When a writer is paid the fees for employment or for the sale of a screenplay, the check almost never goes directly to the writer unless he is not represented by an agent or agency. If the writer is represented by an agent or agency, the check goes to the agent or agency; the agency then deducts 10 percent and issues a check to the writer for the fees minus the 10 percent.

To be able to do this, Rider W provides that an agent obtain written authority from the writer to accept money on his behalf. Rider W also provides that if the agent collects money on behalf of the writer, the agent or agency must make faithful accountings and prompt payments to the writer of his compensation, less any agency commissions. Most agencies turn around money in two days. In addition, the agent or agency cannot commingle the client's money with the agency money.

6

Lawyers: What Do They Mean When They Say That They Are Looking for Someone with Passion?

WHY A LAWYER?

The question might more properly be phrased "Is there any time that one shouldn't have a lawyer?" The answer to the question, though apparently self-serving, is that the only time you do not need to have a lawyer is when you really don't have any business and aren't making any money in the entertainment industry.

If you retained anything from the discussion in the introduction, it should have been the terms "business" or "industry." What makes entertainment an industry is the amount of money that is being passed around. The tremendous sums being exchanged means that the potential to be abused or "taken advantage of" or, if you prefer, "screwed" is great. Unfortunately, this means that sooner or later you will need to have someone representing you in a manner that one can only term as "legal."

Entertainment lawyers are different from other lawyers because entertainment law is the farthest outpost in the practice of law.

However, given the enormous increase in entertainment and entertainment-related products (multimedia and interactive), it appears that some formerly very white shoe (conservative) law firms are now creating or expanding to include entertainment departments or practices. The reason, of course, is that where the money is, there are lawyers.

The role of an entertainment lawyer is multifaceted. A lawyer is generally not able merely to sit back and prepare the contracts for a client. The reality is that the lawyer is often called upon by the client to provide a variety of tasks, from reviewing contracts to helping the client obtain agency representation. Like an agent or manager, the lawyer is often required to provide a client with contacts. This may mean introducing the client to agents who might be interested in the client's work. It may mean educating the client as to who might be interested in the client's work. It also may mean introducing the client to some of the attorney's other clients.

Although this last statement creates that well-known phrase "conflict of interest," many clients specifically engage an attorney because they want to be in business with the attorney's other clients. When this is the situation, the attorney must be careful to inform the client of the risks of two individuals being represented by the same attorney. The reality is, however, that many clients really do not care about the "conflict" issues and prefer to pursue the possibility of getting into proximity with people who could significantly advance their careers. As one individual recently stated at an entertainment legal conference, "The whole business is one big conflict."

Some clients have a very close relationship with their attorneys because they use them to function in a manner that is close to that of a manager. In these situations the clients rely on their attorneys to inform them not only concerning business functions but concerning the next step they should take in their careers. In this vein, I have known attorneys who have read proposed screenplays to ensure that the offered role is correct for their client, and I have also known attorneys who have reviewed a writer-client's work to ensure that it was comparable to the caliber of the writer's previous work.

Given the crossover role of an entertainment attorney's work, it occasionally happens that an attorney becomes an agent or manager. Attorneys have also become very successful producers. (Arnold Kopelson and Gary Goldstein are two who come to mind, but that's another story.) Simply stated, after concerning themselves with crossing the i's and dotting the t's, it occasionally occurs to some of these creative people that being an agent, manager, and/or producer may be a whole lot more fun than being an attorney. In addition to getting involved in the creative side of a career, they also rid themselves of the liabilities that ensue when things do not go as planned and also the potential of malpractice. But I digress. Occasionally it also happens that clients decide they no longer need anyone on "their team" other than an attorney. This can occur at the time a client reaches a point in his career when it seems unnecessary to require the services of an agent or manager or when a client has remained completely responsible for his career for so long that an agent or manager was never necessary or desired.

How Do Emerging Writers Find an Entertainment Attorney?

This is not as easy as it may seem. Estimates are that in major cities there is one attorney for every one hundred people. However, the number of attorneys who are practicing entertainment law with any type of regularity is very small. The problem with finding an attorney who is knowledgeable in this area is that there are primarily two major areas where entertainment law is practiced: Los Angeles and New York. Since Florida is fast emerging as a "hot" film industry and Tennessee has a tremendous country music scene, I presume there are qualified entertainment attorneys in these areas.

"Qualified" has a specific meaning. It is one thing for an attorney to know the area of the law and to have the capacity to negotiate a client's contract or to review a client's potential legal problems with some degree of competence. It is another thing to be able to put your client in business with other people in the entertainment industry or to have the capacity to jump-start a client's career. Is it necessary to have an attorney who can put you in business with other individuals? No. However, as a client, you must understand what role your attorney will perform for you.

That being said, there are a few methods you can use to contact an entertainment attorney. One is the tried-and-true method that I suggest in every area of this chapter, which is to ask your other friends for rec-ommendations. If you do not have friends who are currently working with an attorney, I suggest that you contact the referral service of the local bar association (for example, the Los Angeles County Bar Association) and ask to be referred to an attorney who practices enter-tainment law. The Beverly Hills Bar Association and the Los Angeles County Bar are the two primary organizations in Los Angeles to which entertainment attorneys belong.

In addition, many cities have organizations that have a referral panel of attorneys who have agreed to work with artists on either a pro bono (free) basis or for a sliding scale according to what the client can afford. There is, for example, California Lawyers for the Arts in San Francisco and Los Angeles, Volunteer Lawyers for the Arts in New York, and Texas Accountants and Lawyers for the Arts in Houston. Most of these organizations also offer inexpensive but very informative legal and entertainment seminars on topics ranging from copyright to how to find a manager. (A list of these organizations and their addresses is included at the end of the book.)

WHAT FACTORS SHOULD I CONSIDER BEFORE AGREEING TO HAVE AN ATTORNEY REPRESENT ME?

Factor Number 1: What is it that you want the attorney to do for you? If you are looking for someone to review your contracts and negotiate your deals, it is prudent to ask how much experience the attorney has in this area. If you are truly seeking an attorney-manager, then it is a good idea to ask the attorney if he has ever performed this service for a client and if he feels comfortable performing this role.

Factor Number 2: Do you want to get into business with this attor-ney as your attorney, or are you actually attempting to get into busi-ness with this attorney's other clients? This is a rather sophisticated question to ask yourself because you may not really know who the attorney's other clients are. If you believe, however, that your potential attorney represents Ms. Fabulous Director and you are counting on representation from this attorney as the fastest road to get your work to Ms. Fabulous Director, it is important for you to know that this may not be the way the attorney chooses to play ball. Many attorneys feel that this type of service might go straight into the gray area known as an "ethical dilemma" and might border on another gray area known as "conflict of interest" (especially if business does transpire between you and Ms. Fabulous Director).

Factor Number 3: Is the big-time attorney going to be representing you, or are you actually going to be represented by a junior associate? Here is the ruse: You are lured into bringing your work to the big-time attorney with the idea that you will be represented by the force, power, and connections that have represented all the "big names" in "the Industry," but you subsequently find yourself represented by a junior associate. Hmmmm. Well, truthfully, this is the way most work is done within the industry even if you are describing agency representation. You must determine whether this scenario fits in with the manner in which you choose to be represented.

Factor Number 4: Are you comfortable with the style of this attorney? Some attorneys operate on the "scorched earth policy"—they will take no prisoners. Some attorneys operate as the great conciliators, making sure that everyone comes away from the table satisfied. It is important for you to make a decision as to the style of representation with which you are comfortable. It is important to remember that the entertainment industry is a small world. If you ruin someone in a deal (and, truthfully, as an emerging writer the chances of this happening are slim to none), you may find yourself at a later date being on the other side of the deal when you require the good graces of this individual. Whatever style of representation you choose, it is important for you to be with someone you trust.

Factor Number 5: Do you truly need representation at this time? Funny as this question may seem, many individuals decide to retain the services of an attorney light-years before they really have anything for the attorney to do. This is partially out of vanity, because they want to appear to have someone "on their team." It is important to understand that although many attorneys will perform the attorney-manager functions described above, many attorneys are not comfortable (or are not capable) of performing this function.

Factor Number 6: Can you afford not to have representation at this time? One thing you should understand is that agents do not generally negotiate a contract any further than what is known as "the deal points" (the money, the credit, the time for the writing to take place). The job of reviewing "the fine print"— those never-will-happen contingencies such as who will pay the lawyers if Mr. Producer gets sued for copyright infringement because of your screenplay (and you might be surprised by the answer to that question)—are not generally covered by agents. Another situation that is not generally covered by agents is who will rattle a saber if the producer does not pay you for your work. In this scenario one tends to find the agent running for cover because he does not want to risk ruining his relationship with the producer that has taken so long to build. Consequently, you will need to employ an attorney.

Your should probably employ an attorney around the time that you receive your first contract. At this time you can begin to build a relationship with those individuals who may be with you for the rest of your career. And trust me: As your writing fees grow, so will your need to have an attorney at your side because you will be speaking about the individual who will be participating in an ever-enlarging portion of your compensation, the compensation you receive after your work is done known as back-end compensation.

How Do I Know if My Attorney Is Fulfilling His Obligations to Me?

Is your work getting done? As obvious as this may seem, it is important that your contracts be negotiated and that the things you ask your attorney to do be done in a reasonable amount of time. If this is not achieved, life can get difficult. In addition, it is important that your attorney give you information concerning the direction he is going on your behalf and the results of the work he has done on your behalf. If you have requested that your attorney attempt to put you in business with other individuals who can advance your career (agents and managers, for example), then it is important that your attorney give you a regular accounting of the individuals he has contacted on your behalf.

Does your attorney or attorney's assistant return your phone calls? One of the primary ways that clients become dissatisfied with attorneys is the area I term "lack of communication." Perhaps this might more aptly be called too little or no communication, but it is probably the area in which attorneys receive the most criticism. The problem may be described as follows: Attorneys field a generous amount of phone calls on a daily basis. In addition to performing their work functions, such as reviewing contracts, structuring deals, reading and answering letters, and reviewing legal problems and advising clients concerning them (all of which takes an enormous amount of time), attorneys have an obligation to keep clients informed with regard to the progress of their work. If an attorney has a large client base, with active legal problems, it is difficult to do. It is particularly difficult if the attorney has clients who do the following: call every day just to chat, believe they know more than the attorney concerning how to handle their particular legal problems, believe things should move at lightning speed when the reality is much slower, take it upon themselves to negotiate their own contracts (and inform the attorney of this after the contract has been negotiated), and believe it is the attorney's responsibility to get them out of the holes they have dug. (*Note:* This is a clear reason to drop a client.)

An attorney does have an obligation, however, to communicate with clients on a regular basis, particularly if the attorney is working on a legal matter for the client that is "active." How "regular basis" is defined is something that must be negotiated for every attorney-client relationship, but generally it means that a client's question, query, or phone call should receive a response somewhere between two hours and two days after it is received. It is recommended that the return call come closer to the two-hour side of things, but contingencies do exist where it is impossible for the attorney to respond this quickly. If you feel comfortable in the relationship and feel that your attorney responds to your inquiries and questions within a reasonable amount of time, then your relationship with your attorney is probably healthy.

Note to Eager-Beaver Clients Who Want to Talk to Their Attorney for No Particular Reason at All: Most attorneys work six- to seven-day weeks, averaging twelve- to eighteen-hour days. Obviously, this includes weekends and hours that extend long after 6 P.M. There are those attorneys who would like to have a personal life that include beings other than a cat (if the attorney is lucky). Accordingly, try not to call the attorney's phone service at 10 P.M. on a Sunday night to leave an "urgent–must-return" message unless you clearly have a problem that cannot wait until the morning. Try not to disturb your attorney's first vacation in five years unless your problem is so important that your work will be seriously compromised if your particular attorney does not handle it. And try not to disturb your attorney's honeymoon (unfortunately, this is done frequently) unless your problem is so overwhelming that the sky will fall.

HOW DO ATTORNEYS GET PAID?

Attorneys are usually paid with money. However, this question really goes to the arrangements the attorneys make with their clients in terms of how and when the money is paid.

Hourly Basis: Most attorneys are paid on an hourly basis. The range for these hourly services in a large metropolitan area can be from $175 to $600 per hour. Attorneys tend to charge in increments of a quarter of an hour or a tenth of an hour. This means that if you speak with your attorney for ten minutes, you will be charged for one-fourth of an hour if your attorney charges on a quarterly-hour basis. For example, if your attorney charges $200 per hour and you are charged .25, you will owe your attorney $50.00. Needless to say, the hourly basis of payment is subject to a great deal of criticism because it can get costly pretty quickly, especially if you require services that are labor intensive. Some attorneys will lower the hourly rate if the client is poor, if the cause is especially worthy (such as the client having a very bright future), or if the client can provide the attorney with a large and consistent amount of business. (This is not you; what we are talking about here is the client that is a corporation or an insurance company.) However, depending on the direction in which the attorney is taking his practice, you may be able to negotiate with the attorney to change the normal billing method from the per-hour basis.

Flat Fee Basis: In this situation the attorney agrees to do all the client's work on a particular project for one fee instead of on an hourly basis. This can work to the client's advantage especially if the work requires a great deal of time and the client has negotiated a low fee. However, an experienced attorney will generally negotiate a high enough fee to compensate him adequately if the project should take a great deal of time.

Percentage Basis: A good portion of the attorneys working in the entertainment industry work for a client in exchange for 5 percent to 10 percent of the client's gross compensation. This is similar to an agent because the attorney takes a hit in the early part of the client's career by working for practically nothing while banking on the fact that the payoff will come later in the client's career. Most (but not all) attorneys, though, do not get involved in a client's career on a percentage basis until the client is in the league of regularly receiving large contracts. The reason is that a percentage of nothing is nothing.

Contingency Fee Arrangement: In this arrangement the attorney agrees to receive compensation for services rendered only if he wins the case. If he wins the case, the attorney will take a portion of the money awarded to the client in the range of 20 percent to 40 percent of the overall award. The attorney banks on the fact that damages will be awarded and hopes to receive an award that will adequately compensate for his services. If the client is awarded $3,000,000, the attorney might receive between $600,000 and $1,200,00 for services rendered, a not inconsiderable amount. If the client is awarded nothing, the attorney receives nothing for his services, but he might have made arrangements to have the client pay for the costs associated with filing the lawsuit, such as copying documents, jury fees, and so forth.

The contingency fee arrangement tends to arise only in personal injury cases and cases involving litigation where there is the possibility of large amounts of money being awarded to the client. Accordingly, this situation does not generally arise in the context of entertainment work unless you are run over by your computer. (Just kidding.)

WHAT ARE THE CLIENT'S OBLIGATIONS TO THE ATTORNEY?

It is a given that all clients lie, but we are concerned here with what clients lie about and how much they lie. It is a good idea for a client not to lie to his attorney concerning things the attorney is attempting to negotiate because it is much more difficult to negotiate aggressively on a client's behalf when the lie is discovered (when the attorney discovers, for example, that the writer has already agreed to work for an amount that is half the usual rate). It is also a good idea for a client to inform his attorney of an impending contract before signing it. It is also a wise idea for the client to keep his attorney informed of general career progress so that he may coordinate everything with agents, managers, accountants, and so forth. In this way the attorney will not appear to be behaving like a loose cannon.

ATTORNEY FEE AGREEMENT

You may be wondering what a contract with an attorney looks like. This is one arrangement in Hollywood that is not usually done with a handshake. Most states require that both parties enter into an attorney-client arrangement once it appears that the client will pay more than $1,000 in fees to the attorney. The following is a typical attorney-client fee agreement. The italicized remarks will assist your overall understanding.

SAMPLE: ATTORNEY FEE AGREEMENT

Ladies and Gentlemen:

We are very pleased that you have selected our law firm to represent you. We will diligently and professionally represent you and will at all times strive to achieve the most favorable result, although we obviously cannot make any representation as to the success of these efforts. The purpose of this letter is to set forth the basis on which the firm charges for legal services and related matters. *(The above statement is the attorneys' CYA [Cover Your A—] statement. In defense of my brethren, I will say that as many times as an attorney reminds his clients that one cannot ever predict the outcome of the work he is doing for them, they do not listen. Everyone has heard too many verdicts that range to the millions, and everyone thinks their particular pot of gold is waiting for them just around the corner.)*

In handling entertainment and corporate matters our charges in the first instance are based on hours worked. This firm's hourly charges are currently $___ to $___ per hour for name partners, $ to $___ per hour for other attorneys, and $___per hour for paralegal services. If you require our services in other areas in which we practice, rates for those services would be discussed and worked out at the time the services are required. You will be informed prior to any increase in hourly rates. The applicable hourly billing rates are those in effect at the time of the rendition of services. *(As stated previously, the hourly method of billing is the primary method of compensating attorneys for work. The current range in prices in a large metropolitan area is about $175 for a junior attorney in his first years of practice to $600 per hour for an attorney who has been practicing for many years and is very, very experienced in a given field.)*

Although hourly billing rates are a primary factor in determining the amount of our fees, we reserve the right, with respect to any particular matter, to bill you on a reasonable fee basis determined not only on hourly rates but also on the difficulty and importance of the matter and the results achieved. In those instances where we bill you on the "reasonable fee" basis, we will at your request inform you of all factors used to compute the fee. *(Once in a blue moon an attorney is able to achieve a fabulous result for a client with very little effort. Usually this is based on a combination of efforts, due mostly to luck, the skill of the attorney, and some unforeseen event that weighs heavily in the favor of the client. When this happens, an attorney will want—and, might I add, deserve—to be compensated in a manner that may or may not be reflected in an hourly fee, such as $1,000 not covering all the attorney's efforts when he has sold a script for $750,000. This is when the client will be billed according to the "reasonable fee" basis.)*

We will endeavor to keep your legal fees down by having various tasks handled by professionals with lower billing rates, depending on the demands of the individual task. *(Many firms try to have non-attorneys, called paralegals, perform a variety of tasks for the client in situations in which the work being done is routine and does not require the expertise (or expense) of the attorney. This is beneficial to the client because it helps to keep the overall cost down.)*

Additionally, when we do the production work on a picture or television programs, we may charge a flat fee (rather than an hourly fee), subject to prior discussion and agreement with you. *(If the attorney chooses to bill a client on a flat-fee basis, as explained above, something close to the previous statement will be inserted in the fee agreement rather than the information concerning the hourly fee basis.)*

Additionally, we charge you for cost disbursements and related overhead costs made on your behalf for items such as long distance phone, fax, and messenger. We also impose finance charges of .0833 percent per month, or 10 percent per year, on any unpaid balances that are not timely paid, that is, within thirty (30) days of the last statement issued. All payments received shall be applied first to finance charges, next to disbursements, and finally to fees. Within each of these three categories, payments shall be applied to the oldest balance first. *(Here is a shock. Many people do not realize that attorneys are paid in two categories: for the attorney's services [fees] and for the costs. Costs are for the above-listed items: faxing, messenger, the cost of filing a docu-*

ment with the court, parking, long distance telephone calls, and anything the attorney must pay for out of pocket. Fees are for the hours of service that the attorney must put in to perform the services the client desires. Most people do not realize that all attorneys charge for costs no matter what the outcome of the service performed by the attorney. This means that when you see those advertisements on television in which attorneys advertise "We don't get paid unless you do," what you may not be able to read in the small print is that the attorney is still going to ask you to pay the "costs" of the services.)

You have agreed to pay this firm a retainer in the amount of $___, payable concurrently with your execution of this letter. The amount of this retainer shall be applied against our legal fees and costs as they are incurred on your behalf. *(Most attorneys ask the client to give the attorney money up front, called a retainer, before the attorney's services begin. This is to avoid the nightmare of trying to obtain payment from a client who is not happy with the result.)*

If any dispute arises between us with respect to any statement for fees and/or costs, either you or we shall have the right to require that the dispute be initially submitted to arbitration (which shall be binding arbitration) in ___ County in accordance with the rules of the State Bar of ___, before a single arbitrator selected in accordance with those rules or the rules of any local Bar Association within ___ County which is operating under the auspices of the State Bar or, if none, in accordance with the arbitration laws of ___. The arbitrator shall have the discretion to order that the cost of arbitration including the arbitrator's fees, or other costs, and attorney fees shall be borne by the losing party. *(All attorneys know how cumbersome the legal system is, especially when it comes to convincing a jury to decide that an attorney deserves fees to be paid at all, much less what he has charged. Accordingly, most will decide to forgo going to trial and engage in what is known as alternative dispute resolution (ADR). The most popular form of ADR is what is known as arbitration, which is basically an informal trial that takes place before one person, called an arbitrator rather than a judge. The beauty of this system is that it is cheap, quick, and much easier on the men-*

tal health than going to trial. I recommend it for all circumstances in which it appears that one must resolve differences through "the legal system.")

Either you or we may terminate this agreement at any time that written notice to the other is provided; however, that termination shall not affect our rights to receive payments of fees and cost disbursements that have accrued prior to such termination. *(Yes, yes, yes. A client may fire the attorney at any time. Hmmmm . . . for attorneys who have worked their brains out to get an entertainment client's career off the ground, this does not always go over well, especially if the client decides to "terminate" the relationship just as the client's career is taking off. However, such is life. For attorneys, the converse is true: Attorneys are not generally allowed to "terminate" the relationship once a client's case is close to going to trial. This can be a problem, especially if the client is refusing to pay the attorney.)*

Finally, please be advised that we reserve the right to destroy clients' files after a period of five (5) years after a matter is, in our opinion, completed. You may, of course, request such files by notifying us to such effect prior to that time. *(Generally, attorneys are required to hold on to files for a period of time after their work is finished. A client may obtain his files at any time during this period because they belong to him. After the time has elapsed, the files will be destroyed because all this attorney work takes paper, and paper takes up space.)*

The foregoing reflects our practices with respect to the charging of fees and the like. If you have any questions or disagree with any part, please call immediately. Otherwise, please sign and return the enclosed copy of this letter to confirm your understanding of this agreement with these practices. *(By all means, if a client doesn't get it—that is, he is not sure how he will be billed for something—he should feel free to call the attorney and have him explain it.)*

7

Managers: What Do They Mean When They Say That They Are Looking for Someone with Passion?

WHAT IS THE ROLE OF A MANAGER?

The evolution of the entertainment industry from a national or regional concern to a global business with permutations in untold markets has left agents scrambling to wear a dozen different hats. Agents, once architects of careers, now find themselves in the position of doing everything from finding independent financing for a client's project to investigating the interactive options for a client's commercial. It's a lot to do, and many agents find themselves overwhelmed. Hence, the care and feeding of clients suffers, and many directors, actors, and, yes, even writers have come to the decision that they need a new individual on their team: a manager.

Managers and management in the 90s entertainment industry has evolved far beyond the person who checks to ensure that the client will receive organic apple juice in his trailer. Managers are emerging as the new engineers of the client's career and are filling a void left by agencies who are off searching for options in cyberspace. Simply stated, managers provide a day-by-day relationship with a person charting the grand outline of a career. Rarely is an agent capable of performing this type of service. In addition, an agent will not take the time to raise from the ground the career of someone who is emerging or one for whom it may take a tremendous amount of time or work before the agent realizes a commission.

The ability of a manager to work with a client from the beginning of his career and to shape it every step of the way makes for long-forming relationships in which there is a great deal of trust. Given the bonds that grow between clients and managers, it is not unusual to find them going into business together. Some managers in the entertainment industry are now producing their clients' work and occasionally entering into production deals with their clients in both film and television. By contrast, agents cannot do this because the laws regulating the agency business do not allow agents to go into business with a client.

One important consideration: Under the existing labor commission guidelines and the law, managers cannot obtain work for their clients. This is the area that agents cover. In reality, managers frequently obtain work for their clients. This situation generally comes to light when a manager has obtained a great deal of work for a client but has not been paid. The manager usually has to sue the client, and then the client offers as a defense that the manager was acting as an agent (shock!) and had obtained work for the client for many years (shock!). Needless to say, the client will pretend that he had no idea that the manager was behaving in such a shameless fashion, and usually as a reward for this unprofessional behavior the client is able to retain the portion of the client's income that rightfully should be labeled "manager's commission."

WHAT DUTIES CAN I EXPECT A MANAGER TO DO FOR ME?

The scope of the management-client relationship is much broader than the agent-client relationship. As stated previously, the manager can be the individual who shapes the writer's career; she can be the person who creates the heat that enables the career to begin or be resurrected if it has stalled in midstream. The manager may be responsible for the selection of writing assignments that the manager feels will enhance the client's career. The manager may also be responsible for the creation of publicity and the choice of publicists to help the writer become known to the entertainment community. In addition, the manager may enlarge the writer's group of supporters in the industry by ensuring that the writer is introduced to significant directors and producers.

The manager may also explain the workings of the entertainment industry to the writer-client, including the common practices regarding compensation and privileges generally extended for writing services similar to the ones for which the writer has been engaged.

Another function the manager may have is helping the writer acquire the proper "support staff," which may include agents, accountants, attorneys, and other persons or firms whose services are required for the development of the artistic career and business affairs. This function is very important because the writer may not be able to obtain agency representation or become acquainted with entertainment attorneys and/or accountants in the business without the contacts of the manager and her ability to open doors for him.

How Does Someone Become a Manager?

There are no real qualifications for an individual to become a manager. They are not required to be licensed and generally do not go through a training program in a management company. Most managers come from a background in the entertainment industry, generally as a production executive or an agent. By the time they become managers, therefore, they have the knowledge and contacts necessary to foster a writer's career.

How Does an Emerging Writer Find a Manager?

As with agents, finding a manager is mainly a referral business. If you have a friend who is represented, the best thing you can do is have your friend tell his manager about your wonderful creativity. Alternatively, you might ask anyone you know in the entertainment business to recommend a good manager and to give you an introduction. Barring the above tried-and-true methods, there is always the option of sending a query letter to a manager or management company describing yourself and your work. If you do not know a manager or management company, I suggest that you obtain a copy of *The Hollywood Agents and Managers Directory,* published by the same folks who gave us *The Hollywood Creative Directory.* You can obtain a copy of agents and managers book by writing to The Hollywood Creative Directory, 3000 Olympic Boulevard, Suite 2413, Santa Monica, California 90404, or telephone (310) 315-4815, or fax (310) 315-4816.

WHAT FACTORS SHOULD I TAKE INTO CONSIDERATION BEFORE I AGREE TO HAVE A MANAGER REPRESENT ME?

One of the first decisions to be made is whether you truly need a manager. As stated previously, managers do not officially obtain work for their clients. Under the laws of California, only agents can find work for clients, even though managers do generally participate in finding and generating work for their clients. A key question, therefore, is what function a manager would actually fulfill for you. If you are the type of person who likes to have day-by-day counseling on your career and would like to have someone who designs your career with you, then having a manager would fulfill a needed role for you. On the other hand, if you are the type of person who wants to be in charge of your own destiny and believes that an agent can provide you with enough of a direction, then a manager may be wasted on you.

If you do decide that your potential will best be served by adding a manager to your team, your best bet is to decide with your manager the specific functions she will perform for you, such as helping you find an agent, having your work reviewed by studio and production executives who would respond to your work, and reviewing your work with you to ensure that it is at its best (before it is read by others). You should also decide how and by when you will know that these functions have been performed. As with agents, managers are not miracle workers, and every career has a different chronology as to when it will take off. A manager may give you excellent service and may make every conceivable effort to start your career or create the perception that you are "hot," but if your career does not take off, it may not be the manager's fault.

HOW DO I KNOW IF MY MANAGER IS DOING A GOOD JOB WITH MY CAREER?

Do you frequently hear from your manager? Given the nature of the manager-client relationship, you should hear from your manager constantly. After all, this is someone to whom you have handed your career. If your manager does not call you on a regular basis, you can assume that she has lost interest in your career, has too many clients, or has rather unprofessional business habits. You should not be the one who has to initiate all the phone calls. A person who has made a decision to become the captain of your career should be in contact with you on a regular basis.

Are you receiving exposure within the entertainment community? Clearly, the role of a manager is to create a profile for you within the entertainment community and, in doing so, to make you a hot item, one with whom people will want to work. To do this you will need to attend a certain number of meetings with agents, producers, and other individuals who must first learn about you and then either work with you (as in agents) or hire you (as in production and/or studio executives). In addition, your manager should begin to put you in business with other people who can aid you in your career, such as lawyers and accountants. If within a certain amount of time—six months, say—you are not meeting a few people and receiving agency representation (if you so desire) or gaining access to other people who can help you with your career, then it might be prudent for you to reassess what role your manager is playing in your career and decide if she is fulfilling the functions you set forth.

Is your manager fulfilling the functions you decided she should fulfill? Need I say more? If you and your manager came to some understanding at the beginning of your relationship regarding the duties and functions that she was to fulfill, then after a certain amount of time has elapsed, you will know whether she has fulfilled them. The answer is simple: yes or no.

HOW MUCH DO MANAGERS GET PAID?

Here's the rub. Agents working in the entertainment industry are generally regulated by licensing agencies; managers are not. Whereas agents are not allowed to take more than 10 percent from your gross income, managers may take more. The standard compensation for managers tends to range between 5 percent and 15 percent. Sometimes managers take as much as 30 percent. If the manager ends up producing your work, the manager will generally take an additional fee.

That being said, it has been my experience that good managers who can take an individual's career from nowhere to somewhere deserve more in the ball park of 50 percent of the client's gross income. Managing is a terrifically difficult job, and the manager takes the risk of seeing no money out of the deal for a long time. It takes years of creating contacts and knowing the landscape of the entertainment industry to create a career for someone. In addition, for all the enhancements that a manager can give to someone's career, the job of managing tends to be a rather thankless task, with managers who have done the near impossible not receiving the accolades they deserve, or even thanks from their clients.

WHAT ARE THE CLIENT'S OBLIGATIONS TO THE MANAGER?

Working with a manager is similar to working with an agent: The writer has certain responsibilities in the relationship, such as a duty to do whatever the manager says is most advantageous to foster a career. After all, the manager is the person you have designated as the one who will create your career.

In addition, the client has the responsibility to do well at whatever meetings the manager creates for him and to do the best writing he possibly can at all times, and specifically when the manager is able to find an assignment for the writer. This is the client's end of the deal: If the manager obtains an opportunity for the client, it is the client's job to hit a home run every time.

A LITERARY MANAGEMENT AGREEMENT FOR REPRESENTATION

At a recent conference of entertainment attorneys and managers, one prominent manager remarked that manager-client contracts are not worth the paper they're written on. The reason is that the relationship between manager and client is clearly one of a close and personal nature, based on mutual trust. Once the trust is gone, the relationship can rarely continue. Despite the previous statement, the following is a standard manager-client contract, with italicized comments to assist you.

SAMPLE: LITERARY MANAGEMENT AGREEMENT

1. This firm has agreed to provide you with our personal management services for a period of two years from the date of this memorandum. During that time, we agree to provide you with our guidance and advice regarding all aspects of the development of your career as an artist in the entertainment industry. Our advice and guidance will include but not be limited to the following: the selection of artistic properties; publicity, public relations, and advertising; the selection of other artists to assist or accompany you in your career or in individual projects; common practices in the entertainment industry regarding compensation and privileges generally extended for artistic services similar to the ones for which you are engaged; the selection of support staff and counselors, including agents, business advisors, legal counsel, and any other persons or firms whose services are required for the development of your artistic career and business affairs. *(The problem with this*

paragraph is that there is no method for the writer to be released from the contract in under two years. Accordingly, my recommendation is that a writer and potential manager make a decision that either party may be released from the contract if specific circumstances happen or do not happen within a given period of time. For instance, the typical agency contract releases the writer if he does not receive work in any four-month period. This paragraph presents an opportunity for the writer and manager to spell out exactly what the manager is going to do. For example, both writer and manager could both agree that in a four-month period the manager will obtain ten meetings with ten agents or production companies; ensure that the executive producers on four top TV shows have received and reviewed the writer's work; ensure that the writer's agent is submitting the writer's work for staff positions for all the shows in the new season; and have the writer's feature work sent to twenty companies.)

2. You authorize us to act for you by doing the following: approving all advertising and publicity; approving and permitting the use of your name, likeness, voice, sound effects, caricature, and literary, artistic, and musical materials for the purposes of advertising and publicity and in the promotion of any and all products and services, executing for you in your name and/or on your behalf any and all agreements, documents, and contracts for your services, talent, and/or literary, artistic, and musical materials, collecting and receiving sums, as well as endorsing your name on and cashing any and all checks payable to you for your services, talents, and literary and artistic materials, and retaining those checks and cashing all sums due to us under this agreement; hiring, firing, and directing for you, and in your name, talent agents and employment agents as well as other persons, firms, and corporations who may be retained to obtain contracts, engagements, or employment for you. This firm is not required to make any loans or advances to you or on your behalf. *(The problem with this paragraph is that it gives the manager the power to do things, without informing the writer, that should be done by the writer. No agreement should be entered into on a writer's behalf for any-*

*thing without his prior approval. In addition, the writer must
be informed of any check that comes to the manager's office
before it is cashed. Also, no one should be hired or fired without the writer's prior approval. Please be advised that the
source of many lawsuits has been the abuse of power given to
managers to cash checks.)*

3. You agree at all times to devote yourself to your career as an
   artist and to do all things necessary to promote that career and
   to maximize your earnings from all endeavors in the entertainment industry. You agree to use reputable theatrical and/or
   other employment agencies to obtain engagements and
   employment, but you shall not engage any talent or employment agency without our consent. We shall keep you advised
   regarding all offers and overtures that we receive on your
   behalf from any talent and/or employment agents. You shall
   keep us advised regarding all offers of employment that you
   receive, and you will refer any inquiries regarding your services to us. You shall instruct any talent engaged by us to
   remit to us all compensation, in the form of cash or other
   property or interests, received by that agent as compensation
   for your services. *(I suggest that the sentence "but you shall
   not engage any talent or employment agency without out consent" be deleted because this is giving entirely too much control to a manager.)*

4. You have not retained our personal management firm under
   this agreement as an employment agent or a talent agent. This
   firm has not offered or attempted or promised to obtain
   employment or engagement for you, and this firm is not obligated, authorized, or expected to do so. You shall refer any and
   all inquiries from potential employers to your talent and/or
   employment agent and/or attorneys, and also inform us as to
   any such inquiries. *(This states that the manager will not be
   obtaining employment or be seeking engagements for you. As
   stated previously, this is in accordance with the law; however,
   the reality is something else.)*

5. We are not entering into a partnership by virtue of this agreement. In all matters covered by this agreement, this firm shall
   act as an independent contractor, and, as such, this firm may

appoint or engage any other persons, firms, and corporations that it may choose to perform the same or similar services for others, as well as engage in any and all other business activities. *(I suggest that you delete "this firm may appoint or engage any other persons, firms, and corporations that it may choose to perform the same or similar services for others, as well as engage in any and all other business activities." This is much too wide and opens the door to allowing all sorts of money to be spent and charged to you without your prior approval. If the manager will not agree to deleting this line, then I suggest that you add the following line: "However, this firm has no authority to appoint any other person(s), firm(s), and/or corporation(s) to perform the same or similar services to be covered by this contract for the writer without the prior approval of the writer.")*

6. This firm shall not be required to devote its services exclusively to you. This firm shall only be required to render reasonable services that are covered by this agreement. If for any reason this firm is unable to promptly render such reasonable services when you request us to do so, we will immediately notify you of that inability and the reason for it. This firm shall not be deemed to be in default of its obligations under this agreement unless and until you give written notice describing the exact service that you require, and then only if we do not begin, within fifteen (15) days after we receive that notice, to provide the requested service. Nothing in this agreement shall be construed to require any member of this firm to travel or to meet with you at any particular place or places unless we agree to do so and also agree regarding the responsibility for the costs and expenses of that travel. *(The problem with this paragraph is that it says nothing. What are the "reasonable services" to be performed by the manager? What does that mean? The "obligations" the manager is to perform are so vague that you would never know when or if he was in default. Also, because it has never been established what the "exact service" is that the manager is to perform, the writer does not know if he has the right to tell him to do something that may or may not be a service that he said he would per-*

*form in the agreement. In addition, the last sentence drives me
crazy: "Nothing in this agreement shall be construed to
require any member of this firm to travel or to meet with you
at any particular place or places . . . ." Does this mean that if
you desperately need to see him somewhere in the town in
which both of you live and work that he will not come unless
he agrees to do so? This sentence must be altered to reflect
some agreement as to the locations and distances that the firm
will or will not travel, in what circumstances the firm will or
will not be expected to travel, and when, if ever, you will be
expected to pay for traveling.)*

7. As compensation for the services covered by this agreement,
you shall pay to us, when received, a sum equal to ten (10)
percent of any and all gross earnings or other consideration
that you receive for your activities in the entertainment industry. For the purpose of this agreement, "activities" in the
entertainment industry shall include, but not be limited to,
your employment in any and all of the following: motion pictures, television, radio, music, literature, talent engagements,
personal appearances, public appearances in places of amuse-
ment and entertainment, records and recording, and publica-
tions. Following the expiration or termination of this agreement, you agree to pay us ten (10) percent of your gross earnings for any and all resumptions or engagement, contracts,
and agreements that many have been discontinued while this
agreement was in effect and resumed within a year after its
expiration and termination. The term "gross earnings or other
consideration" shall include, without limitations, salaries,
earnings, fees, royalties, gifts, bonuses, shares of stock, shares
of profit, partnership interests, percentages, and the total
amount paid for a package of television or radio programs
(live or recorded), motion picture, or other entertainment
packages earned or received by you or your heirs, executors,
administrators, or assigns or by any other person, firm, or corporation on your behalf. If you receive, as all or part of your
compensation for activities in the entertainment industry,
stock or the right to buy stock in any corporation, or if you
package or own all or part of an entertainment property,

whether as an individual proprietor, stockholder, partner, joint venturer, or otherwise, our percentage shall apply to all of that stock, the right to buy stock, individual proprietorship, partnership, joint venture, or other form of interest, and we shall be entitled to our percentage share thereof. If you are required to make any payment for an ownership interest as described in this agreement, we will pay our percentage share of that payment if we want our percentage share of that interest. *(This sentence makes it clear that no matter what the circumstances, the manager or management company is entitled to its 10 percent. This also speaks to the fact that no matter what form the compensation takes, be it stock, business, or option to buy, the manager or management company does not lose its option to obtain its 10 percent.)*

8. This firm shall have the right to assign its rights and obligations under this agreement to a corporation that acquires all, or substantially all, of the assets of this firm. *(The firm may have the right to assign its assets and liabilities, but it should not have the right to assign your contract. What this means is that if the management firm should find itself facing a major debt, then the firm would have the right to consider your contract "an asset" and assign it to whomever it owes the debt. You should not agree to this paragraph without adding the sentence "with the permission of the writer.")*

9. Any and all disputes that may arise between you and this firm regarding the terms of this agreement shall be submitted to final and binding arbitration. *(Once again, alternative dispute resolution, in the form of arbitration, raises its head. Clearly, if this firm runs into a disagreement with you, these individuals have wisely chosen to pursue all differences through arbitration, which, as I stated previously, is a smart alternative to taking anything or anyone to trial.)*

This agreement is dated and effective as of _____.

Very truly yours,

I do hereby agree to the foregoing:

8

What Can I Do if I Don't Have an Agent, Attorney, or Manager?

GIVE YOUR SCRIPT TO EVERYONE

The purpose of having an agent, lawyer, or manager is that he will ideally have the contacts to get your career off the ground and obtain work for you. However, even when you have a "team" of them working for you, it'll still be part of your work as a writer to meet people and let them know about you and your work. You'll do this for your entire career because a portion of your work as a writer will be to create and maintain the contacts that can sustain a career. The bright side of not having representation is that you'll never be under the illusion that you don't have to pound the pavement to meet people, but you also clearly fall into the category known as "Give Your Script to Everyone."

"Give Your Script to Everyone" does not mean that you should send ten copies of your urbane parody of *Citizen Kane* to your dry cleaner. It does mean that you should give your work to anyone connected to the entertainment industry, such as an assistant director you meet by chance, the agent's assistant who is a friend of a friend, and the writing instructor at your community college. Why? You never know where these people will go or with whom they are connected. If your work happens to find an advocate among one of these individuals, your work could be given to someone who would know what to do with it. This could be a beginning for you or even propel your work to an unknown height. (I know one writer who gave his work to a creative writing instructor at his art school. The instructor called a former student, who happened to be a literary agent. The rest, as they say, is history.)

GET A JOB IN THE ENTERTAINMENT INDUSTRY DOING ANYTHING

Before you continue reading this paragraph, consider whether the place you are living has an entertainment industry. Next, consider whether you want to move to an area that has an entertainment industry. If the answer to both of these questions is no, precede to the following paragraph immediately. If the answer to one of the above questions is yes, consider this action the "get your foot in the door" alternative. Once you have any job—be it temping, typing, or being an assistant—once again, learn as much as you can in this position. Then "give your script to everyone" and find as much information as you can about who might be interested in your work. As off-the-wall as this may seem, this approach works. I know writers and production executives who began their career as typists at studios, asked a zillion questions, and then found information concerning people who could help them in their careers. Now all of these individuals have careers as writers in the entertainment industry.

JOIN AS MANY ENTERTAINMENT-RELATED ORGANIZATIONS AS YOU CAN (OR CAN TOLERATE)

Nauseating. Nauseating. Nauseating. If you're like most writers, the idea of joining a group makes you crazy. Or sick. Or depressed. To think that this should be done to help get your career off the ground seems like a shameless waste of time or just plain shameless.

Obviously, this is a variation of "give your script to everyone." Only this is more along the lines of "find the right people" so that you can "give your script to everyone." Needless to say, the entertainment industry is loaded with organizations with popular causes that help everyone feel better about what they are doing for a living. So find one that you can tolerate. If you are not in Hollywood (and that might just be a blessing), get involved in a local film society or writers group. Trust me: The film industry does not exist only in Hollywood. There are film societies, film festivals, and writers groups everywhere.

FIND A PRODUCER TO SUPPORT YOUR WORK

This was discussed under the chapter on agents. Producers need to find new material constantly, which clearly means the obvious: new sources of writing. Invest in a copy of *The Hollywood Creative Directory*.

GO TO FILM FESTIVALS AND INFORMAL ENTERTAINMENT INDUSTRY GATHERINGS

Many remote little burgs such as Palm Springs, Telluride, Santa Barbara, and Park City are discovering the joys of film festivals that provide major cash infusions, sometimes during an "off season." The benefit to you as a writer is entirely different: a chance to visit with members of the film industry in a relaxed setting.

As you may know, a film festival generally clumps together directors, producers, and agents, all looking for "the fresh new talent." Why not let it be you?

These events are an opportunity to relax and be with people you might not otherwise have an opportunity to meet. Go to these festivals. Be bold. Strike up conversations. Give your work to everyone.

ENTER YOUR WORK IN AS MANY CONTESTS AS POSSIBLE

The beauty pageant approach may not be for everyone (but, hey, it worked for Michelle Pfeiffer, and look at her now). The good thing about entering these contests is that the people who read for them tend to be agents or producers who are looking for new talent. If they like your work or if you happen to win one of the contests, you are likely to have both aggressive young producers and aggressive young agents chasing you. (A list of entertainment-related contests for writers is located at the back of the book.)

Section 3

WRITING FOR THE ENTERTAINMENT INDUSTRY:

Why Should I Write the Next *Pulp Fiction* When I Really Want to Write for "The Young and the Restless"?

Now that you have learned how to protect your stunning masterpiece, ensured that you will not be sued by your loved ones for basing your exposé on their lives, discovered when you may or may not have an agreement, and found (or decided not to bother with) "representation," the next step is to understand how writers work in the entertainment industry. This section is divided into four chapters: Writing for Film (Chapter 9), Writing for Episodic Television (Chapter 10), Writing for the Entertainment Industry (Chapter 11), and Why Write for Television When You Can Write for Cyberspace? (Chapter 12). It includes interviews with writers, agents, and a producer (a former literary manager) working in different areas of film and television. It also includes a non-WGA contract (without the compensation and working conditions guaranteed by the WGA Minimum Basic Agreement).

Hopefully this section will help to eliminate basic misconceptions about writing for film and television and you will learn what kind of work exists for writers, how this work is obtained, and what working conditions are available for writers in the entertainment industry.

9

Writing for Film

Employment as a Writer

Writers make money writing for film by two primary methods. The first method is through accepting writing assignments. In a writing assignment a writer may be hired to (a) develop a pitch into a screenplay by writing a treatment, a first-draft screenplay, and a set of first revisions with an option to hire the writer to write a second set of revisions and a polish; (b) rewrite another writer's work; or (c) polish another writer's work (basically, punch up the dialogue).

The second method is through the sale of a spec screenplay (one that the writer has written on his own) or the film rights to a novel or other literary property. (For example the author Michael Crichton has made a great deal of money selling the film rights to his novels *Jurassic Park, Disclosure,* and *Congo.*) Although aspiring writers read and dream about the sale of the million-dollar screenplay, the reality is that most sales are for far less, if at all. Another reality is that most writers working in the film industry do not make their living from the sale of a spec screenplay but through writing assignments.

A screenwriter creates a career for himself by writing something everyone wants to read. By *everyone,* I mean all producers, directors, actors, and creative executives. Once the work becomes noticed by these people, agents usually take notice. Although the work, generally a screenplay, probably won't sell, its value is in obtaining writing assignments for the writer.

If the work is very hot, the writer generally receives a phone call from a production or studio executive (or several production companies and several studio executives) who wants the writer to come in for a "general meeting." The purpose of this meeting is to "meet and greet." It is hoped that the writer will "bond" with the executive and not alienate anyone in the room.

If the "general meeting" is successful, the writer may find himself receiving a call to come into the studio so that the production executive can "discuss" a project. The project may be an idea the executive has, a book that the company/studio would like to transform into a movie, or another literary project that the studio would like to develop. The executive will have the proposed project delivered to the writer so that the writer can read the project and develop his pitch. Once the writer has created his pitch, the executive will have a "pitch" meeting with the writer.

In the "pitch" meeting, the writer will present his view to the executive of how the project can be developed into a feature film. Generally, the executive (or executives) is not looking for a summary of the project but is looking for a fresh view of the project, something that "stretches the envelope" or presents a way of seeing the project that he has not previously envisioned. If the executive likes the "pitch," he will usually ask the writer to return to pitch the project to another executive who is higher on the food chain.

If the "pitch" meeting with the more senior executive is successful, the writer may actually be hired to write the project. Before the writer is hired, however, the studio may want to see a second screenplay from the writer (especially if the writer has no previous writing credits or has not done previous work), something that shows the writer can consistently create good work or write in the genre (comedy, action-adventure) of the proposed film. After this comes all sorts of wrangling regarding the writing fees for the writer (that is, how little he can be paid), the amount of time necessary for the writer to deliver the different drafts of the work, and other terms and conditions regarding the writer. If there is a basic "meeting of the minds" regarding the writer— that is, all parties can come to an understanding regarding the agreement for writing services—the writer will actually begin writing.

Once the writer has the project, it is important that he do fabulous work. If the writer does well on the project, this can be the launching pad for further work. If the writer blows the project—such as getting fired early (generally after the first set of revisions)—then he will remain an "unproven commodity." Although this may not be the end of the writer's career, it will be very difficult (note: difficult but not impossible) to obtain the next assignment for the writer.

If the writer does well on the assignment, he can use the project as a reference for another one and begin to become a "proven commodity." It should be mentioned, though, that there are very few proven commodities—writers that studios and production executives always think of when they want someone to write for them. But if the writer becomes a proven commodity, he may become one of the lucky few hired to rewrite and polish other writers' work for enormous sums of money. In addition, if the writer becomes very successful or creates a spec screenplay that everyone wants, he may have an opportunity to do what approximately 95 percent of all writers want to do: direct a film (but that's another book).

WRITING FOR FILM: INTERVIEWS WITH JANE ANDERSON AND GARY GOLDSTEIN

The methods by which writers enter into the entertainment industry are all different. Their stories present different paths taken by writers to reach their goals. The following interview with screenwriter Jane Anderson presents a writer's perspective concerning writing for film. Producer Gary Goldstein, a former literary manager, offers a different vision.

INTERVIEW WITH JANE ANDERSON

Screenwriter of *The Positively True Adventures of the Alleged Murdering Texas Cheerleader Mom* (Emmy awarded), *It Could Happen to You,* and *How to Make an American Quilt.*

How did you start your writing career?

I was working as an actress in New York City. I found that I was breaking my back to audition for parts that were horribly written, and I decided that rather then break my heart over bad material I'd start writing my own. I became a comedienne and wrote one-woman shows for myself. I then was brought out to Los Angeles to be on the "Billy Crystal Comedy Hour"; this lasted about three weeks. After this, I was trying to make my career as a comic and managed to get a job on "The Facts of Life" as a staff writer. I took this job because I wanted a parking place in my life.

I was a very good comic, but I found that I kept hitting walls in that career. As soon as I started writing, I knew that I was a writer because jobs just kept coming to me.

How did you get the staff writing job on "The Facts of Life"?

I had a small part as an actress on "The Facts of Life," and I had already written a spec script for "Night Court." I went up to the producers of "The Facts of Life" and said, "Hi, I want to write for your show." They said, "Well, give us a script." I gave them a script but didn't know that they [the producers] had fired four writers that week and were looking for more writers. They read my script and hired me.

I lasted for about a year. I'm not built to be a staff writer; I don't enjoy that kind of work because I'm a much more private writer. I'm not good at sitting around a table and punching up a script with jokes. But what I did learn was very valuable: I learned how not to be precious with my writing because when you're a staff writer on a show, you're asked to write ten pages that day, and then they'll look at them and throw them out and ask you to write another ten pages. You learn very quickly that you can't hold on to what you've written, you have to move on. This has really helped me with the rewrite process. It was an incredible lesson.

After "The Facts of Life," did you work on another TV show?

After that I wrote a full-length play, and from that play I was hired by Grant Tinker to create sitcom [a situation comedy], a TV show.

They came to me with any idea and asked me to write the pilot. The show was called "Raising Miranda," and it was picked up. So I found myself back in the television world and thought since I was the creator of the show that I would have enormous artistic control over the show, the look of it, the style, and that maybe I would have the power to demand that they not have a laugh track on this piece. I quickly learned that I was yet again a hired gun. I was part of the staff on the show. I forget how many episodes it was, and it ran for a season, and then it was canceled. I was deeply relieved that it was canceled because yet again I found myself in a staff situation where I wasn't happy because it wasn't the style that I was used to writing.

I have enormous respect for staff writers. I think even though everybody wants to be a feature writer or a playwright, a novelist, I think every form takes a very special and particular talent. And staff writers have to be very fast, and they have to be sprinters. They have to be quick, and they have to be able to stay up until five in the morning and still be funny. I really do admire that. I'm a different kind of writer, and I think part of the journey of finding success as a writer is to know what your skills are and if you are equipped to be a screenwriter, which is a completely different form of discipline than writing for TV. Both are valid.

What kind of equipment (skills) does a writer need to be a feature writer?

I think the first thing is that you need to have something to say. And something large enough to say, that will last the length of a feature film. Your ideas have to be large. You have to have the ability to sit by yourself for days and months, developing your ideas, researching your ideas, struggling with your characters. You have to be an architect as well as a creative writer. By an architect, I mean you have to be able to envision the entire structure of this piece you are writing. You have to build the skeleton, you have to know how to engineer the pipes and the electricity and the frame of your screenplay. And then you have to have the ability to fill it in with character and emotion and detail.

When you are writing sitcom, you have your producer, your executive, your network dictating what the episodes are going to be, and you fill that out for them. When you are writing an original screen-play or even an assignment, you have to in your head play director, cinematographer, set decorator, and acting coach. And you have to coordinate all of these in a very organized way, and it's not sprint-ing, like writing sitcom, it's more a marathon runner. It takes three to six months of your life to create this piece.

When you think about the development of your career, is there some-thing you did that allowed you to develop into this feature film writer, this "marathon runner"?

Being a playwright helped because writing a play is almost the same process. Writing a play means that you go down into the cellar of your head and that you are committing to a long piece for several months of your life, and I basically learned it through that.

In the beginning of my writing career, I wrote short pieces, and I built up to longer pieces until I could handle a three-act structure.

How did you get an agent, and what has been your experience with agents?

I can't even remember how I stumbled on my first agent. I really can't. As I remember, I got the job first, then I ran around looking for someone to handle it for me. Somehow I started working with The Gage Group [an agency in Los Angeles], and I fell in love with Martin Gage and Jonathan Westover.

Not long after I began working with The Gage Group, my career was starting to take off. And I thought, well, The Gage Group is a small agency, and it seems that all the important writers are with larger agencies, like CAA and William Morris—you know, these big packagers—and in my ignorance I thought, well, I should go to a larger agency and maybe my career will take off even more. I did briefly, and I found that after an agent is finished wooing you and telling you how much he respects your work, he goes about trying to sell you down the river. The larger the agency is, the less time they have or care to take to understand what you really are as a writer. I remember making it very clear to them that I didn't want to make a career out of writing for TV, that I wanted to write movies. And the first thing that this agent did in this big agency was try to get me a huge multi-year deal writing for television. I think that a lot of agents push for that because it's such a low-maintenance career. They make a ton of money and don't have to worry about you. It's hard work to develop someone's career as a screenwriter. It's iffy. You put out a script a year if you're lucky . . . . And I went back to The Gage Group and I was nurtured and taken care of, and they respected the direction I wanted to go in. And the rest is history.

You want to find an agent who knows your writing rhythm and what you can handle, and won't overload you with assignments because overloading is as dangerous as unemployment. It can kill you just as quickly.

Do you remember what your transition was from writing for television to writing features?

I remember that I very deliberately sat down and wrote a screenplay. I had to be very focused because I kept getting offers to write for television. I had enough money to survive to write the screenplay. That screenplay started going around, and I got interviews out of that, and I could go to pitch meetings. And that was basically my transition. It was hard because I could have written for television and had a comfy job.

You must have had enormous discipline to do that.

Well, I loved what I was writing. And that is the great difference. You don't resent it. It's like raising a kid takes everything out of you, but if you love that child with all your heart, you don't mind cupping your hand so that the child can vomit onto you when you are driving in a car. If you love what you are doing, you don't even notice how difficult it is. For me, writing for sitcoms was soul-killing—not for other people but for me. I wasn't meant to do it, and there were times that I would wake up in the morning and have to hack out my script for the day for a TV show, and I would want to die. But writing my very own script and writing what I believed and writing what I loved, I didn't even notice how hard it was.

And that still applies now. If I have to take an assignment and it turns out to be the wrong assignment for me, I feel this horrible weight on my shoulders. And then my work starts to go sour. That's why you should be very careful what assignment you take, even though in the beginning you're tempted to take anything that's thrown your way—rewrites . . . . That rewrite for "The Ghost and Mrs. Muir," "Gilligan's Island" . . . these things are thrown your way, and you think, well, it's a big opportunity.

I remember when I was with my former agent, I was asked to write a feature and it was for a big star, but it was a subject that didn't interest me at all, and I didn't like what they wanted me to write. I knew I couldn't fulfill that assignment properly because it wasn't me. My agent thought that I was nuts for turning it down and urged me to take it because she said that it would be good for my career. I knew in my heart that if I took the assignment I might ruin my career because I would do such a lousy job on it. You have to listen to your gut when someone pitches you an assignment. If you suddenly feel as though you want to go crawl and take a nap, you know that you shouldn't write this thing.

When you are brought in for a meeting concerning a writing assignment, what tips do you have for successfully pitching the project?

I like to bring in visuals. There is a piece that I have been pitching lately, and it's a period piece. Because most executives are terrified of period pieces and have no sense of history, I have found this great old turn-of-the-century photograph book with visuals in it. One had a photo of this young boy that is the image of one of the characters. So I go in, I open up the page, let them look at the person on the page. They start staring at it, their imaginations start turning, and they immediately relax.

You want to break up the verbiage of trying to explain the story because you can put someone to sleep in the room if you are just telling the plot. I structure my pitches this way: I'll go in, and first I tell them what the movie is about, the essence of it, that one-sentence pitch that gets them excited, the log line. With this particular thing I'll say, "This is an end-of-the-world comedy or a comedy about the end of the world." Then I crystallize it, and I say to them, "This movie is about what it would be like if you were told that the world was going to end in a week and all the things you would want to do that you wouldn't have to be accountable for." I remember when I was in New York City during the blackout and it was like the world was coming to an end, and everybody did either really destructive things or really wonderful things. And sometimes an exec will remember being in the blackout, and he'll say, "Yeah, yeah, I remember being in the blackout." And I'll say, "I remember during the blackout Zabars opened its doors, and everybody got to get free deli," and the exec will say, "Yeah, yeah, I remember that. That was great." And immediately they feel personally involved with the story. I then will start introducing the characters because characters are never a thing that you can immediately get a grasp on. And then I will tell them the story, and I'm very careful when I tell them the story not to let that part go on too long because you can't tell it beat by beat or else you get the snores again. I will tell a somewhat detailed description of the story, and then at the end I'll ask them if they have any questions. And then they'll start saying, "And what about this and this?" And then they'll have their answers. So you let them verbally take part in the pitch with you so they aren't sitting there. You don't ever want them to have an opportunity to daydream about their girlfriends or what they are going to have for dinner that night or the fact that they didn't get a first credit on their movie. You don't want their attention to ever stray. That's why you always encourage them to ask questions. You tell just enough so that they are titillated enough to give you the "so what about" questions.

How can a writer successfully work with studio executives when going through the development process?

Your best defense is to know your material better than anybody and to stick by your vision. If you're really clear about what the movie is about, then you're in the position to guide them through the process rather than having them tell you what to do. As soon as you depend on them to come up with the solutions, then you're sunk, because executives, no matter how well meaning, usually don't know what they want. And they will change their minds at every meeting. And you have to protect yourself from being asked to write extraneous drafts of a movie. That's the worst thing that happens. They especially get the new people to write them for free, which I find absolutely untenable.

When you have that meeting where they tell you what they want, what kind of movie they want, then you very clearly tell them your vision and get them to sign off on that vision. Then I go back and write an extremely detailed outline, usually about thirty pages. I go beat by beat. I include dialogue so that they can tell what the tone is, and I give them the outline before I ever do a script. They can use that outline to change the story or do whatever they want. And that is a safer way to do it, when they have a script they can take apart, because once you write a script, you are married to what you have written. You can let go of beats in an outline, but you can't let go of scenes in a script. You get them to sign off on the outline, you do whatever adjustments that they want, but you have in writing that they agreed to and signed off on your vision of the story. After you have written a draft of the script, if they come back to you and say, "That's not what we wanted," you can show them the outline they signed off on. And then you are in a position to say to them, "If that's not what you wanted, then you should have told me at that time. If you want a different movie, then you are going to have to pay me for a new draft." And that's how it's successfully done.

When you come to the stage that you are working with directors and actors, how can you incorporate their suggestions into your work?

I think, if you are lucky enough to get a film produced, and you are lucky enough to work with a director, I suggest that you let this person be your ally, unless the person doesn't even want to know from you and goes off to write it himself, but I won't even talk about that type of director. The kind of director who respects writers are your allies in the process, and I find it very much the most valuable of all [allies.] I learn more from working with Michael Ritchie than going to any class. Working with experienced directors is just an utter delight because they will teach you what is needed to make a great movie. So I love working with directors.

Actors, they feel lucky to work with you, but there comes a point in the process where the director doesn't want you around. I've worked with a few actors, and the really great ones have limited suggestions. When they don't have great suggestions, I just say,

"Talk to the director." You know, you pass the buck. Screenwriters rarely get to work directly with the actors, so I don't have a lot to say about that.

What advice do you have for emerging writers?

Your first script might get you in the door and get you into meetings, it might get you a rewrite assignment, it might get you a job that you thought you might never have. I did write a script that did not get made; I call it "your social introduction script." It's your calling card; it gets you into the studios. There are rare instances of that five-million-dollar sale of that first script, but that's not anything anybody should expect.

I think writers are so isolated. [They should see] if they can find anyplace to work their craft in a group and get objective feedback that isn't connected to a budget or an executive. Writers groups, I think, are the most helpful when they're about bringing in pieces of your script and reading it and getting feedback. I don't like writers groups that are bitch sessions.

Because we're so isolated, we tend to be abused in dark rooms in this industry. We think it's only us who's being beaten up or rewritten or changed or screwed over. Then we start to talk to other writers, and we hear their horrible stories in the torture chamber of the executive's office, and we start feeding on each other. We have to be careful not to get into a kind of victimhood. It's healthy to air our souls and talk about what's been done. But then you have to let go and move on. You don't want to make a profession out of being a victim.

I also believe that distance is a very important thing to have. A writer must be able to get away from the work and get some distance from it. You must be able to let your work sit for one week or one month, and then be able to go back to it. Time really helps the writing process. If possible, you should ask for a grace period to put some distance between you and the work you have just completed. Hopefully, you can get this grace period before you get notes back from the work you have just completed.

One other very important thing is that a writer must find a technique for taking criticism. This is part of the craft of writing and a very important technique to develop if a writer is hoping to work within the film industry.

INTERVIEW WITH GARY GOLDSTEIN

Producer of *Pretty Woman, Under Siege, Under Siege II,* and *The Hunted* and former literary manager.

Tell us about your evolution from attorney to producer.

Growing up in San Francisco in the 60s and having attended U.C. Berkeley during the maelstrom of the late 60s and early 70s, I'd come to harbor a rather romantic notion about becoming a criminal defense attorney. It echoed the reformist ethic of my upbringing. To my chagrin, however, I found almost immediately I was not well-suited to the task. I realized the one thing I really fantasized about was the world of writers and writing. So I ran away to Los Angeles, thinking I'd become the Maxwell Perkins of the screenwriting trade, fantasizing a latter-day Algonquin Round Table. Again, I was sorely surprised.

When I arrived, I knew virtually nothing of the business [the entertainment industry] and proceeded to interview with quite a few places, primarily studios. I couldn't get a job because I knew no one and knew nothing about the business. So I naively said to myself "Oh well, I'll just start my own company." Having been told "management" was a relatively new and unregulated area, I immediately started a literary management company. The first few years were lean, to say the least, but eventually I learned and focused primarily on writers because that was my first love.

I managed writers for almost ten years, the first six years just managing, and the last four producing as well on the side. About two years ago, I realized producing was far more challenging and fun than representation and I dissolved the management company. J.F. Lawton, who'd been a client since the very beginning [the writer of *Pretty Woman, Under Seige, The Hunted, Mistress*] was the impetus for my producing.

During the writers' strike of 1988, which virtually shut down the entire business for almost a year, Jonathan [Lawton] came in the door one day with a script in hand and said "You've nothing to do and I have a script that I want to direct. Why don't you raise some money and we'll make this film and you'll produce it." I raised two postage stamps worth of financing and we did, in fact, make the film, *Cannibal Women in the Avocado Jungle of Death*.

It was guerrilla filmmaking at its finest. Neither of us knew what we were doing. I think we made thirty company moves in eleven days—Riverside, Malibu, Hollywood. It was insane. The poor actors and crew—we didn't pay anybody much of anything.

We used my offices as our production office. We crammed thirty people into a couple of offices and were crawling all over each other. We had two weeks. We prepped the film, shot it in eleven days, cut it in one week, and ran of to Sundance for the production lab.

While it was a matter of the blind leading the blind, we completed the film with what little time and money was available to us and had a riotous time. A feminist spoof of *Heart of Darkness*, the film is quite funny, made money, and to this day runs constantly on various cable outlets. And that is the story of our first film.

When you were a manager, how and where would you find new writers?

At the 7-Eleven. Particularly in Los Angeles, wherever you go, just whisper the phrase "I represent writers." I took a midnight flight to San Francisco and went to rent a car at Hertz. At the counter, there's a fellow in his sixties and, to complete the rental form, asks my occupation. Absently, I respond "literary manager." With twelve exhausted and unhappy people behind me, this guy instantly disappears and returns with an old duffel bag filled with scripts, insisting I begin reading one right there and then while he finishes filling out the rental car form.

Everybody is a writer. I find writers and writers find me in a myriad of ways. By attending screenings or parties or by staying home. Early on, it was imperative that I get out and spread the gospel. As time passed, word of mouth became more important. Clients would speak to their friends, attorneys and executives would refer friends and clients, or the salesperson at a store would regale me with tales of a boyfriend or girlfriend's writing prowess. I largely operated on the basis of referral. We generally declined blind submissions [e.g. letters addressed to my company clearly as the result of a company listing in one of numerous entertainment directories]. But if some-one I knew had read and responded well to a screenplay I was always happy to read it.

In the beginning, my theory of management was a bit different; literary management was a rather new idea at the time. Historically, personal management began with in-front-of-the-camera talent and had existed for some long while, albeit not as long as "agency." Literary management—any non-actor management (director, writer, writer-director, writer-producer etc.)—was basically a new idea.

Agents have been around since H.M. Swanson, who was the first literary agent. Swanson started representing many writers under slave contracts to the studios by telling them "You have to have someone negotiating for you." This was many, many years ago, I believe during the thirties. So while agenting has been around a long time, management is newer and has mostly grown up around the idea of the actor and the actress.

During the early 80s, there were only a couple of small literary management companies. There was one other and then there was mine, and mine was a total fluke. I started it because no one told me writers don't have managers, so I assumed that they could. And there was one other village idiot doing the same thing. And yet now its become very common. Most, however, began with actors and later branched into the literary areas.

While there are a few larger management firms (e.g. Brillstein-Grey, SandDollar etc.), they're mostly actor-based. By definition, people who go into management tend to be more entrepreneurial than agents and run smaller shops. More recently, more and more companies that manage actors have gone into managing writers. So then they can "package," which is, of course, a gimmick, and usu-ally not true. Nevertheless, it's good business and feels "appealing" to prospective clients.

Management is odd given the wide range of styles embraced by each company. Confusing the issue somewhat is the fact of more and more managers becoming manager-producers. They are piggyback-ing their clients and producing, which is essentially how I began.

This is a convenient way to enter the producing ranks, but is appropriate only if the client has expressed a desire for you as manager to also become their producer.

What role do you think a manager plays in a writer's career, as distinguished from the agent?

I think it's very simple. Agents live within a very specific economic model: they sign revenue streams. If you don't hold the promise of producing an income rather quickly, most agents are probably not going to sign you at least not an established one. When I say an agent, I'm talking about respected agencies–be it CAA or Morris or ICM or UTA or the numerous, more modest-sized companies–who require good business incentive to sign a client. Their attitude often is, let Brand X sign you and do the hard work for a couple of years to build you up. Then when you're ready, when the more established agency thinks you're just about to really peak, they'll steal you. And they do. They're pretty effective and it can be as simple and willful as that.

Most agencies, even the mid-size companies, are not necessarily in the business of finding, discovering, nurturing, and developing new talent. That's not their raison d'être. They're bookers. Not to paint a black hat on the agent and a white hat on the manager, since this would also pervert the truth. Nevertheless, as a general model, the manager will hopefully be more inclined toward younger talent. My philosophy, and that of a number of managers I know, was to find and develop "green" talent–that writer who demonstrates strong craft, though is very naive about the business and who may to date, have never been represented, let alone sold or optioned a screenplay or been produced.

Initially, I sought out younger writers, recognizing the business reality that water seeks its own level. I was new to management and I needed writers who were more eager and willing to take a chance. Later on, however, that philosophy stayed the course for selfish and pragmatic reasons. As a whole, I'd found younger writers more appreciative and enthusiastic, nicer, and easier to represent. They hadn't developed a lot of bad habits. Over the years, I'd been approached by numerous writers who were leaving larger agencies and wanted a manager. In most instances, I declined even though their resumes were more impressive, simply because I sensed a poorly handled history which meant I would have to move through the town cleaning up messes and being continually surprised by what I'd failed to know entering into the relationship. I wanted writers who work hard, haven't learned skepticism or bad business habits, and walk into a room knowing they've a strong support system. It simply made my work more rewarding and enjoyable to develop and guide careers from the outset.

While this may not be the paradigm for all management firms, this was my experience and seems to be at the heart of the difference between agency and management in general. The other item worth noting, perhaps, is that in theory the manager is responsible for fewer clients and thus can be more available to the client on a regular basis.

How does an emerging writer start the process of getting known in the entertainment industry?

Give your scripts to anybody who will read them. Anybody. Not the clerk at the 7–Eleven, but anybody reasonably related to the business. If someone is a second assistant director who has worked with thus and such group, let them read it. You never know who knows whom, and people move around and graduate very quickly in this business. So-and-so's assistant last week is now the casting director, is now the. . . . It's wacky how rapidly people can change positions.

Writers often worry about protecting their material. Stop worrying. Put a copyright notice on it, register it with the Writers Guild, and then say "The hell with it," because until you are established, you have to take a little risk. If you know another writer and he or she is represented and the writer is happy with their agent, let your writer friend read your work. Let them submit it to his agent on your behalf. Just run with your imagination, anything that makes sense, as long as it's not too nutty. But I would say, get your material read by anyone who will read it for the first couple of years. There's no science to it, no direct path to travel. Scripts circulate in the oddest of ways and your job is to create the greatest opportunity for your work to get read. Once you've been produced and have a team of agents, lawyers, managers, business managers, publicists, chiropractors, herbalists, and psychics, then you can exercise a certain greater discretion about how to introduce each new piece of work to the larger community.

Now that you are producing, has the method by which you receive scripts changed at all?

No, it's still random. The more films I get produced, the more [scripts] I receive through the agency system. But not as many as you might think. I still discover a lot of material on my own. The mid-level agents like me a lot, we work really well together and they know my penchant for working well and closely with their writers. Occasionally I'll be sent material from an ICM [International Creative Management] or a CAA [Creative Artists Agency]. But by and large, CAA is an enclave unto itself. The town has such a desperate appetite for good material, that the agencies don't part with their clients' material readily, they don't make gifts of it. The larger agencies have a lot of hungry mouths to feed, numerous large talent clients who have either vanity production companies or real production companies, as well as directors with or without their own production entities. Thus they tend to submit their writer clientele's output to non-writing clients in order to "package."

Packaging basically means "writer beware." Agents always sell themselves with "Come with us, we package." It can be a good thing, but rarely for the writer. If you are a big established name, you may enjoy a certain enhanced protection. But in a majority of cases, the actor(s), director, and/or producer are far weightier clients than the writer and their needs get addressed first. When it comes to the nitty gritty of creative deal terms or as the financial pie is being divided, the writer generally is the one the agents fight for the least.

Likewise, to the extent agencies do submit "spec" material to outside producers, the tendency is to embrace producers with large deals on the various studio lots. As a practical matter, these producers should have a stronger "voice" with their respective studios and stand in a better position to encourage the acquisition of a screenplay. By choice, I'm an independent producer working with various different studios and independent film production companies. So while I do receive one or several "spec" scripts weekly, this represents a smaller part of my effort compared with studio-based producers.

The majority of my film projects begin with a script from a writer I've known and worked with previously or someone they've referred to me. Beyond that, people, ideas, and scripts come over the transom by way of agents and entertainment attorneys and, increasingly, directly from executives at the studios or independent production companies. I also secure rights to books and remake rights to older American and European films and then bring in elements, including the writer of my choosing.

When should writers option their script, and what should they be cautious about?

Be careful about optioning your scripts. Option your scripts to someone if you've done your homework and you think these are legitimate people and the terms of the option are fair. There are all kinds of lousy deals being offered to writers.

In a perfect world? Don't option your material. In an ideal situation, you [a writer] find a producer or director or star whose take on your material you like and then you decide to team up with them. And you go forth into the world together. Let the free marketplace system work to your benefit. If and when an independent company or a studio or any kind of financing entity acquires the material, you'll both make your own deals and you'll be reasonable, and you won't kill the deal. But you or your respective representatives will make your own individual deals. That way, there's no conflict. They're not meddling in your business, and you're not meddling in theirs. That's hard to pull off. Most producers are going to say "Well, I'm going to invest the next twelve to twenty-four months of my life trying to set this up"—taking meetings, phone calls, sending letters, scripts, xeroxing, and the like—and they want to know they enjoy exclusivity. Without an option, your partner [producer or otherwise] has no assurance you or your agent aren't working at cross-purposes with other individuals or companies, or 'shopping' the deal the producer brings to the table. It's more about exclusivity than it is the economics of the situation.

But to the extent a deal [usually an option agreement] is required, be certain to seek experienced advice to insure fairness. There are many variables and there is no standard deal and there are even many different deal structures. It may depend upon whether it is a small art film or a highly castable studio film. So while I'm not advocating you not option your material, I think it essential you find your way to sound advice from an attorney or agent who's been the architect of more than one or two such deals in the past. A good advisor will also emphasize deal points other than money, especially for a younger writer whose remuneration will likely not be tremendous at the outset. How and when can you, as writer, be replaced on the project? Are you being guaranteed at least one rewrite, if not something greater than that, the idea of having any given studio as my "home" is less appealing. I have eclectic tastes and I don't know any studio that would like even a majority of the projects that appeal to me.

My attitude about studios is that they are smart. They are all bleeding-heart liberals, except when it comes to business, and then they are deathly dangerous. The studio always comes out ahead. With all but a few of the richest producer deals, the producer usually pays dearly for every dollar that they take from the studio. The studio takes overhead and advance monies out of your producing fees, they may charge things against your film that shouldn't be, and so forth. Also, it's the psychology of it. I hear a lot of frustrated producers saying "God, I can't get an answer out of my studio, they won't set this project free so I can take it somewhere else." As an independent, if people know that I could take my script anywhere, they all tend to want to know about it. And they are more respectful, and we end up striking fair deals from an arms-length stance.

The good news is I live a healthier, simpler life, with no one to answer to other than myself. For any creative person [writers, directors, producers]—and this may well apply to agents or other "noncreative" players—the more you create about yourself a sense of competition, the better. Hollywood or the film business is all about hope, expectation, and anticipation—what's just around the corner, and less about what's here and real. What might such and such person create tomorrow? That certain agent might find the hottest new writer with the most brilliant screenplay ever written. Hope springs eternal. People really pay attention because of that.

My particular bias is such that if a studio "owned" me and knew they enjoyed exclusivity vis-à-vis the universe of my producing efforts, it's a little less exciting. So I pay my employees, my rent, and my option monies and, so far, I'm happy doing it that way.

What are your feelings about writers who want to be directors?

Simply put, they're crazy.

As a producer, there's nothing better than working with a talented writer-director. I'd rather work with a writer-director than a separate writer and director any day of the week. If you go into the project seeing eye-to-eye creatively and you know what you are going for, then its easier and cleaner to have the writer and director be the same person. The more people that are involved the more difficult it can become. Any film project becomes populated with studio executives, agents, actors, producer(s), director, writer(s), and various others. The room can quickly come to feel quite crowded.

If the writer-director and the producer have a pretty clear point of view about their film, they can negotiate those waters more readily. The goal is to foster an atmosphere of true partnership and teamwork and yet fight constructively with your partners to protect a creative vision. So I love writer-directors.

As a practical matter, establish yourself as a writer before you jump into directing. There are a lot of people who write their first script and say that they want to direct it, and they slow their progress. While there are no rules per se, for most I'd urge a focus on the writing side until achieving a certain success. Then pick carefully the script that is both highly personal and potentially commercial as a vehicle for your directorial debut.

Stories abound of the aspiring filmmaker who wrote a script, secured financing, made a brilliant film, and launched a career. To some extent, what's right for any individual depends on why they write. If you really like writing, if writing is something that you want to be doing for years and years, then I encourage you to seek your success before entering the fray as a director. If writing merely serves a greater good, that's a different matter. It's a highly personal choice—temper your choices with just a tad of practicality and then proceed.

The general trend very much favors the writer-director. The auteur era as we've known it is at a close and the pre-eminence of the writer-director is being increasingly acknowledged.

The traditional path that I see (for writers who want to be directors) is three produced scripts, and the fourth produced script the studio will let you direct.

The path from writer to director is, first and foremost, unpredictable. Ask ten directors how they came to direct their first film, even their second, and you'll hear ten extremely different tales. Any attempt to formulate a definitive strategy will likely have holes in it. Nevertheless, we can try to generalize. Let's begin by ruling out the world of independent filmmaking, which would make impossible any intelligent response. In the realm of the studio, certain behaviors seem to repeat and thus be susceptible to this sort of discussion.

While there's no magic number, I'll go along with your notion that if a writer has several scripts produced, especially if the films were successful, that writer will find a greater receptiveness to his or her aspirations (directing, producing, acting, etc.). This is different than the writer whose work has been purchased and/or developed on one or more occasions by one or more studios. The realistic touchstone becomes films actually produced. In that event, particularly if one studio has enjoyed several successful working experiences with the writer, the studio may entertain letting the writer matriculate. More so if the writer is aligned with a strong producer on that studio's lot. In some instances, studios are known to get their pound of flesh or, more politely, a quid pro quo in the form of one or more other pieces of writing the studio may need before actually handing over the reins.

This simply echoes a simple business reality, also true of Hollywood. It is a business of relationships. Find successful producers to champion your cause and spend time writing brilliant work and becoming the darling of certain studio executives. You can even make a study of which studios, which executives and which producers have a history of launching first-time directors. You can create your opportunity. It's all about shared history and success and knowing how to instill confidence in those around you.

Frank Darabont is a most respected writer who'd optioned and subsequently adapted a book, *The Shawshank Redemption*. Rob Reiner at Castle Rock Pictures wanted very much to direct it himself. The writer was offered several million dollars to step aside. Given his determination and feeling this one was "it" for him, he stayed the course and did eventually direct under the aegis of Castle Rock and earned an Oscar nomination along the way.

If as a writer you feel a strong desire to direct a particular story, stick to your guns until you find someone to champion you. There are many producers, myself included, who will support a first-time director who really comes across in a room. If the quality of the writing speaks for itself and the need to direct is burning a hole in your soul, make your wishes known. Be realistic and scale your plan accordingly. A major star will rarely star in your feature debut, but reach as high as you can and try for the exception. If you're great in a room, tremendously persuasive and passionate, and exhibit creative leadership, this is what people want, actors included. If you can get into a room and convince a "viable" actor, you'll get a shot at directing your project. As the junior executives of MGM chairman Alan Ladd Jr. were wont to say, "Bring someone in Laddie's office, give him five to ten minutes, and he'll tell you if they are a director." While wholly subjective, the idea and approach has merit.

How important is it for a writer to network?

Networking is annoying. I'd rather stay home. I can think of a million things that I'd rather do than hang out with the film crowd. But it is essential. The earlier in one's career, the more important. It's a vital part of one's evolution in the film business.

Join organizations if you are inclined. If you're politically inclined, seek out the Hollywood Women's Political Committee, Women in Film, or the myriad other groups fostered by the entertainment community. Likewise, there are other organizations for a host of appetites, from charities for children, homeless, and AIDS to environmental organizations. And they're awash with folks from the film community.

Though it's unfair and stating the obvious, women should be even more aggressive networkers. Discrimination does exist and it affects all of us who weren't born into the business. Women especially. Perhaps a tiny bit less so for women writers than directors, producers, executives, or the like. Writing may be the one area where there's a tendency towards a meritocracy. What's on the page speaks pretty clearly. You may get paid less than the guy, but that's changing just as it has for actress pay scales.

You're going to get a million "no's." You're going to hear "no" until you're blue in the face. And you must ignore it. You can't hear that word if you want to be in a creative enterprise. You join these organizations, get out there, and meet agents and other writers. It's important to meet your peers, especially for writers. Writers are unique in that they don't meet their peers in the ordinary course of their work. They've no idea what other writers are about, or how to interact with them, or how to act as a group. It's terribly important to meet other writers, exchange ideas, and learn from one another's experiences. Likewise, there are a significant number of producers, development people, and others who are receptive to meeting writers. Force yourself to do it.

Just assume that everyone you deal with in the film business is as insecure as you might imagine. Don't be afraid. Just go out and be yourself and meet as many people as you can. The more people you know, the shorter the distance between where you are and where you desire to be. Just know how to approach people–think of what they do and what they need. Your talent aside, people want to work with those they know and feel comfortable with in a room. You never know where you'll meet that one person with whom you can work successfully and whose professional friendship you'll come to value for many years.

Jonathan Lawton is the single most important creative person in my life. A great friend over the last fourteen years, Jonathan's a wonderful gentleman and extraordinarily talented. I've no doubt we'll collaborate on films until either of us gets fed up, or we die. While not "networking," we met in an unusual way. I'd bought Macintosh computers for my office, and because I was computerphobic, I called a writer friend and confessed I hadn't even opened the boxes, let alone plugged them in. The friend urged me to phone Jonathan, reputed to be a wiz computer genius. He turned out to be a lovely guy, 23 years old at the time, earning a living as a film editor and computer guru. Several weeks later, he'd programmed the office and taught us all how to join in the twentieth century. He changed my life. Along the way, he'd learned my business and subtly led me to ask if he was, in fact, a writer. As it turned out, he had more than half a dozen completed screenplays hiding in his apartment, never read by a living soul. His work was extraordinary and we've been working together ever since.

One of the great and wonderful things about this business is that you will meet strange and bizarre people in strange and bizarre ways. Many will go in and out of your lives, and others will stick. You just have to create the opportunity.

If you're not comfortable in Hollywood settings, go to film festivals where people are skiing and drinking hot toddies and are more relaxed than normal. It's a question of how much energy and how aggressive you want to be about finding people.

Start early. It's a small town filled with an endless array of people and the more you know the better off you will be. You'll gain perspective on the kinds of people you're drawn to and will align yourself with over time. Writers tend to stay home or in an office and write. So fight inertia and circulate.

Can a writer rely on his agent to do the important networking for him?

As a manager, even if my client had an agent, I always felt one hundred percent responsible for moving their career forward. By the same token, I feel every member of the team should feel that way. The person who should feel the strongest about that, of course, is the creative person. A writer should rely on his or her agent or manager, but not use them as a shield to protect them from the larger community. Many writers complain they create the bulk of the opportunities that come their way. While agents and others should be producing opportunity and result, the above "complaint" is simply a reflection of reality. The agent opens doors and makes introductions, but it is the writer who goes into the room and "sells" themselves. Likewise, it's the writer's responsibility not to insulate themselves but to be social creatures in the context of their profession. We all find opportunity by virtue of our relationships. It's human nature and the film business is not exempt.

As a producer, how closely do you think producers and writers should work together and what are your usual habits when working with writers?

It really depends on the writer. My preference is to work very, very closely. My style is that of a very strong collaborator and editor.

By way of example, I've a project entitled *Maelstrom* on which the writer and I completed four rewrites during the last year for the studio. In between official deliveries to the studio, the writer and I would do multiple rewrites, mini-rewrites. We'd spend approximately six hours together, once a week. Each week was a cycle and during each cycle we would create a whole new rewrite. Each week the writer would deliver the newest revision which I would read overnight, making my notes. We'd then spend another six hours or so going over my notes, and then he would go away for another week and create yet another whole new rewrite. We would do this repeatedly, constantly, every week. And after enough of those, he would move far enough and create a draft which we felt was ready for the studio. And, like Sisyphus, we would start over and do it again. While not the norm, some producers enjoy working that closely with the writer.

I experienced the far side of that process on yet a different studio project. After one meeting with the studio, the writer disappeared, literally left town, returning six weeks later to deliver a draft. We had no input and no conversation. This was the writer's choice and not terribly pleasing to me. Nor to the studio who saw the work as falling short of our stated goals.

It depends also on how experienced the writer is and to what extent the writer welcomes collaboration. J.F. Lawton is such a sophisticated, experienced writer that I ordinarily only give my notes and reactions after he's fully completed his draft.

Any final advice for emerging writers?

All writers should want to become great writers. I think that most writers should forget about the business, don't read the trades, and

stay at home and write and write and write and write until you find
your rhythm. Eventually, you will write something that everyone
will stand up and shout about.

THE NON-WRITERS GUILD OF AMERICA CONTRACT: WRITING FOR FILM

OK. Life does not always proceed as planned. As with many writers
who desire to write for the entertainment industry, somewhere along
the road to glory is the opportunity to write in a situation that is less
than perfect. By less than perfect I mean a situation in which a writer is
handed a contract that does not meet the basic compensation and
working conditions of the Writers Guild of America Minimum Basic
Agreement—in other words, non-WGA contracts. If you are a member
of the WGA, this is not addressed to you. As you know, it would be
foolish for you to accept a contract similar to this, and if caught, you
would pay the piper—or the WGA (see the chapter on the WGA,
specifically Working Rule 8). If you are not a member of the WGA,
however, the following represents the type of agreement that might be
presented to you in the early stages of your career. For purposes of
comparison with what you will receive later in your career (a WGA
agreement), here is a typical non-WGA agreement, with my comments.

SAMPLE: THE NON-WGA AGREEMENT

This Agreement is made and entered into as of _____ by and between _____ (hereinafter referred to as "Producer") and _____ (hereinafter referred to as "Writer"), with reference to the following:

Producer desires to engage the services of Writer to write an original treatment, first draft screenplay ("First Draft"), second draft screenplay ("Second Draft") third draft screenplay ("Third Draft"), and final draft screenplay ("Final Draft") and revisions thereof (the Polish) (hereinafter collectively referred to as the "Screenplay") suitable as the basis for a feature-length theatrical motion picture, as a specially commissioned work made for hire. *(Clearly this is not a WGA agreement because the Producer is asking for four drafts, an original treatment, and a polish from this writer!!!!)*

Writer desires to be engaged by Producer on the terms and conditions contained herein.

I. **Engagement: Service.** Producer hereby engages the services of Writer to write a Screenplay as an independent contractor performing a specially ordered or commissioned work made for hire. Writer shall deliver the Screenplay as and when required by Producer, with such work to be completed in accordance with the comments, notes, instructions, and directions of Producer according to the following schedule. *(Well, the writer is bound to this Producer and clearly will not have any rights of copyright in this work. With this production, the writer may not want any copyright in the work, however, because I doubt that a work of quality can be accomplished on the schedule set forth below.)*

II. **Schedule for Performance.**

A. First Draft Screenplay

Start of Services: Upon execution of Certificate of Authorship

Writing Period: 3 weeks

Reading Period: 7 business days

      B. Second Draft Screenplay
         Writing Period: 2 Weeks
         Reading Period: 7 business days
      C. Third Draft Screenplay
         Writing Period: 1 week
         Reading Period: 4 Weeks prior to principal photo-
           graph
      D. Fourth Draft Screenplay
         Writing Period: 1 week
         Reading Period: 2 weeks prior to principal photo-
           graph
      E. Polish
         Writing Period: 1 week

(Obviously this is a jam-it-out-and-shoot-it company that is making product as fast as possible, with no concern for the writer or writer's schedule. This is not a good schedule if you are a slow writer, but it may beat working as a temp typist if you need the money.)

III. **Compensation.**
      A. In consideration for all services performed and to be performed by Writer hereunder, for all rights, licenses, privileges, and property conveyed or agreed to be conveyed pursuant to this Agreement, and all warranties, representations, and covenants herein made by Writer, Producer agrees to pay to Writer and Writer agrees to accept as a flat fee the sum of *Four Thousand Dollars* ($4,000.00) payable twenty-five percent (25%) upon Writer's execution of this Agreement and seventy-five percent (75%) upon delivery of the Screenplay. *(Needless to say, the money is far off the WGA scale. In addition, the prospect of receiving only 25 percent at the commencement is a cheap way to deal with the writer. Also, the "guaranteed" services include only the first draft, which puts this writer in the position of turning in a great first draft and having the producer say "adios" because he has received a working draft that is suitable for his production.)*

B. In the event Producer elects, in its sole discretion, to have Writer perform additional services on the First Draft of the Screenplay, in consideration for all services performed and to be performed by Writer, for all rights, licenses, privileges, and property conveyed or agreed to be conveyed, and for all warranties, representations, and covenants herein made by Writer, in respect of each state of such additional services, Producer agrees to pay to Writer and Writer agrees to accept as a flat fee:

1. For the Second Draft of the Screenplay, the sum of Fifteen Hundred Dollars ($1,500.00) upon delivery of said draft;

2. For the Third Draft of the Screenplay, the sum of One Thousand Dollars ($1,000.00) upon delivery of said draft;

3. For the Fourth Draft of the Screenplay, the sum of One Thousand Dollars ($1,000.00) upon delivery of said draft;

4. For the Polish of the Screenplay, the sum of Five Hundred Dollars ($500.00) upon delivery of said Polish.

5. Producer shall be entitled to elect not to proceed to an additional stage of the screenplay at any time. Upon such election, Producer shall have no further obligation to pay Writer any amounts, except for a stage for which Writer has completely performed the services. *(As stated previously, the money for the above services is very little and far below the WGA minimum compensation. In addition, the writer is to be paid only when each draft is turned in. Also, the Producer has the option "not to proceed to an additional stage of the screenplay at any time," which means that the writer could "be fired" at any time. Most likely the writer who agreed to this contract would find himself not receiving more than $4,000 from it.)*

6. In the event that the Producer produces the Screenplay, and the budget is greater than Three

Hundred and Fifty Thousand Dollars ($350,000.00), then in addition to the sums provided for in Paragraph 3 A-B (1–4), Writer shall be paid an amount equal to two and one-half percent (2.5%) of the amount provided in addition to Three Hundred and Fifty Thousand Dollars ($350,000.00); however, the total Purchase Price shall in no event exceed One Hundred Thousand Dollars ($100,000.00) regardless of the amount of the budget. This amount will be deferred and paid to Writer from Producer's Net Profits. *(This is an area where most writers get totally screwed—that is, accepting a significant portion of compensation for services in the form of "deferred compensation." As explained in the WGA contract, a writer will rarely see any "net profits." To accept "net profits" from "producer's net profits" means that you will see less than nothing because this refers to a percentage of the amount remaining after the studio or another financier receives full recoupment of the gross funds necessary to pay negative costs, payment of deferments, if any, and thereafter deducting continuing distribution costs and fees. The remaining income can then be further reduced by as much as 50 percent or more of the net profits that a studio or other financier retains as compensation for supplying financing and completion advances. What is left is generally not more than 40 percent of 100 percent of net profits as the "producer's share.")*

IV. **Credit.**

A. The granting of, and the form, placement, size, duration, and all other matters relating to, any credit accorded Writer hereunder shall be determined by Producer in Producer's sole discretion. *(The likelihood of receiving credit for the work is not too high in this situation. As stated previously, if the work is not something the writer wants to be associated with, then the writer should use a pseudonym. If some of the compen-*

sation (such as a bonus) is tied to receiving credit, however, this could be a problem.

V. **Grant of Rights.**

A. Writer hereby grants to Producer all right, title, and interest in and to the Screenplay and all other results and proceeds of Writer's services hereunder, and the Screenplay shall become the property of the Producer, which shall for copyright purposes be deemed the author thereof. Producer shall have the right to obtain copyright of the Screenplay in its own name or otherwise, free of any claim thereto by Writer, including, without limitation, in connection with any right of droit moral or any similar right, all of which are hereby waived by Writer. As used herein, the term "Screenplay" shall include the treatment, the Screenplay, and all drafts, all revisions, rewrites, and polishes hereof created by Writer, and all parts thereof, including but not limited to the theme, plot, characters, story, and setting contained therein. *(Clearly, the Producer will own everything that the writer even thinks about this production, and the writer will have no claim of copyright on this work.)*

B. Writer hereby conveys, grants, and assigns exclusively to Producer, forever and throughout the universe, all right, title, and interest in and to the Screenplay and all other results and proceeds of Writer's services hereunder and any and all parts thereof, including but not limited to all motion picture rights, television rights, video rights, CD-ROM rights, interactive media rights, book rights, remake and sequel rights, the title and theme thereof, the ideas, performances, characters, and characterizations, and all other materials therein contained, whether or not said rights are now known, recognized, or contemplated. *(The Producer owns every derivative work which is remotely based upon the screenplay or any work the writer has done for the producer.)*

C. Producer may make any changes in, deletions from, or additions to the Screenplay or any photoplay, production, or other material based on the Screenplay and all other results and proceeds of Writer's services hereunder which Producer in Producer's sole discretion may consider necessary or desirable. As between Writer and Producer, the title of the Screenplay is the sole property of Producer and may be used as the title of any photoplay, production, or other material, although no other part of the Screenplay is used therein. Producer may use one or more other titles for the Screenplay or any photoplay, production, or material based thereon. *(The producer may do anything he wants to this work.)*

D. Writer's grant of rights in this Agreement is irrevocable and without right of recision by Writer.

Dated: _____   By: _____

For: _____

Dated: _____   By: _____

"Writer"

10

Writing for Episodic Television

EMPLOYMENT AS A WRITER

Writers make money writing for episodic television in only one way: by obtaining a position on a television show. Although some writers free-lance by writing and selling spec episodes (episodes the writer was not hired to write but sold to the show independently), and a few (and I mean a few) special individuals are able to create television shows without having significant experience as a writer on a television show, the primary method by which writers make money writing for television is by obtaining a staff position on a television show. (By episodic television I am distinguishing between a weekly television series where the program shows once a week and long-form television, which are movies-for-television and TV miniseries.) The emerging writer who hopes to write for television must have some sample scripts that show an ability to write for the medium. It is best to have at least two sample scripts from two different shows, and it is generally best to write for your favorite shows. When writing a sample script, it is important to know the show inside and out: You should know the characters thoroughly and the activities these characters would logically engage in. You should know the plot line, the direction the show has taken, the location, the genre. In general, you should be an expert on the show. In addition, you should (I mean <u>must</u>) choose a show that is not only currently on the air but is currently "hot" and not fading from glory.

When you actually write the script, remember to be as imaginative as possible with the plot and to push the envelope as far as you can with the characters.

Although the primary method by which a writer has her script read by the producer of a television show is by receiving the script through an agent, the industry is filled with individuals who have obtained positions on television shows without having an agent (see the interviews that follow). The methods by which these aspiring writers have gotten their scripts to producers of television shows include taking an internship with the show; obtaining a production assistant position with the show; becoming a secretary with the show; winning a contest; and making friends with the writers or producers for a show. There are obviously a thousand different methods to have your work read, but you need to be creative.

In the event that you write a script that gets you into a meeting with a producer (generally the executive producer) of a television show, do yourself a favor: Go into the meeting with several pitches for possible episodes for the program, and know the show as if it were a matter of life and death. Needless to say, with the intense competition for positions on a television show, it is not wise to insult a supervising or executive producer with your lack of knowledge concerning his show.

The position in which a writer joins a television show generally corresponds to the amount of experience the writer has in television. In dramatic television, a writer's title on the show generally changes for every year the writer is a member of the show's writing staff. These titles are regulated by the Writers Guild of America, which sets the base salary level and the credit that a writer receives.

The following are the basic positions that a staff writer on a dramatic television program might occupy:

Staff writer. This is an entry-level position. The staff writer generally does not receive on-screen credit (that is, the writer does not get a credit byline on the television screen when credits for the show are run) but does receive credit for the individual episodes the writer creates for the series. The staff writer generally receives a ten- to twenty-week contract with an option to renew, and is generally, but not always, paid for scripts that she creates for the show against a weekly salary. The writer's minimum weekly salary is set by the WGA. The staff writer works with the rest of the writers to create the story arc of the show and is responsible for individually writing several of the outlines and episodes during the season.

Story editor. If the staff writer remains on the show for one year, she probably will be bumped up to the next higher title, which is story editor. The story editor receives on-screen credit. The writer who becomes story editor generally has a ten- to twenty-week contract with the show with an option to renew the contract. The story editor's responsibilities are to write outlines and teleplays. Additional responsibilities are varied. The minimum amount for the story editor's salary is set by the WGA, which considers the story editor a "writer in an additional capacity." The story editor is expected to write several scripts for the show and is paid an additional amount, usually WGA minimum, for each episode she writes.

Executive story editor. If the writer remains on the show for yet another year, the writer will graduate to the position of executive story editor. The responsibilities of the executive story editor are similar to the story editor's with varied responsibilities. The executive story editor receives on-screen credit. The minimum salary is set by the WGA, which also considers the executive story editor a "writer in an additional capacity." The executive story editor is expected to write several scripts for the show and is paid an additional amount, usually WGA minimum, for each episode she writes.

Co-producer. In the position of co-producer the writer begins to be involved with casting and editorial choices. The responsibilities of the co-producer include duties similar to those of executive story editor, plus casting.

Producer. There are several kinds of producers, both writing and non-writing. The executive and supervising producers of the show are involved in all casting and editorial positions.

Executive producer. The executive producer is a title with various definitions and therefore the following might be considered generalizations. The executive producer is generally the individual who puts together the entire show, from concept to stars (as in actors), to decisions concerning who will produce and hire the initial group of staff writers for the show. The executive producer writes the pilot episode, is often known as "the show runner," and is the producer responsible for seeing that every aspect of the show runs smoothly. All final decisions concerning casting, editorial choices, arc of the story, location, concept, and direction of the show are decided by the executive producer. Usually, the only authority above the executive producer is the network itself.

The executive producer status is a position of extraordinary creativity. Unlike film, in which writers aspire to be directors, writers in television aspire to be executive producers.

WRITING FOR EPISODIC TELEVISION: INTERVIEWS WITH STEVE KRONISH AND LAWRENCE MEYERS

INTERVIEW WITH STEVE KRONISH

Steve Kronish was the executive producer and creator of "The Commish" and the executive producer of "Wiseguy."

How did you begin your career writing for television?

I came out to California in 1973, and I went to U.S.C. and got a master's in journalism. I've always wanted to be either a United States senator or Tom Winker, and obviously I failed on both counts.

I just started writing. The first TV scripts I wrote were "Mary Tyler Moore" scripts, and "Bob Newhart" scripts, and of course none of them sold. The U.S.C. degree was kind of a backup in case things did not pan out, although I'm not sure that a master's degree helps you much in getting a job in the newspaper business anyway.

I started writing those half-hour comedy scripts and did not sell anything. Then a friend of mine got me a job working as a talent coordinator for some local TV shows at KCOP Channel 13. I did that for about a year and a half. Out of that experience I wrote a play about a green room situation at a television talk show, and that was produced at an equity waiver house on Santa Monica Boulevard. In the interim—this is now about '78 or so—I was working as an assistant golf pro at a country club in Woodland Hills.

Some of the members helped me finance the production. One of the members had a son who was a feature producer at Universal. He saw the play. This is now–actually I am skipping way ahead, but it was in '81, I think, that the play was produced. And in the interim I had been writing more "Mary Tyler Moore" scripts, all that kind of stuff. . . . It had dawned on me that there was probably going to be not too many things more useless than a "Mary Tyler Moore" script once "Mary Tyler Moore" went off the air, and, obviously, eventually she did.

I guess I wrote a couple of features, spec things, that never went anywhere, but this producer came to see the show. He called me up about two and a half days later and said that he was working on a Cheech and Chong movie. He wanted a script that he could use to board—that is, to create a schedule. I didn't even know what a board was, but he promised me two drafts of the script—and at $7,500 a draft, which was more than I was making for a year working as a golf pro. He wanted the script in a week, so I took a week off from the club and wrote this script, gave it to him, and got my $7,500. He said that it was fine. I did not hear from him again about the second draft and the second $7,500. Finally I found out that he had gone to Europe to do the movie with Cheech and Chong, and not with my script. He did not steal my script, but I never got the second draft and I never got the second $7,500.

I sat down to write him a letter in which I was going to say that I felt kind of taken advantage of and lied to, but then I thought, well, if I do that, there goes that contact, and I did not have many contacts to burn. In fact, he was about it. So I wrote him a thank-you note, and I did not hear from him again for two years. And then Labor Day weekend of 1984, I got a call from him. He was working on a movie at Universal, and the studio hated the script; but they had a start date of a month from that time, and would I take a look at it. So I did, and I came up with some ideas on how to do something with it. In the interim they were trying to get some name people to do a rewrite on it, but they said, "Why don't you come in and rewrite a couple of scenes, and we will pay you for a polish and see how it goes?" I went in and I wrote the scenes, handed them in, left, and figured, well, I have $6,500 for that, which was sound money, and that was great, and that was that.

That evening I got a call from the production secretary asking me to come back to the studio and if I had a passport. I realized that since I lived in North Hollywood and Universal was in Universal City, I did not need a passport for that. Something was up.

I got back to the studio, and the directors very casually said, "Well, you know, when we get to Paris, we'll work on this scene and this scene." Twenty-four hours later I found myself looking at the Eiffel Tower. I was supposed to be in Paris for two weeks and then go home, and my wife was going to come over and meet me. We were going to blow all the money and just see Europe a little bit, but we wound up being in Paris for three weeks and Berlin for four weeks. It was great, an unbelievable kind of thing. The picture was called *Gotcha!* which starred Anthony Edwards, who is now starring in "E.R." and Linda Fiorentino. I did not get a screen credit, but it was basically a page-one dialogue rewrite, and it was a silly kind of little movie. But for me it was the first thing that made me actually believe I was in show business.

About six months after that, the director of that show, a guy named Jeff Kanew, called me because he had been contacted by Universal, and they said they wanted him to write and direct an episode of "Alfred Hitchcock Presents," when it was an NBC show. This was in '86 now. He said, "You know, I do not want to write it, and if they like it, I will tell them you did it, and you will get the money and everything." So I wrote this script, and I think for the first and only time in my life they shot the draft, and without any changes. The supervising producer of the show basically was thinking, "Now who the hell is this guy?" He called me in and put me on staff. I think that was in the summer of '86. I've been working ever since.

My first staff job was on "Alfred Hitchcock Presents." That lasted one season, although our lead-in was a show called "Amazing Stories" which was a Steven Spielberg show, and I think on the forty-four-episode order when it began. We were the second half-hour in that one-hour block. I thought, well, Spielberg is the lead-in, I am going to be working forever. This is going to be great, and we were, actually. "Hitchcock" was doing better than the Spielberg show in the ratings, and my boss was telling me to go buy a house, everything was going to be great. My wife and I were looking for our first house. We bought it in the morning, we signed the papers for the house, and my parents had come out from New York to celebrate the event. We were leaving to go out for dinner and the phone rang. It was this producer, and he said we had just gotten canceled. I said, "I just bought a house. You told me to buy a house." I went for three weeks or so thinking I was going to be evicted before I moved in, but from that job I worked for a year on a show called "MacGuyver" at Paramount.

Were you a staff writer on "MacGuyver"?

At that time, I think, I was a writer-producer. The opportunity came up to do a show that was just beginning called "Wiseguy" for CBS. I started as a producer on "Wiseguy" and wound up being a co-executive producer on that show. I was there for three years.

Do you think persistence is an important part of being successful as a writer in the entertainment industry?

It was, yes. I think every now and then you read about the overnight success, but there are very few. Had I known it was going to be as difficult as it proved to be for me, I am sure I would not have done it. I think that one of the other things that I had going for me was that my parents were always supportive of what I was trying to do. If I had to fight them as well as everybody else, I do not think I would have been able to do it. But then there were a few times when I said that I was coming home, I could not stand it anymore. And they said, "You can do it." I know that was difficult for them because I think to this day that my mother thinks my living in California is just a passing thing. I know it was very tough for them to say that, but they did, and I know that I could not have struggled through the difficult periods without knowing that at least they were supportive. That was really important, and it is something that a lot of people do not have. I was lucky, as far as I am concerned. I mean, I was very close to going into the advertising business. I was close to going into the restaurant business. I was looking at myself—I was thirty years old or thereabouts. All my friends from school were accountants and lawyers, and getting on with their lives, and I was pretty much unemployed. I do not come from a background where being unemployed is the norm. So that was difficult, and even to the extent that now—being hopefully between jobs and not at the end of the road—that is something sort of foreign to the way everybody lived when I was growing up. You had a job, and that was it. You got a job and went to work every day. There was no such thing as "Are you working?" Nobody ever *not* worked. It was a given you were working. I think that it takes some getting used to emotionally, and some people, probably myself included. . . have in the back of their minds that the last gig you got is the last gig you are going to get, that the last script you wrote is the last, that you will never get another idea. . . .

That seems to be a fairly common thread among people in this business, and many actors are probably more neurotic than most writers, but writers are fairly neurotic, too, I think, as a group. And. . . whether the product is good, better, and different, I think you still try to make it as good as it can be, and that involves putting something of yourself into it. When it is rejected, it hurts—probably not as much as actors because it is somewhat less personal. There are no absolute factors that determine what is successful and what is not successful, and sometimes merit does not have much to do with it. So, for me, this is an unusual period because, like I say, I have really kind of been working without a break for quite a while. So this break—although it has been only two months–seems like a year to me. . . .

Depending on your own personality and your philosophy about how you are going to live, that can be fine or it can be tough. . . . I will get through this period, and it will be okay. I have four children now and a house—all that stuff—so I suppose I am a little less casual about the ups and downs of it, and I hope that within the next few weeks I will know where I am. I think that people from school or younger people I have talked to would ask, "When did you feel that you had made it?" My standard answer is, "When I feel that way, I will tell you." I do not know that it is the kind of business that really ever enables you to feel totally comfortable.

When and how did you get your first agent?

First of all, besides my current agent I have had only one agent. I started working with him in 1984. Up until about four or five months ago, he was my first and only agent.

Going with my current agent was a fairly major thing for me. I felt I needed a certain amount of clout that I did not think my former agent had—although I think he is a really good agent and I cannot point to any failure on his part. I mean he in fact made some very good deals for me. But I have known my current agent for a few years. We belong to the same golf club, and he was with a big agency at that time, and I felt that I needed to make a change.

The reason I stayed with the one agent that I had for eight years was that he wanted me when nobody else did, and that meant a lot to me. It was really only when I felt I needed to do something for my own career and my family that I felt I had to make a change. Otherwise I would have stayed with him.

Ultimately, I think you are your own agent in terms of the work you do. If you do lousy work, the best Mike Ovitz cannot sell you. I think I was able to develop a reputation within some circles of somebody who is reliable, a hard worker and all that kind of stuff. It had nothing to do with whether my agent was good or not and what kind of deals he made. It was what kind of performance I gave when I was on the job. But. . . having said that your stuff will get read, it probably will, but it does not mean that getting an agent is easy. It is probably one of the most difficult things to do in the business just because of the sheer volume of people trying to get in versus how many agents there are. An agent does not want to have a lot of clients who are not working. It does not do him any good and does not do them any good. He keeps getting calls asking, "Why aren't I working?"—and there is no point in signing people if you cannot do anything for them.

I think when somebody is starting out, he submits all the scripts, and I think secretaries read them, readers read them. If it's really good, it does go up the ladder. But still it is a tough process, and in some respects it's easier to get a job than an agent.

Do you remember any particular meeting that you had in your early days or any particular pitch in your first big meeting where it clicked for you what you were supposed to do in the room?

I think that probably the best thing that happened to me along those lines was watching Steve Cannell pitch. I remember we were at

NBC; it was Cannell, David Burke, who was also a co-executive producer of "Wiseguy," and myself. We were going in there to show them sort of a cop show that was about a kind of psychological profiling unit of the FBI. The show was a very short-lived series called "Unsub" for NBC. That was, I think, in '88 or '89. The key thing I took away from that was Cannell's ability to get to the heart of a character. He talked more about characters than about plots. But it was as if he was on stage. He was mesmerizing. I do not think David Burke or I said a word in the meeting. I think we were just learning from someone who really knows how to do it.

I think that when I went in to pitch "The Commish" to Kim Le Masters, who was at that time president of CBS (which is where "The Commish" began, although it did not ultimately air on CBS), I felt that it was important to try to present it in as short a period of time the essence of the character of "The Commish." So rather than get into any elaborate plot pitches or even what we would do with a pilot episode, I told them a couple of stories about this character and the way he handled certain situations that were designed to be very theatrical and funny. I think it helps if you can be funny in the room because these guys hear thousands of pitches, and you have to grab them, just as when you are writing a spec script, because their attention span is short and they have heard it all before anyway. So you have to present it in a way that makes it entertaining, and if they are laughing, my experience is you have gone halfway to getting them on board with you.

"The Commish" was designed to be a wider kind of show. I felt that I really had to present that in the pitch. It worked. There were some funny stories, and Kim was laughing. I think he saw it as I did and as Cannell did, as a way to do a different kind of cop show, that also had family aspects to it. He was a guy who would rather get the job done in a lighter, funnier way than come in with guns a-blazing. That was not the idea of the show.

I think the advice I would give somebody—which I would hopefully take myself in writing a spec script—is that you have to get them in the first ten pages or else they are going to put it down because there is just too much other stuff to read. I would also try to get my pitch appointment early in the day. I definitely would not want to pitch first thing after lunch. I don't think I would want to pitch at the end of the day. Mid-morning would be great, but right after lunchtime is death. Everybody is nodding off, it's a killer. I'm sure people have been successful at it, but I think you are really climbing a greased pole when you have that two o'clock appointment.

When emerging writers or young writers came to pitch to you, can you think of a few pitches that stood out?

Most of the pictures I have heard are obviously within the context of the shows I was working on. I think that if you are going to pitch for a show or if you are going to write a spec script for a show, the thing that is absolutely vital—and it always shocks me that a fair number of people don't do it—is that you should try to know the show as well as you possibly can. No one is going to know it as well as the people on staff who are doing it day in day out.

I think the thing that stands out more than any one particular successful pitch is the large number of unsuccessful pitches that were unsuccessful because the people did not really know the show or did not really know the way the main characters would behave. It seems unbelievable to me because as a freelancer that is your job. You have to know.

From a staff point of view, we are really hiring a freelancer to hopefully relieve some of the pressure of doing the scripts under the time constraints that we have. If we have to beat the thing out with him or her, then what do we need the person for? We're doing it ourselves anyway. It always surprises me how many people would come in with this. . . and it was like they did not want to do the work required because it was spec, but unfortunately you have to. So I think that no one particular pitch stands out in my mind, and the overwhelming memory that I came away with after four years on "The Commish" and three years on "Wiseguy" was an overall negative impression concerning people who did not take the time to learn the show. If somebody called up who was coming in to pitch a week from a particular day and wanted to see scripts or wanted to see tapes, we would send them out. It was not like we were trying to be secretive about what it was we were doing or what we felt was the essence of the show. We were trying to help these people because it ultimately meant helping ourselves.

When you were creating "The Commish," can you remember why you would select somebody to be on staff?

I was looking for somebody who had some show running experience. He or she did not necessarily have to be an executive producer. Someone who had been a supervising producer or something like that with some experience in post-production and that kind of thing would be good.

As far as just straight writing, I was looking for someone who could tell a dramatic story with a degree of humor. There are not many shows that allow a writer to do that, or there weren't many at that time. So a lot of what I read were spec features that people had written. I felt that it would be relatively easy to work with someone to get the dramatic side of the equation out of them, but I think someone can either write with humor or they can't. The people I tried to work with were people who had a strong humor component in their work. We hired one guy once who had done only comedies. We figured we could all get the cop stuff. I think one of the things that made "The Commish" was that we did do funny things and we told stories that were less heavy on the cop stuff and more heavy on the personal stuff, the family stuff—things that had nothing to do with what he did for a living. It is one of the things that I think the network was never particularly crazy about, or the percentage that we wanted to allot to the non-cop stuff. Judging from the mail we used to get, it was what our audience liked most about the stuff.

I am the first to admit that David Milch and Dick Wolf tell much better cop stories than I do. That really was not the emphasis in my mind of the show. When I first conceived of the show, I wanted to do one that was 50 percent cop and 50 percent "Honeymooners." It never quite worked out that way. That is what we were going for. If we had been given the chance to do a fifth year, I would have liked to have done one or two shows that had no cop stuff in them at all but were strictly human stories. When you get to the fourth and fifth years, you have to assume that there is an element of the audience out there that has invested in us and our characters, that they will watch them even if you deviate somewhat from the normal pattern of your storytelling.

We did a show last year that was really all about a period of time from when the Commish's wife found the lump in her breast until they determined that she was okay. So it was like a three- or four-day period where everybody was trying to live normally because the odds were that it was nothing—but you do not live normally. That show got a lot of reaction because Tony (the Commish) screwed up at work. We knew that once that cancer story was introduced, it was going to take over whatever crime story was being told, and that was really the point. It was supposed to.

Had we tried to tell that story in the first year, I would have gotten a lot more resistance from the network, and it probably would not have gone over quite as well because the audience hadn't had time to live with our people for four years.

To get back to your original question, I was not looking for people who were limited to telling intricate "plotty" stories with a lot of cop stuff in it because that was not our show. I was much more interested in somebody who told a story that was moving from an emotional, human point of view, and we figured we could always come up with a cop story; we would come up with something. If we could get people to feel something about our characters—that is what I was trying to go for. That's the kind of writer I tried to find, and for the most part I think I was reasonably successful at it.

Were there a lot of people on staff who had film school experience?

No. They were not excluded, it just worked out that way. I would not exclude anybody because they went to film school. Of those on staff (I am trying to go back to "Wiseguy"), I can't think of anybody who started out wanting to be a television writer. We had one guy on "Wiseguy" who was a playwright; another had been a lumberjack, a prison guard, a bartender. There were a couple of times when we would all just sit around at the end of the day, with a drink or something, and talk about where we thought we would be and where we were. I can't remember anybody who said when he was a kid that he sat around dreaming of writing television shows. I don't think there was anyone who ever thought that. Not that there is anything wrong in wanting to be that—we just had all taken the scenic route.

Could you describe the experience on any of the shows you worked on of how the writers worked together to create a typical episode?

I always felt that when it came to breaking a story, it seemed to go better and easier in a group. Sometimes the number of that group varied; sometimes it got too big, and you had so many opinions that you could never get anything done. I found that the optimal number was three or four.

Somebody would usually come in with kind of an idea—you know, like to do a show about Rachel getting breast cancer or they think Rachel has breast cancer. So we sit down, and three or four of us beat it out. Then usually the person who had the original idea would go off and write it by himself. It is weird—you generally use the traditional three-act dramatic structure, but we have four acts, so it gets a little squirrelly.

Only when we were under time pressure did we team up. In those cases, one guy would write two acts and then the other guy would write two acts. Hopefully, at that point you could get a script in a few days.

What I tried to do, somewhat to the consternation of my staff, was when one season ended, I tried to get a leg-up on the next one. On "The Commish" we knew for the first three years that we were picked up before that season ended. So I would try to use the hiatus period to at least have everybody write a script so that we would come back to work in the middle of May with four or five scripts in some state of readiness.

It was my experience that no matter how far ahead you are when you begin the season, you are staggering toward the finish line at the end. Human nature takes over, and they can shoot faster than we can write, and invariably one or two scripts are junk and have to be worked on and worked on.

In a normal scenario, a writer would usually have a couple of weeks to write the script once the story had been beat out. Again, under crisis conditions, that time period got a lot shorter, and if there was really a problem, that is when we would team up. . . . Occasionally we would do a script with four people—you know, each guy took an act. Then it became a question of trying to blend it all together after the four acts had been written.

We got to the point toward the end of "The Commish" and "Wiseguy" where we knew each other; we all kind of knew what we were trying to accomplish, and so it worked reasonably well. Normally we would break the story as a group and then write them individually.

We usually worked with a big white board, kind of creating the outline together. Once we felt it was right, then the guy would go off and do it. I did not generally have to do an outline once we had essentially done one as a group.

Basically you would break the story, get the beats [acts] together, and then you would work together on the white board creating the outline and send whoever was up out to write the episode?

Yes. Generally they had about two weeks to write it. Some of that depended on what their other responsibilities were. The sole responsibility of a staff writer was writing. He did not have to do any post-production stuff, he did not have to cast, he did not have to be involved in any of the other things.

The way I tried to run it was to have everyone who was involved in the show be involved in as much or as little of the overall production as they wanted to be as long as their other work was getting done. So an assistant could sit in the editing room and watch the process if she or he wanted to become familiar with it, as long as their stuff was being taken care of. I think that is why, particularly with assistants, most of them take the jobs—not because of the fantastic salaries they get, but because it gives them the opportunity to be involved in this kind of thing. In most cases it is the career path they would like to follow, and so I felt that the more they saw the process, the more they would learn about it. Most of them took advantage of that.

In terms of the writers, generally if a person had nothing else to do but write, I would say he or she should be able to write a script in a week if the story is beaten out and that is all you are doing. If there are other responsibilities, then you might have a little more time.

It proved to be a job and half for me. There were long days. I am sure that other people probably could have handled it more efficiently than I did. For me it seemed never-ending. The only time I can remember really relaxing during the season was when the last script had been written and they were starting to shoot it, because when you are in the thick of it, there is never really any letup.

I think that is one of the great things about television, unlike the feature business: What you write today is going to be seen in six weeks. You can work very hard on a feature script and ninety-nine times out of a hundred it never gets made. On TV—assuming you are on staff on a show—it is going to get shot, and there is something energizing about that. But also once in a while you wish you could say, "Stop. Do not shoot tomorrow because this thing is not ready." But you can't. You just have to live with it. I remember reading once when Joe DiMaggio was playing in his prime for the Yankees; he was the most valuable player and everything. He was taking extra batting practice one day, and one of the other players said, "Why are you doing this? Look who you are," and he said, "There may be somebody out there in the stands who has never seen me play." The point was that he did not want to embarrass himself, and he wanted everybody who saw Joe DiMaggio to see the Joe DiMaggio he wanted them to see. I think that was kind of analogous to us, and certainly we did not succeed all the time. I think what kind of drives you is the knowledge that on any given night someone who has never seen the show before might see the show, and you want them to come back. You want it to be as good as it can be because your name is on it, because your friends watch it, people in the business watch it, and obviously millions of people you do not know watch it, and you want each episode to be something that will cause somebody to say, "Hey, did you see that show last night?" Or if they see it for the first time, they will watch it again next week. That, I think, is the overriding pressure I always felt— that every week it had to be the best it could be, and you know that every week it's not going to be the best it can be.

I always felt that out of twenty-two shows if you did five great ones and ten or eleven good ones, you were going to do a couple where you wished there was a nationwide blackout. Hopefully it won't get to that point, it won't be that bad, but you are never able to revel in the shows that are really good or mourn with the shows that are terrible because there is just no time. You just have to keep on going.

I think when you get criticized either by your actors or by your crew or by other people—"everybody's a critic"—I think that is the one thing where your own protection is your staff or yourself or whatever. You just feel like saying, "If we had just had another three days, we could have turned this thing around," and "Yes, we tried as hard as we could, and this was the best we could do and not screw up the next three shows."

I think Steve Bochco's (creator of "Hill Street Blues," "LA Law," and "NYPD Blue") greatest genius is that he has been able to attract the best writers in town. It is my assumption that he is not there until 3 A.M. every night, somebody else is—you know, David Milch is or the people who work for David Milch. It is very difficult. . . you'd think that it would be a buyers' market, just by virtue of the fact that in our business there are not that many shows. The real cream of the crop is hard to find, and they generally want to go on the shows that are going to win them an Emmy. And I don't blame them.

What is a great writer for TV, or what would your dream writer be like?

Well, I'm not sure if there is any huge difference between a great writer for TV, a great writer for features, or a great writer for theater, but I do think that there is an intimacy in television that features cannot have because nobody wants to see a sixty-foot nostril, and that theater cannot have because the people at the back are sitting far, far away. We can show people's lives; we can be very emotional. We can do really great small moments. We cannot compete with features in terms of their special effects, but I think we can compete with them—and in some cases surpass them—because people are sitting so close, generally speaking, to the screen and we are in their house. So I think that someone who is really a great TV writer—I am talking about one-hour dramas—would be somebody who is able to create those little memorable moments.

David Burke, who worked with me on "Wiseguy," was one of the best I have ever worked with at doing that. On "Wiseguy" he created some moments with Ray Sharkey and Ken Wahl that were absolutely riveting, yet they were small. Things were not blown up; there were no shootings.

I think that whenever we tried, either on "Wiseguy" or on "The Commish," to get exceptionally plotty, we fell all over ourselves. We could not remember what we were doing, but when we were able to come up with scenarios that were basically driven by the emotions of the characters and their relationships, it became easy to follow, it became much more fun to write—because like any other writer, you find things in your own life that may not be in their entirety analogous to situations that you have experienced but that usually have something you can draw on to make those moments real. As writers we have not been cops, we have not been detectives, we have not solved crimes of an intricate nature, but we have lived with crazy uncles or brothers that we could not stand, or fathers or mothers that were, you know, whatever the nature of those relationships were, and I think those are the things that made those shows work. Again, on "The Commish"—in a much lighter tone than most memorable shows—there were shows that had a great emotional component, and when they were over, nobody remembered what the crime story was. We put Tony in a position that an audience could empathize with because they had been there. I think that my dream writer would be somebody who was driven much more by those basic human emotions rather than somebody who could tell a cop story with twelve plot scripts. It moves too fast, and I think you have to grab them emotionally; otherwise they are making a sandwich someplace.

INTERVIEW WITH LAWRENCE MEYERS

Lawrence Meyers is the executive story editor of "Picket Fences."

How did you start your writing career?

I began writing rudimentary scripts for super–8 films when I was a teenager, gradually learning the importance of script as I made more complex films during my undergraduate and graduate studies.

What was the transition from film student to writing for the entertainment industry?

The single best piece of advice I have ever received was given to me by a well-known director who taught a class I attended at U.S.C. film school. He said, "Write as much as you can—television scripts, movie scripts, whatever." I took this advice very seriously and sat down to tackle my first feature spec script that summer. Simultaneously, that same director offered me an opportunity to pitch an idea for a television show he executive-produced. The pitch was later purchased, and a few months later I wrote the script—my first paid writing job. Well, the TV script never got produced, and the feature is collecting dust on a shelf. I'm too embarrassed to show it to anyone. But the point is that I just jumped into writing. It's hard not to be inspired when a successful person whom you respect tells you how he got into the business. I didn't have a flashy, bold student film to show around, so writing had to be my ticket in. And so it was.

How did you get an agent?

I've always been frustrated when other people get asked this question and they don't provide the step-by-step details as to *how* it actually happened. So allow me to indulge.

I got lucky. In short, I was lucky enough to meet an established industry person whom I impressed. That person set me up with an agent.

U.S.C. film school was worth its weight in tuition during the years I attended. The year after the Big Director taught there, a Big Producer taught a feature screenwriting class there. The day I read my first scene to the class, the Big Producer went bonkers for it and all but promised me an agent right then. A few weeks later I was handed a contract for the above-mentioned TV show and asked the producer to refer me to an agent who could look it over for me. I met the agent, who worked at a large agency, and he asked about me and my work. He agreed to look over the contract for no charge, and we kept in touch. After the semester ended, I read a short story that the producer had the rights to and had been trying to make into a feature. I formulated a pitch, and the producer liked it. A meeting at a major studio was immediately set up, and I pitched the studio.

The producer was impressed with my pitch, probably called the agent to relay the news, and two days later I met with the agent. He signed me.

What was been your experience with agents?

The most important thing to remember is that this business is about one thing and one thing only: money. A veteran writer once told me, "None of these people [in the industry] are your friends. The only thing they care about is whether you can make them money. You are a commodity to them, and that's it." Once I learned that, I understood agents a lot better.

I am generally cynical about people in the business. I think that almost everyone is ultimately out for himself. However, if you are lucky, you may find people who in addition to looking out for their own best interest are also looking out for yours. Ideally, your agent will genuinely care about nurturing your talent and getting your career off the ground. This is in their own best interest, after all. The real test for an agent is how much he does for you when you are starting out or if your career takes a nosedive into Death Valley. If he sticks with you and really works for you during these periods, you are in good shape. I am fortunate that in the three years it took to really get my career moving, my agent didn't give up on me, and as of this writing, my career isn't in the toilet. Thus, my experience has been generally good.

For people just starting out, I highly recommend seeking representation with a small- to mid-sized agency. While the agent worked very hard for me in television, I just couldn't get the attention of the feature division of a large agency. They had bigger clients who earned them much more money with less effort than I did. I can't blame them. It's a big business and I was a small player. Beginners will burn bright in the agent's eyes at first, but if something doesn't happen very, very quickly, they may be lost in the shuffle. Such was my plight. I am now at a smaller agency and still with the agent, and I feel I am being better serviced in both TV and features.

What do you believe was your big break?

Getting an agent was a major step. But as far as work is concerned, I've had two. One was landing a story editor position on the Emmy-winning "Picket Fences." The other was landing my first feature film assignment, writing for the same Big Producer who introduced me to the agent.

What has your experience been writing for television?

Much better as a staff writer than as a freelancer. As a staff writer on "Picket Fences," I think I may be rather spoiled. I am surrounded by six of the most talented, professional, intelligent, and friendly writers I have ever met in the business. The environment is supportive, and I am treated as a respected veteran. I have great latitude in creating stories that I can personally relate to and that have emotional resonance for me. My writing style is not constricted. As a freelancer I am sometimes forced to come up with stories that I may not have an emotional connection to in order to secure a gig. As a "guest writer" on the show, I am more constrained by the producers' vision of the show and must conform to it. As such, there is also a greater chance that I will get rewritten. Since I have learned to work within that system, I have been invited to be more involved in all aspects of the production of my episodes than I would normally expect.

How did you begin writing for film?

Spec scripts first, then I was asked to write a script that the above-mentioned Big Producer had an idea for. We successfully pitched the studio, and I had my first gig.

What tips do you have for successfully pitching the project at a meeting concerning a potential writing assignment?

There has been no formula for me. In TV I prepare a logline and brief story concept, followed by a one-page pitch with the major story beats in case they are interested in hearing more. Usually they love the premise, and we start spitballing right there—and the story ends up being totally different from what I had prepared. For film I work up a twenty-minute pitch (keep it short; these people have short attention spans) with major story beats. I rehearse it with a dramatic storytelling flair and go in to pitch. My theory is that producers and studio execs hear these things all the time—they are similar to bored students in a chemistry class. You have to be dynamic, as well as have commercial elements, to use them to maximum effect. The most important thing to remember is this: *They want you to have a great story with marketable elements.* They want you to come into the room with the next *Forrest Gump* or *Raiders of the Lost Ark.* If you go in believing that you do and tell your story with such conviction, that will help. Also, the Big Producer once told me that "the Sell is in the set pieces." When you sell, have three great set pieces, and this should help. I also try to present the story in an organized fashion: I give a logline, a few sentences on the main characters and their flaws, the story, the theme, and what the characters learn at the end. The worst thing you can do is confuse them. And then I pray.

When you are hired to write a film project, who are your bosses and whom must you please?

Your bosses are whoever hired you, and you must please them— producers, studio execs, stars, directors, anyone else who thinks they have a say—that is, until you're a highly successful writer whom everyone wants. Then you probably have a bit more power. . .

How can a writer successfully work with studio executives, producers, and so forth, when going through the development process on a screenplay?

My feeling is that when working on assignment, it's important to remember you're a writer for hire. Presumably you've been hired for the project because of your expertise as a writer. Therefore, if your bosses are smart, they'll listen to what you have to say when you're presenting your opinion. But while you are the storytelling expert, odds are they are the business experts, so you must balance your vision with a certain amount of pragmatism. If you can still tell a good story and it still expresses some of the things you want and gives all your bosses what they want, then consider yourself lucky. Sure, you want to argue your points and do so forcefully, but let's face it: You're a hired gun. Ultimately they're going to do what they want. Why not try to work *with* them instead of butting heads?

Choose your battles. Fight for the things most important to you.

If the assignment involves rewrites of a spec script that you sold to them, perhaps they'll realize that you have lived with the script for a long time already and they'll defer more to your knowledge. Don't count on it, though.

How do you diplomatically incorporate studio executives' suggestions into your writing assignments and still stick up for your own ideas? What about the "suggestions" of producers, directors, and actors?

The question assumes that the writer has the power in this equation. That is a false assumption. Unless you're one of the few big writers who has a substantial "fuck you" fund, you're not in much of a position to control this project. Producers, directors, and stars, they have more power than you, and the good ones know and value the input of the writer and will work with him or her to keep the story good without the need to massage their own egos. That's the theory, anyway. Otherwise, see number nine.

What advice do you have for aspiring writers who are attempting to write for the film industry?

Don't.

But if you're *really* serious about it and you're sure this is your passion, then I'll repeat the advice I was given: Keep writing. Always. Use your intelligence and entrepreneurial spirit to find ways to get your material read. Study movies and TV. Understand the medium you want to work in. Learn about the business. Move to Los Angeles and get immersed in the business. Call production companies, tell then you are a film student fresh out of school and you have a script. They'll tell you to send it over since they don't want to miss out on the next Spielberg. Go to film school and meet all the guests that visit. Be mature when you speak to them and not some slobbering fan. They hate that. Write them an intelligent letter afterward telling them how educational their visit was and try to establish a line of communication with their office. Network through friends and family to find people who are—or who know others who are—working in the industry. Write spec scripts, get a job as an intern at a production company (companies are always looking for interns they can exploit for free), and once you're working there and get to know the development people, hand them your script. If they don't like it, keep writing and keep learning about the business while you're there. (You can quit your nonpaying job there now. They were exploiting you; you tried to exploit them, but they were too stupid to like your script. Move on.) Get a job as a writer's assistant on a TV show. Write a spec for that show (I know four people who got in this way). Did I say keep writing scripts? Write query letters to agents and entertainment attorneys to try to get representation. But don't be stupid about it. Don't just jump into things without being ready for battle. Have two feature scripts and/or at least two TV specs ready to show. The same goes *before* you get a job as an intern at some company or studio. Don't give up. These things take time.

Most of all, use your head. This business is not as closed as people think or would like you to believe. In no particular order, you must have luck, talent, chutzpah, and persistence. You can't control your luck, and you're either born with talent or you aren't—and in many cases it doesn't matter. A spec script can sell even if it's written in crayon as long as it has a great idea—or so I'm told. You *can* control chutzpah and persistence. Be bold. You have to be or you won't survive in the industry anyway. Better get used to it early. But most of all, don't give up, and don't let rejection get you down. I've heard this from all the big shots: If you have talent, then you'll make it. Go for it.

TOP TEN GENERAL RULES I LEARNED THE HARD WAY

1. Everyone in this business is out for themselves.
2. Always, always, always watch what you say and who you say it to. Think before you speak. What goes around comes around.
3. Shut up and let them do the talking.
4. Less is more.
5. Be patient.
6. TV is about process, not product.
7. Think long-term.
8. Always look them in the eye.
9. Don't let rejection get you down.
10. Trust your gut–especially about people.

A WRITERS GUILD OF AMERICA CONTRACT FOR A STAFF WRITING POSITION ON AN EPISODIC TELEVISION SHOW

The following contract is typical for a staff writing position on an episodic (weekly) television show. Annotation of the terms is provided as a means of explanation only and is not intended to be legal advice; therefore, as with the WGA Contract for Film, if you are handed a contract for a staff writer's position on a television show, do not attempt to negotiate it yourself. Please consult an agent or an attorney, or both. Please.

SAMPLE: A WGA TELEVISION CONTRACT

Agreement between ("Studio") and ("Artist") in connection with the above-referenced Series.

I. **Services/Term:** Studio hereby engages Artist to render services as a term writer for twenty (20) weeks commencing ("First Period"). *(A contract for twenty weeks is considered "week to week and term employment" under the WGA Agreement. Under this contract a writer will be paid a guaranteed weekly salary for twenty weeks. After the twenty weeks, the studio has an option to renew the writer's contract. For the "first period," this writer will be a staff writer on the show.)*

II. **Options:** Artist hereby grants to Studio exclusive and irrevocable options for Artist's exclusive services as specified below:

A. **Second Period:** Studio shall have the option to engage Artist as a story editor for the remaining episodes produced in the Series year commencing the first business day of preparation of the next episode following completion of the First Period ("Second Period"). Such option shall be exercised, if at all, in writing not later than the last business day of the First Period. *(After the twenty weeks of the "first period," the studio has the option to hire the writer for the "second period" for the remaining episodes produced in that broadcast year. If the option is exercised and the writer is hired, the writer will be bumped up in salary and position to "story editor.")*

B. **Broadcast Year:** Studio shall have the option to engage Artist as an executive story editor for all episodes produced for the broadcast year. Such option shall be exercised, if at all, in writing within ten (10) business days following Studio's acceptance of a written network order or by ____, whichever is earlier. *(If the show is picked up for another year [not canceled], the studio*

> *has the option of hiring the writer. If the studio exercises the option and hires the writer, the writer will be bumped up in salary and position to "executive story editor.")*

III. **Series Services:** During the term, Artist's services shall be exclusive to television. Artist warrants and represents that any services to a third party shall not interfere with Artist's first-priority Series obligations. Artist shall render all services customarily rendered by a term writer or story editor, as applicable, in the United States television industry. Such services shall be performed consistent with Studio's directions, practices, and policies. Artist warrants and represents that Artist has no obligation, nor will Artist incur any obligation, which might interfere with Artist's Series obligations. *(The writer is to be exclusive to the studio and will not do anything that will interfere with the performance of his obligation to the series.)*

IV. **Compensation:** Subject to Artist's complete performance of the terms and conditions of this Agreement, Artist shall be entitled to receive the following compensation:

A. Broadcast Year:

1. First Period: ___ per week, which shall be credited against any compensation due to Artist in connection with assigned script services. *(WGA scale for a staff writer with a twenty-week contract is $2,209 per week. This writer will probably receive scale plus 10 percent (for the agent), or approximately $2,430 per week.)*

2. Second Period (if option exercised): ___ per episode. *(If the writer's option is renewed in the second period, the writer will become a story editor for the remainder of the broadcast year. A story editor is designated as a "writer employed in an additional capacity" under the WGA agreement, and scale for this position in a term up to and including nine weeks would be $4,804 per week. Generally, the writer's agent will have negotiated for a salary that is $1,000 to $1,500 above the WGA scale.*

B. Broadcast Year (if option is exercised): ___ per episode. *(If the show is picked-up for a second year and the studio decides to renew the writer's option, the writer will be an executive story editor for the entire broadcast year. Similar to the story editor, the executive story editor is designated a "writer employed in an additional capacity" under the WGA agreement, and scale for this position in a term up to and including twenty weeks or more would be $3,602 per week. Generally, the writer's agent will have negotiated for a salary that is $1,000 to $1,500 above the salary the writer received for the story editor position.)*

V. **Credit:** Artist shall be accorded screen credit on each episode Artist actually completes performance, as follows:
   A. Broadcast Year:
      1. First Period: Per the WGA.
      2. Second Period (if option exercised): Story Editor.
      3. *Broadcast Year (if option exercised)*: Executive Story Editor.

(Credit on television is regulated by the WGA. In the staff writer position, the writer will not receive on-screen credit (that is, the credits that run after the show will not read "staff writer"). However, the writer will receive screen credit for every individual script he writes. If the writer's option is renewed and he becomes "the story editor," the writer will receive on-screen credit as the story editor on every show. In addition, if the show goes on to another year and the writer's option is again renewed, the writer will receive on-screen credit as the executive story editor on every show.)

All other aspects of credit will be determined in Studio's sole discretion. All credits are subject to applicable guild approval and customary licensee approval. Casual or inadvertent failure to accord credit as provided herein shall not be deemed a breach of this Agreement. Artist shall not be entitled to seek injunctive relief for a failure to accord credit. Studio agrees, upon receipt of written notice from Artist specifying any such failure, to promptly take such steps as are reasonably practicable to cure such failure with respect to future copies of the applicable episode.

VI. **Scripts:**
  A. First Period Scripts: Artist's weekly compensation during the First Period shall be credited against any compensation due to Artist in connection with assigned script services.
  B. Guarantees: Subject to Artist providing services for the applicable episodes in each broadcast year, Artist is guaranteed the financial equivalent of the following number of scripts (story and teleplay):
    1. Broadcast Year: One script for the First Period, and if Studio exercises its option, two scripts for the Second Period.
      a. Three scripts based on production of twenty-two (22) episodes.

Scripts may be written by Artist solely or with other assigned writer(s).

  C. WGA Minimum/Script Service Agreement: Series scripts assigned to Artist shall be compensated at WGA minimum. Artist's episodic script services shall be rendered pursuant to the standard Studio agreement, which Artist agrees to execute prior to commencing each such writing assignment. *(The writer is guaranteed that he will write a certain number of scripts in each period. Except in the first period, when the script is credited against any compensation due to the Artist in connection with assigned script services, the Artist will receive the WGA minimum for each script of $22,984 [for scripts of the length that are broadcast on ABC, CBS, NBC, and FBC]. This will be in addition to the weekly amount the writer receives for a story editor or executive story editor position.)*

VII. **WGA Agreement:** To the extent applicable, this Agreement shall be subject to the provisions of the WGA Agreement. Studio shall pay directly all applicable pension, health, and welfare contributions. Studio may allocate any of the fees hereunder for Artist's services as compensation for a writer also employed in additional capacities under Article 14 of the WGA basic Agreement. *(This agreement is a WGA agreement, and the studio will directly pay to the WGA any necessary pension, health, and/or welfare contributions.)*

VIII. **Office and Secretary:** For as long as Artist is rendering exclusive services hereunder, Studio shall provide Artist with an office, computer, and a shared secretary.

IX. **Ownership:** Studio shall own all of the results and proceeds of Artist's services as a "work-for-hire" for use in perpetuity throughout the universe in all media now known or hereafter devised, subject only to any applicable requirements of a collective bargaining agreement. *(This is a work-for-hire agreement, and the studio owns all of the writer's work—in every existing format and in those formats that may be created in the future—that the writer creates in connection with the series.)*

Dated: _____   By: _____

Dated: _____   By: _____

Social Security # _____

11

Writing for the Entertainment Industry

The following interviews with agents and writers explain how a writer gains employment and works in different areas of the entertainment industry—soap operas, feature animation, and long-form television.

WRITING FOR SOAP OPERAS

INTERVIEW WITH BETSY SYNDER

Betsy Synder was a writer for five years on the soap opera "General Hospital." The following interview with Ms. Synder presents her experiences and perspective concerning her employment as a writer in this area of the entertainment industry.

How did you begin your career writing for soap operas?

I moved to Los Angeles from the East Coast after I graduated from college and met a group of people who were working in various positions on the soap opera "General Hospital." My friends told me that I was the perfect person to be the secretary to the head writer for the show. I interviewed with the producer for "General Hospital," whose sister happened to be the head writer, and got the job as the head writer's secretary.

I was very lucky to get this job because the show usually promoted someone from its pool of unpaid student interns into this position. I believe that I was chosen for this position because I had been an English major in college.

As the head writer's secretary, my job was to synthesize and write the long-term story notes. Fortunately, the writers liked my notes. As the younger writers were promoted, I was promoted and became an assistant to a head writer, or what is known as a writer's assistant.

The beauty of being a secretary or an assistant was that it was like being in a soap opera writers' training-camp. I had the opportunity to see how the show was created and how it was structured.

How did you make the transition from writer's assistant to soap opera writer?

During the time that I was working as a secretary, I was encouraged to become a writer's assistant but not encouraged to become a writer. I felt that I could write for a soap opera, but I did not think that my bosses would promote me to become a writer on the show. I began working with another woman, who became my writing partner, to generate soap opera scripts.

My partner and I began showing our work to a writer on another soap opera. After reading our work, the writer told us that he thought our strength would be in creating outlines for soap operas, or as what is known as breakdown writers. We created a few outlines and gave them to the writer. The writer showed our work to the head writer of his show, who was impressed with our outlines: We were told that the head writer was thinking of offering us a writing position. However, the head writer of "General Hospital" heard that we were possibly going to be offered a position on the other soap opera and told us that he would promote us to a writing position on "General Hospital." Subsequently, my partner and I were offered a job as breakdown (outline writers) on "General Hospital."

What was it like to write with a partner?

One thing that I learned from working with a partner is that you are wrong as many times as you are right. Working with a partner was a give-and-take experience. At a certain point I found that we were finishing each other's sentences.

My partner was the continuity person [someone who reads through everything and makes sure that all writing on the show is not too repetitive and that all scenes are progressing] on "General Hospital" when I joined the show. It was my partner's promotion from writer's secretary to continuity person that created the opening for the position I first got.

I think the partnership was great in the beginning because we both had little confidence in our writing. We needed each other to create scripts and keep each other going. The partnership was a way to make us write scripts because it made us have a designated time and place when we would work. At one time we took a vacation at the same time so that we could write a great sample script.

I worked with my partner for three years. Then the partnership was dissolved because we both had enough confidence to write alone.

Did you eventually get an agent?

At the time that I was offered the writer's position on "General Hospital" I did not have an agent. My partner and I got our jobs through our own efforts. On "General Hospital" one agent represented all of the writers on the show. One of the other writers on the show called the agent who represented everyone after I was offered the writing position, and the agent agreed to negotiate the contract for me. The agent then became my agent. I didn't actually meet my agent (in person) until one and a half years later.

Is there a specific background which soap writers have?

These is no particular background which makes a great soap writer. I have seen doctors, teachers, and musicians become soap writers— the writers come from everywhere. However, one common element that I have noticed is that all soap writers must respect the soap audience and know that the soap audience does not take it as a joke. To be successful at this, you must know that there is a large soap audience that watches the soaps religiously and takes the shows very seriously.

How do the writers work together to keep all the story lines in a soap opera going?

The process begins with the producer and the head writers creating the long-term story. In the long-term story, the producer and head writer determine the direction that the characters in the soap are going over "the long term" or perhaps the season.

After the long-term story is created, the head writers create "the thrust"—a weekly projection that is an overview of the week. The thrust is then broken down into five breakdowns, one for every day of the week (Monday through Friday). The breakdowns, or outlines, are created by the breakdown writers. (My partner and I were breakdown writers on "General Hospital.") The breakdown consists of six acts and a prologue. To create the breakdown, I would take the narrative of the thrust and create a scene-by-scene outline that generally consisted of fourteen pages double-spaced. The structure of the breakdown was very important because it was from this that the other breakdowns would counterpoint with different story lines and character development. My partner and I wrote two break-downs per week.

On "General Hospital" the thrust would go out on Wednesday, and on Thursday all of the breakdown writers, including my partner and I, would meet with the head writer to see if we had come up with ideas that were acceptable to the head writer. After this Thursday meeting, we would have one day, Friday, to actually write the breakdown. The breakdown would have to be finished by Saturday because the producers were given the entire weekend to review the breakdown. On Monday all breakdown writers had to meet with the producer and head writer. The purpose of this meeting, the revision meeting, was to go over the breakdowns and see what did and did not work. The revision meeting could last eight to twelve hours, and then all of the breakdown writers would have to go home and work as long as it took to incorporate all the revisions into the script so that we would have it on the desk of the head writer by Tuesday morning at 8 A.M. or the following morning. If the breakdown was accepted, it would be sent to the dialogue writers. The dialogue writers would have one week to write the script and then turn it back in. After that, the editors would usually punch up and edit the script, and then it would be sent to the actors. However, as far as the breakdown writers were concerned, on Wednesday the next thrust would go out, and the whole cycle would start again for us.

What is the hierarchy of writers on a soap opera?

Basically, the positions that a writer on a soap opera will occupy are the following: The two entry-level positions that a writer can have on a soap opera are **breakdown writer** and **script/dialogue writer**. Both positions are at the same level, and the difference is the actual work the writer is doing. A breakdown writer—the position I held—participates in creating the five scene-by-scene outlines per week that are the structure and basis on which dialogue is built. A script/dialogue writer will take the breakdown that the breakdown writer has created and build in dialogue to the step-by-step outline.

A breakdown writer or script writer does not receive on-screen credit—that is, the writer does not get a credit byline as breakdown writer or dialogue writer on the television screen when credits for the show are run. The staff writer makes no editorial decisions concerning the writing of the show and has no decision-making authority over the casting.

The breakdown or script/dialogue writer generally receives a twenty-week contract with an option to renew. Needless to say, all writers live in fear that their option will not be picked up. The **associate head writer** assists with the head writer's duties. Oftentimes the associate head writer must generate the story line for the thrust.

The position of **head writer** has huge responsibilities. The head writer has the job of generating the story doc [the master plan of all plots and subplots that will fill a certain time span], with three or possibly four stories going at one time for which the head writer must generate all the story beats. In addition, the head writer must meet with all the breakdown writers, go through revision meetings with them, create the thrust, and develop the long-term story and character ideas with the producers.

To become a head writer, experience in the field helps, but talent and an ability to bring a fresh approach to the field also help.

An **executive producer** is someone who has had a great deal of successful experience in the industry. The executive producer is involved in everything, from the writing for the show, including the long-form character plot, to working with actors to develop their characters. The executive producer is also involved with the music, the sets, the wardrobe, and the overall look of the show. In addition to all this, the executive producer sits in on the writers' meetings and reads everything. The executive producer also reviews the thrust and makes revisions to it.

Due to the amount of responsibility the executive producer has, the individual chosen for this position generally has a great deal of experience in the industry. However, there is a trend in the soaps toward looking outside the soap industry for fresh talent to invigorate things.

As a writer for the soaps, you must know that the soap audience does not take it as a joke and must be very respectful of the soap viewers.

What are the advantages and disadvantages of working in this medium?

Writing for the soaps represents steady work for a writer if you find yourself in a situation in which you are well thought of, and you have the gratification of seeing work on the screen quickly. Also, it's lucrative.

The disadvantages are that you don't have time to see if what you write is what you want to say, and your writing can be very formulaic. There is a time restriction, and at times you can find yourself falling into a formula without being very creative. You can be pigeonholed in the industry as a "soap writer." However, that is something one can overcome.

What recommendations or advice do you have for the writer who wants to work on a soap opera?

Get an internship with a soap opera if you can. This is a great way to get noticed and an invaluable method of learning how the soaps work. On "General Hospital" the paid staff positions are usually filled from the intern pool. Take a course on how to write for the soaps, then attempt to write some sample scenes and build up to a sample script. If possible, try to enlist the aid of an agent who works with soap writers.

Writing for Feature Animation

INTERVIEW WITH PHILLIP LAZEBNIK

Phillip Lazebnik was one of the screenwriters of the Disney animated features *Pocahontas* and the *The Legend of Mulan*. The following represents his experiences writing for feature animation.

How did you begin your writing career?

I've always written, since I was a child, probably because my father is a writer also. He's a professor of English at Stevens College. I always wrote musicals for the family and so forth . . . . I always wrote, and I always enjoyed it, although I never thought of making a career out of it. I wrote a very bizarre musical in high school for my Humanities class, which was inspired by the autobiography of Harpo Marx, which was my bible in high school. It was a rip-roaring success in my Humanities class, and I said, "Hey, this is fun."

In college [at Harvard], I majored in ancient Greek and classics. I was at the time primarily doing music, playing the piano and the violin. As much as I enjoyed that, I enjoyed doing theater even more. I expanded my musical [from high school] and put it on at Harvard, and I founded a theater society, the Harvard Premiere Society, and wrote and produced two more shows that were pretty big events, and I totally did everything. At Harvard, at that time, you couldn't major in theater. Anything that was useful was taboo—which was great because that meant I had to do everything myself. It was also a little misleading because my musicals would always sell out. We'd make loads of money that we would put back into the theater so that we could have an even bigger production next year, and I came out of Harvard thinking, "This is an easy way to make money."

Did you continue to write for the theater after you graduated from college?

After college I won a fellowship to travel around Europe for a year. After I got back, I thought that my brother Ken and I, and Kingsly Day, who is a friend and fellow writer from Columbia, Missouri, should form a theater company. So we formed the Chicago Premiere Society, and it was devoted pretty much exclusively to writing musicals.

Kingsly and I had written a musical, "The Joy of Socks," which was about the assassination of President Garfield, and other such things. It was riotous good fun. And so we said, "Well, hell, we'll just write five more of these and have a season." And I didn't know anything about setting up a theater company whatsoever . . . . So armed with a tiny bit of money from our parents, I went to the two places I had heard of in Chicago, Second City and David Mamet's theater company.

At Second City I played a few of our songs, and they said "Great, we'll give you a Monday night showcase." I said okay. I thought that was what we deserved. I didn't know that was quite a generous offer. And then I went to the St. Nicholas Theater Company, which was David Mamet's theater company—he still had a theater company back then—and I said, "Could I see the managing director? I'd like some advice about starting a theater company." And the director just took me in and gave me all this advice. He happened to be Peter Schneider, the president of animation at Disney.

We put on our showcase at Second City, which was a lot of fun, but then we learned the hard facts of life, which is it's tough out there. We rented a little storefront—very tiny, you could barely get fifty chairs in . . . . We made the sets, the stage, the platforms, everything, ourselves, and just set to for our first season. Every six weeks we'd have a new musical. And we'd build the sets, and we'd rehearse while we were performing the first musical and writing the third musical. And it never occurred to us that if a show was successful we could extend it, so we were always under this horrible time crunch. And it was all very rudimentary. The spotlight would be me in the back holding a flashlight and so forth.

Far from making lots of money, we found that if we were lucky, we had fifteen people in the audience every night. So we very soon had to have full-time jobs. I was a typist, later a word processor, so I had an eight-hour day, as we all did, and then went to the theater and worked eight hours a night—and continued this for several years. The shows got good reviews in general, and the audiences kept growing, though never enough to make any money. Finally we got tired of dealing with plumbing and inspectors and so forth, and we gave up our theater building. We just produced in other theaters.

We started having some success. Our first big success was "Byrne Baby Byrne." That was when Jane Byrne was mayor of Chicago, a rather flamboyant character, and we wrote a political satire that played in Zanies Comedy Club in downtown Chicago. It was a huge, huge success. It ran for three years. It was constantly in the gossip columns and got loads of publicity. The governor came to see it. There were lines around the block. It was a big deal, and we actually made money from that. Then after that we wrote a musical murder mystery, "Summerstock Murder," which was in three acts, etcetera, in which in each act we were doing a different kind of musical. The first act we were doing an operetta, the second act was sort of a Cole Porter musical, and the third act was kind of a Steven Sondheim modern musical. And in each one of them there was a visiting guest star, a fading TV star, a fading movie star, a fading Broadway star—the same actress playing different roles. And it was a murder mystery. It was enormously complicated but again was a big success, and it played for two and a half years, I believe . . . . And in it Kingsly and I alternately played the detective, who was the pianist of the group. We had a tape of an orchestra for the production numbers; we would play the piano during the rehearsal numbers. And that actually got sold to the Rodgers and Hammerstein library.

We went on to do other shows—"Dear Amanda," which was a thinly veiled Ann Landers musical, and then "State Street," which was a humongous celebration of Chicago's history about the Chicago fire and the con artist ring of H. Crosby who came into town with a scam that he was going to build a grand opera house, and he discovered nobody liked operas. So he decided to raffle off the opera house. It was again, very successful, but needless to say, no money was made there . . . . And I'm still writing with Kingsly Day.

As recently as a couple of years ago we wrote a farce called "Tour de Farce" in which two actors play ten characters.

What was your transition to writing for the entertainment industry?

It became apparent that there was not loads of money to be made in theater. We were doing pretty well, but the American musical is in dire straits. As a matter of fact, the American musical theater is really alive only in one place and that's Disney Feature Animation.

So, at the time, my youngest brother was out in Hollywood being a writer, and he said I should come and do that. I knew one other person in Hollywood, the brother of a friend of mine in college, and I called him up. He said I should write a spec script of "Family Ties" because his wife was a writer on "Family Ties." I said okay, and he gave me a sort of shorthand format of the show to help me out. I had about a week. I wrote it . . . and gave it to him, and he called back that afternoon—because he is the one person in Hollywood, I found out later, who actually reads things immediately. He said, "I liked it." I thought, "Well, that's great, I may sell a script." I went back home to Chicago, and he called two weeks later and said, "I'm producing a TV show, and I'd like to put you on staff. Can you move out in two weeks?"

I was astounded, needless to say. On my last day in Chicago I was typing away as a word processor, and then the next day I was in my office with my assistant, the PAs [production assistants], and so forth, writing a television show. The show was "Day by Day," which was a Gary Goldberg show about a preschool. It was co-created and produced by Andy Borowitz. I spent two years on that show, then I went on and worked on the first two years of "Wings."

What was your transition from writing for television to writing for feature animation?

After working on "Wings," I went over to Disney, and I was on two years of "The Torkelsons." Then I got a call from Disney saying, "Are you interested in writing an animated feature that's coming up, *Pocahontas*?" I was thrilled because I loved them, I absolutely loved them, and I said the trouble was that I didn't know my time schedule. They wanted me for eight weeks, so I said I didn't know if I could do it. I turned them down. I felt terrible about it. But then they called back and said, "How about four weeks because we need a script really fast?" So I said, "Sure." . . . They had already hired Carl Binder, who had been there for a while, and Suzanna Grant had come on a week before me, so the three of us wrote a new script for *Pocahontas* in two weeks. Jeff Katzenberg liked it, so they said, "Can you do four more weeks?" And I said okay. I spent four more weeks doing a rewrite of the script, and then the weeks kept extending themselves. In all, I was there a year and a half.

It was a lot of fun. Unlike any other screenwriting job, it was a nine-to-six job. You go in every other day to the office, have loads of meetings. You meet with the artists—it's a very, very collaborative process. But it was a lot of fun.

After *Pocahontas* I went on to *The Legend of Mulan*, which is another feature animated film by Disney . . . and in a month or so I was going off to Dreamworks.

In other words, your rite of passage has been very different from most people.

Yes. When people say, "Ooh, ooh, one script and you got on staff," I say, "Yes. Nine years of theater. I've paid my dues."

In your story, you had so many different breaks, it doesn't sound as if there was one moment that you would point to as your big break.

In terms of Hollywood, there's no doubt that the big break was when Andy called me up [to be a staff writer on "Day by Day"]. I mean, I remember that was when my life changed overnight. And I went from feeling incredibly poor—well, I was incredibly poor. Our daughter had just been born, my wife and I were both working, we had no money, we were in debt, and suddenly I was a staff writer on a TV show. I never, ever felt more fortunate.

At a certain point you must have gotten an agent.

I didn't have an agent at the time [I got the staff writing job]. I got an agent later, which is a lot easier—when you have a job. I've been with the same agent my entire career, Gary Cosay at UTA [United Talent Agency], and Nancy Jones.

The fact is that I understand other writers, but for my personal experience, Gary and Nancy have done everything. Once I was on board I was already a working writer on "Day by Day," but for instance, *Pocahontas* is absolutely due to Nancy Jones. I never would have thought of that in a million years. I didn't know anything about it. Unbeknownst to me, she was plugging me to various places including Disney Feature Animation. It was a wonderful opportunity for me. So I owe a great deal to the agency.

How does writing for feature animation differ from your previous writing?

Well, the big difference is the amount of collaboration. You're working with the artists from the moment go—actually, from before the moment go—because they have been working on developmental logs before you even write a word. And once you write the theme and they board it, they change it. They change it in a lot of different ways, and the idea is to make it better. And then you give your notes, and they change it back, plus the director and the producers and everyone else involved. So it's working with the artists and seeing your scenes illustrated immediately. That's the difference.

As far as the actual writing, we never thought about writing an animated feature, we just thought about writing a movie. In that sense it was the same, but the process was different in that the usual screenwriter writes for three, six months at home, hands in the script, gets notes, rewrites it, gets more notes, rewrites it. Finally the rewrites are over, and that's it. Maybe he's invited to the premiere.

We're on location, so to speak, with the animators, and every day you are having meetings with the artists, with the songwriters, with the producers, with the executives, with the directors, and so forth, and you're part of the creative team that's shaping the film.

What is the process of writing in feature animation?

The process is enormously complicated. After we wrote the initial script, and rewrote, they started handing out sequences, scenes that were ready to be boarded by the artists. For every one that had to be boarded, we would have a meeting in which we would get notes on that scene. And we would rewrite the scene, and we would get more notes. We would rewrite it again. Then it would be handed to the artists, who in a couple of weeks would come back with the scene boarded—which is to say that it is exactly the same way as it was in Walt Disney's era. You have these big bulletin board–like deals—which I'm staring at in my office right now. They hang on the wall, and you use pushpins to tack on the drawings, one after another. It's like a glorified comic book with dialogue strips underneath. And you have a meeting where you go through the scene. Everybody gives notes. We would go back and rewrite the pages; the artists would go back and redo or reorder the drawings, whatever needed to be done. And you'd do this process over and over again, endlessly, and then eventually you'd get closer to the point where you could film the boards, put them on reels with temporary dialogue and music and sound effects. Eventually you're able to see chunks of the movie and then the entire movie on film, on the screen, like a slide show in a way. So you could see the sketches one after another and get a very good sense of how the movie was going.

It's an advantage over a live-action film where you don't really know what you have until you go to dailies. Then you all talk together, and if there is a huge problem, it's basically too late to hire everybody to come back again. Here at every stage you can actually see the movie. It's in a rough stage, but you can actually see through that if you have the experience and see if something is working or not. Often, something that looks as though it is working on the board will fail miserably when it's up on a reel. And the process just keeps on going.

I didn't fully understand the actual animation process for months. It's enormously complex. Once a board is approved and is ready to go into production, then it's workbooked, where everybody goes through and determines exactly what the shots will be. Often a scene will be totally changed then. From there it goes into layout where they decide what the background is going to be. Meanwhile, the artistic director is trying to determine how it fits in the grand scheme of things. In the workbook, it's divided into little scenes. A scene in animation, a cut, is for the animators, so the scene is usually only a couple of seconds long. And then the director has to decide when a scene will begin and when it will end. There is no editing, so you have to decide when the animator starts animating on it. Meanwhile, they've gone out and usually filmed live actors doing the scenes for the reference shoots to help the animators with the motions of human characters. Then they edit those together, so actually they're making two movies at the same time. The animators will make their rough animation, which is just roughly drawn from one proof to the next. And once that's approved, then it goes to clean-up animators, to clean up the lines, the rough in-betweeners, and the regular in-betweeners who draw in all the pictures in between. . . . It gets colorized, and then the pictures are brought back and they're ready to go. And that's just a sketch of the enormous process that goes on. It's overwhelming.

It sounds much more elaborate than the usual feature writing process that goes on.

Yeah, well, but you have less autonomy than you do in television writing. You're just a member of the team, and you have to remember it's a collaborative process. It's not one person's vision, that's for sure.

Do you have any ideas concerning how a writer can successfully pitch a project?

Number one: Be clear. I write everything down that I'm going to say, and then I don't look at it and I pitch. But I've done it, and I know what I am going to say. And I practice. And I rehearse. And I think of the pitch. Like telling a story, you have to understand everything. You have to understand who the characters are, you have to understand what the situation is. You have to assume that your audience knows nothing about what's happened before or what's going to happen after, and you have to be concise: You can't ramble on and on and on. The shorter the better.

There are people who get up, and it's like a stand-up routine. They're enormous entertainers. But I've never thought that was necessary for myself. A lot of writers do. They think if they don't have the people bellowing with laughter that they're utter failures. And it's really tough to get a lot of laughs from these audiences. What they want to know is what's going on. And they want to know it as simply and concisely as possible.

What's it like to incorporate all the suggestions of all of the producers, directors, and animators?

Well, sometimes it's very difficult. Often, the writers have a very clear idea of what we want to do, then we'll go off and compromise, and do something else that's a consensus. Of course that's difficult, but that's part of the job.

What are you going to be doing at Dreamworks?

I have a three-year deal in which I'm going to do everything: film, television, and animation. It's an overall deal. One of most important projects is to write an animated feature, to be determined.

What advice would you give emerging writers?

I don't know if it's helpful to say that you want to be a feature animation writer. None of us on *Pocahontas*—actually, none of us on *The Legend of Mulan,* either—had any experience writing animation before we came over here. It's not really necessary. A writer is a writer. The trouble, of course, is that there is no easy answer, and there's no simple route for becoming a writer. The main thing you have to do is write and keep on writing, and remain proficient.

The most impressive thing in a script for me is to tell a story well, because the vast majority of spec scripts from beginning writers don't. You might think that it isn't hard to tell a story well, but it is extremely difficult to tell a story in which the characters remain consistent, where things make sense, where things don't contradict everything else, and that is interesting and contains conflict and character and all that. It's very difficult, and that's what almost always is lacking in unprofessional scripts. That's first and foremost to me.

WRITING FOR MOVIES FOR TELEVISION AND TV MINISERIES (LONG-FORM TELEVISION)

INTERVIEW WITH JONATHAN WESTOVER

Jonathan Westover is an agent in the motion picture literature department of The Gage Group, an agency in Los Angeles, California. In the following interview he offers his advice and relates his experiences working with writers in long-form television.

When we are talking about writing for long-form television, what formats are we talking about?

We are principally talking about the area defined by television miniseries and movies for television (MFTs). In terms of subject matter, we are talking about life stories, authorized and unauthorized biographies, natural catastrophes, historical events, true crime, fiction, book adaptations, current tragedies and events, and star vehicles (stories created for well-known television stars) or whatever subject can fit into the programming and budget of television. It's constantly changing.

What is the market for miniseries and MFTs ?

Everybody. This is a very healthy market. This area is a very important part of the original programming on television. For the cable channels, it is a very important way for them to distinguish the cable programming from the network programming, and a very significant method for cable channels such as Home Box Office (HBO) and Turner Network Television (TNT) to promote themselves.

What is the audience for long-form television?

The audience for network miniseries/MFTs is mostly focused on the perceived female market. The cables, specifically HBO, Showtime, and TNT, skew more toward a male audience. However, all of the cables and networks are constantly in a state of discovery and change as to how to attract a new audience.

Why would a writer want to write in this market?

One reason is that the writer may actually like the type of work produced in this area. In addition, if a writer is actually able to work in this market, the writer will have a greater probability of actually seeing his work made into a completed project, as opposed to feature films where the project can take forever and has a tremendous possibility of not being made at all. If you are fortunate enough to gain acceptance into the established group of writers in this genre, you will work a lot. Also, writers working in long-form television have the ability to work on topical and timely subjects that do not often get made into feature films. In addition, this area of writing offers roles in television for women that have range, character, subtlety, and dynamics–in short, good roles for women that are not often found.

How can a writer who wants to work in this market get started?

One way is to make a concerted effort to write the type of material that would lend itself to this type of work. An example I know is a writer who took the time to learn the seven-act formula for movies of the week and wrote spec writing samples in this formula specifically geared for the TV-movie-of-the-week market. Another method is obtain the rights to a very hot and topical story. A third method would be to write a spec screenplay that lends itself to the type of topics usually presented in this market.

What a writer is using as a spec writing sample must demonstrate an affinity for this type of work. In addition, if you have something in your background that shows an affinity for the area in which you are writing (for example, if you were on the police force for five years before you began writing or you have a background in medicine or something that brings a new angle to the work), this can help.

How can a writer gain the attention of an agent who specializes in long-form television?

As a writer, it is important to know your market and to do your homework. By "know your market," it is important to understand the type of work that will make it into this format and the type of work that is unacceptable in this format. For instance, big-budget works which require expensive special effects are not the type of work that gets made in this market. In short, if you want to write in this market, do your homework: Get to know the type of work that can be made in this genre and show me something I can send out as evidence of your capability to write in this area.

Can a writer option the rights to a story and hope to set up a project with him or her attached?

If you (the writer) own the rights to a hot story and someone wants it bad enough, you probably can dictate the terms of how and when the project will be created. But if you are attempting to be the writer on the project, you will need to have something, such as a spec screenplay, to show that you are capable of writing the project.

All writers should be warned, however, that if a hot story comes up, there is intense competition for the rights to it. Needless to say, everyone flies to wherever the story took place in an attempt to get the rights. In addition, many people scour the paper and several online services on a daily basis in an attempt to find the situations and/or stories that would make good projects.

What are the disadvantages of writing in long-form television?

If you want to go from this market to writing for features, you may have to prove yourself again in the feature market. One issue used to be that television writers were labeled as "television writers" only and not given a chance to go in a different direction. The division is not that big now, and it is not as difficult to go from writing for television to writing for film.

What is the future of MFTs?

Well, it's a very healthy market that will continue to grow. The most definite thing that you can say about this market is that it is constantly changing.

12

Why Write for Television When You Can Write for Cyberspace?

INTRODUCTION

Once upon a time, "interactive" was the province of computer nerds and engineers who preferred to do nothing more than communicate through the world of electronic mail known as Cyberspace. Now these nerds are billionaires, as they have evolved from working in their parents' garages, to owning corporations with profits larger than the gross national product of many third-world countries. Needless to say, everyone is attempting to catch-up with the former nerds: Everyone, including the entertainment industry.

It has not gone unnoticed to the multi-billion dollar industry which gave us such gems as *Waterworld* and *Cabin Boy* that "interactive," along with providing the world with an enormous new source of product, has a feature destined to make any bottom-line executive happy. Unlike feature films, which generally cost $50 million dollars to make and can take years to show a profit, an interactive game such as *Wing Commander* can be produced for $150,000 to $2,000,000, and can see profits rather quickly. More to the point, in 1994, the "game" industry made $3 billion dollars more than the film industry. Thus we now have Silliwood (short for "Silicon Hollywood"), the approaching convergence of movies, interactive, television, and computers.

What does this mean for writers? Everything, and a lot of it. For those of you who have been faking it for far too long, the following two interviews, with interactive writer/designers Bruce Onders and Jeff Sullivan, and attorney David Hankin, should clarify the mystery of "interactive writing for the entertainment industry."

WRITING FOR INTERACTIVE: INTERVIEWS WITH BRUCE ONDER AND JEFFREY SULLIVAN AND WITH DAVID HANKIN

INTERVIEW WITH BRUCE ONDER AND JEFFREY SULLIVAN

Jeffrey Sullivan ("JS") and Bruce Onder ("BO") founded Digital Arcana in 1994. They are producing and designing *The Outer Limits: On-Line* (working title at press time), a multi-player game environment based on MGM's award-winning science fiction series. They are developing a number of original game ideas with various game publishers. They were also designers of *Spycraft: The Great Game* for Activision Studios.

How did you begin writing for the interactive entertainment industry?

BO We came out to Los Angeles, originally, to be screenwriters. We had been doing some game design work back East, but we didn't have any intention to come out here to get into computer gaming. Also I think our total sales across all game design activities was enough to buy a pretty decent meal. At McDonald's.

JS Bear in mind, the game design we'd done back east was not computer games, it was board and role-playing games. Still, it did give us a tremendous leg up, since it addressed the true fundamentals of game design, which isn't flashy graphics, polygon counts, or animation frame rates—it's the richness of the game world, the variety and enjoyability of the non-player characters, and most of all, the story.

Of course, that was all background. When we moved to L.A., we threw ourselves into screenwriting.

BO We got computer-related jobs to pay the bills. Jeff was an artificial intelligence programmer for a research think tank, and I was a database consultant he hired to do the dirty work.

JS And eventually we started making progress with our scripts. We got a short film made as part of an independent anthology, wrote some episodes of animated shows, and sold a feature, which never got made. All through this time, we'd been avid gamers, but something happened that opened our eyes. We saw a sneak peek at *Myst*, and we were blown away. Or at least I was.

BO I was sort of ambivalent about *Myst*. I'm definitely not the puzzle-solving type. I was impressed with the backstory more than the environment.

JS In any case, when we saw what Cyan was doing with *Myst*, I realized that computer adventures were changing in a fundamental way. For me, and I know Bruce differs in this—*Myst* was a completely organic experience. I played it from start to finish without a hint, and I enjoyed every minute of it. *Myst* crystallized a lot of the thoughts I'd been having about the future of computer gaming. It delivered an experience I found truly superior to most movies or novels, and did so in a wonderfully engaging way.

   Based on the cinematic inklings I saw in *Myst*, I felt that the gaming industry was about to undergo a revolution where screenwriting and game design would begin to merge in meaningful ways, and Bruce and I began plans to take part in it.

   Being screenwriters, avid gamers, and computer geeks, we figured we were a perfect fit.

BO So we started developing some ideas for games and shopping those around. One of the first places we went was Activision. Jeff had been talking to Bill Volk, who was a producer there at the time, and he set up a meeting for us with Howard Marks, the president of the company. We pitched everything we had to them, but basically they were only interested in hot licenses or existing stuff, like their own Infocom titles.

JS We parted ways, with Activision saying they'd like to find something to do with us. Naturally, being screenwriters in Hollywood, we'd heard that before, so we filed it in our back pockets and, with an additional $1.50, could get a cup of coffee.

You can imagine our surprise several months later when we got a call from Andrew Goldman, a producer at Activision. He was working on an espionage thriller, and needed some game design work done. We'd been recommended to him, so we met and showed him some samples—some original interactive work to show our design abilities and a screenplay for general writing, dialog, and storytelling. That work went on to become *Spycraft: The Great Game*, a very interesting project for us. It was a great learning experience in working on multi-million dollar projects—there are still relatively few of them in the industry—and also a stepping-stone to bigger and better things.

Are you represented by agents for your screenwriting and interactive work?

BO No. Right now we're pretty happy with our own marketing efforts. I guess we'd consider having an agent again, but frankly they'd have to sell themselves on us and not vice versa.

JS We looked at the agent scene a while back and were disappointed to learn that most of the agents in town don't know anything about interactive. Even those that are positioning themselves as interactive agents are a very, very mixed bag. Some of them are excellent, but most of them range from moderately to dangerously uninformed about industry trends and practices.

Some of the larger agencies—William Morris, ICM (International Creative Management), CAA (Creative Artists Agency)—have formal interactive departments, but most of them are devoted more to handling companies than individual talent. I suppose that makes sense from a money standpoint, but it was rather disappointing from a personal standpoint.

There are a few agents at these big agencies who are actually handling individual talent like game designers and writers, but they are so few that they're generally pretty booked up all the time.

And of course, we'd like an agent, or at least agency, who can handle both our interactive and screenwriting. And that combination is pretty hard to find. At least, we haven't found it yet.

So reality is that, although some of the agencies are actually alleging that they have multimedia departments, the reality of what they can do for you is very limited?

JS Yes, unless you're a game company who's looking to form big licensing or alliance deals.

No matter who you're dealing with, you need to make sure that they're handling your career the way you want them to. It doesn't matter if you're at CAA if they really don't move you much because they have five bigger clients who land all the contracts.

BO You're going to be your own best marketing tool, whether you have an agent or not. Personally, I'd spend a lot more time finding a knowledgeable lawyer who has done interactive deals before. That's a tall order, too, but I think it's more important.

JS The other thing to keep in mind is that even the most experienced agents are flying blind to some extent in this area. It's not like there's a ton of precedent on deals. When it comes to formal negotiations, I'll go out on a limb and say that about 100% of the agents out there need a lawyer to back them up.

Some very sophisticated agents actually have the lawyer negotiate the fine points of the deal, because there are no boilerplates. As a result, a lot of very important technical and legal issues have to be dealt with properly or you could put the next six months of your life into something and walk away from it with no rights. I cannot stress enough the importance of having competent legal representation. We used to think lawyers were an expensive luxury, but I can't imagine being anywhere but the loony bin if we hadn't used one on our past two deals.

It's pretty easy to find a good lawyer, just ask around—get recommendations from people working in the field. You'll find the same small group of names floating to the top. Go with one of them, and you're okay.

What does a writer do in creating interactive product?

BO Traditionally, what companies use a writer for is either a puzzle creator or a "flesh-out" person. A lot of writers get hired to think up clues to things like math or geography puzzles; for example, for the Carmen Sandiego series from Broderbund. On the other hand, the "flesh-out" people are writers brought in to flesh out a game design by adding or, um, fleshing out characters, creating or, er, fleshing out story lines, and coming up with dialogue. I think one of the places where real writing is starting to blossom is in the more movie-like titles like *Full Throttle* by Tim Schaefer at LucasArts. That is real writing, in my mind, as opposed to thinking of a couple of puzzles involving elves, or "something we can plug in here." That stuff is so dissociated from the process that I don't personally consider it writing.

I also think that the trend is moving toward integrating game designers with writers because the game design, in a lot of ways, is so closely tied to the kind of story you can tell—or can't tell—that it's really part of the same process. I think there's going to be a lot of appeal for someone who can say "listen, I'm a writer and a designer, and I can talk to you intelligently about things like interface and puzzle design, story linearity, as well as character arcs, dialogue subtext, and pacing."

So you're saying that someone who wants to write in this field has to create a greater understanding of what it actually takes to create the product.

BO It's going to be much harder to sell yourself in this field if you don't know what interactive writing entails. I'm surprised by the number of people who want to break into the field, but their total experience is "I looked at *Myst*" or "I played *Doom*." And I'm not just talking writers here. Producers are just as guilty! But don't do the crime if you can't do the time.

JS Don't do it!

Can you describe the process of creating an interactive product and the participants along the way?

JS At a very high level, a **producer** is given the task of developing a title based on some concept someone has brought to the table. The producer then needs to schedule the development of that idea into a game design document, which is the blueprint the production people need to go ahead and build the thing.

BO The producer is the guy who's reporting directly to whoever is holding the purse strings. His butt's on the line, and he is expected to handle the project without much in the way of supervision above his level. He may also be the person who is entrusted with the creative direction, or they may have a **director** doing this, just like on a film. More often than not, I'd say, the producer is also the director.

During development, the **designer**'s working with the producer and any lead production people to get the interface, overall look and feel, and other technical-creative issues resolved. The designer is hopefully also deciding how big the game is going to be—how many worlds, or rooms, or levels. Sometimes it's hard to know how big a game should be. It's easy for the honchos to say "give me 20 hours of gameplay," but what does that mean? Over time you start to get a feel for how long a puzzle or a sequence should take.

JS In a perfect world, the designer's job is pretty much done by the time production starts. However, that doesn't mean the design won't change, because it certainly will. If the programmers just can't get all the features you've designed implemented on time or on budget, then guess what? The design is changed to reflect that. The design will be under constant assault from every direction, and there's nothing to be done about that.

BO If there's a separate **writer** involved, his job needs to be completed before any permanent assets are created. For instance, if you're doing a full-motion video game, you can't shoot the scenes and then rewrite the dialogue or story. Unless you're very silly. I assume that's what they mean when they say "Sillywood." Har har.

JS The **programming team** will be hard at work putting all the core code in place while the design is under way. The lead programmer will be involved in the design, suggesting specific ways to accomplish things in code, or flat out saying that the current technology won't let the design be implemented well enough. In other words, the lead programmer will tell every member of the team what they need to do to make their creative vision a reality. The programmer will work with the producer to ensure that milestones are being met.

BO The **sound designer** and **composer** can usually be brought in late in the game. The sound designer is like a foley artist, creating all of the sounds produced by the program, like that of a door closing or a cow walking. The composer—well, he composes for you.

JS Unless he's dead, in which case he'll usually decompose for you.

BO One of the most important people during production is the **asset mananger**. This is the guy who is in charge of tracking all the different files that need to be created for the game. Everything needs to be date and time stamped, assigned a version number, and named logically and consistently. The asset manager will also be tracking which files are "checked in" and which ones are still being created. He knows when someone is late with a new version, and he knows how much storage is needed to hold the current version of the game.

JS Poor asset management is suicide. You'll lose track of things fast, because on a single game you will be generating many gigabytes of data, all of it unique in very subtle ways. A good asset manager will be able to keep tabs on all of this information, and more.

Is there a particular point when a writer who is not the designer would be hired?

BO Traditionally, a writer might be hired toward the end of the project to "flesh out the dialogue" or come up with a bunch of puzzle clues. But when Jeff and I sign on to a project, it's usually to integrate the traditional writer stuff with the designer stuff. Not only does that give us more input into the whole process of creating a game, but you gotta have those hyphenated titles, man [laughs]!

JS Now that the "Silliwood" confluence of Silicon Valley and Hollywood is all the rage, it's not too uncommon to bring in a writer up front to help shape the game idea. Then he's often sent away while the game designer works up a design (or maybe he's brought in from time to time for meetings to come up with character ideas or plot twists). But still, the non-designer writer is often considered an appendage rather than a vital organ.

How does writing an interactive script differ from writing a traditional script?

JS The first thing you'll discover is, unlike screenwriting, there is no generally accepted format for a game design document.

BO There's also no standard list of items that make up a design document. Sometimes the script is included, and sometimes it isn't. Things like that.

JS So you'll find that producers who hire you will do one of two things. They will either hand you a game design document format that you'll have to adhere to. . .

BO . . . and which may be totally inadequate for the project you're working on. . .

JS . . . or they'll give you complete freedom to come up with your own format. Which is pretty scary when you're just starting and you don't even know what should be in there! But frankly, that's the position many producers are in as well.

BO Over a number of projects, a company will slowly develop a format they will use in-house. Maybe. Independent designers will develop their own format, too, but they will have the advantage, presumably, of working for different companies. So they can grab the best ideas from a number of different sources.

JS The fundamental difference between traditional screenwriting and interactive is that in interactive, things can be gotten at in multiple ways. For example, in a script you have a character, Nick, sneak into the alley and slip inside the warehouse after jimmying the lock. That's the option you took, and it's the only way Nick gets into the warehouse. But in interactive, you might have a dozen different ways into the warehouse, including jimmying the lock, being captured, or even joining with the bad guys and walking through the front door.

Handling this non-linearity in an inherently linear form like paper—or even with a word-processor—is a really tough thing. The things you're writing about, referring to, they're moving targets. It gets very complicated, and the biggest advantage a writer can have— whatever system they're using—is to be meticulous and consistent.

Even though it may seem like it's taking you longer to work when you're constantly checking your references and going back to make sure you're using the right ones, if you don't do that, and you cut some corners, it's definitely going to come back to bite you. After it happens to you a couple of times, you realize you can't afford to be doing this because you lose so much time trying to make up for your corner-cutting.

BO One of the ways many companies get around the limitation of paper is to use databases to hold game information.

We created a design database for a few of our projects, and in some ways it really helps keep track of things. When every reference is a true link to a record—like a reference to a character in a script isn't just your recollection of the character's name, but an actual pointer to his record in the database—you get all kinds of flexibility and power. Changes can be made in one place, and are instantly reflected throughout the whole design. You can ask questions like "what characters have less than five lines?" or "What are all the things that can ever be found in this room?" which are great things to be able to do.

JS   The downside of the database approach is managing the evolution of the design. If you go into the database too soon, you have a real nightmare of keeping track of revisions, unless the system is really sophisticated.

I think we've decided that design databases are good for moving from final design into production, but are actually more of a hindrance early in the design phase. Also, since we're computer geeks, we managed to crib together a set of macros we use with our word processor to let us get some nice things like hot-linked references to scene numbers, auto-numbering scenes and chapters, and stuff like that. It takes care of a lot of the bookkeeping nightmare, which is what a computer is better at doing than I am. Well, that and entering my credit card statements.

How can an emerging writer "break in" to writing for interactive?

BO   Probably the easiest way to break in is to bend over and smile the first time. This has a certain appeal to people like Jeff [laughs].

JS   That'd be funny—if you hadn't set yourself up with an easy punchline.

BO   [laughs] But seriously, it's not really different from Hollywood filmmaking in this regard—producers will try to screw you every way you let them, and on your first deal you can't possibly know all those ways of getting screwed.

JS   On the *fifth* deal, you won't know all the ways! But every deal, you keep learning new ones. And they go into the next contract, so you're always better protected.

If someone outside of the field wants to get in contact with an interactive producer, how should they try it?

JS   The best way is e-mail. Since this field is, by necessity, computer-oriented, almost everybody in it has one (or more) e-mail addresses. E-mail is nice because it lets you be much more specific and detailed than you can get in a phone conversation, but it's non-intrusive. The recipient can read it at their leisure, not when they've got an important meeting going on in the office.

You can often find game-company people on various on-line services—the internet, Compuserve, America On-line, etc.—and they're surprisingly accessible.

The game industry hasn't evolved into this culture of inaccessibility that Hollywood has, although I do see it moving in that direction.

BO If they are completely new to the entertainment industry, one of the best ways may be to get involved with the company in a different capacity.

It's possible to become a tester in the quality assurance department, and make suggestions about game design that make people say "hey, this person is on the ball." People remember that you came up with the idea for making Hubert purple instead of red because people like purple better.

JS [makes the "this guy is nuts" sign] Good example.

BO Hopefully, your contributions are more vital than that, but that's a good way to work your way up.

If you're an existing screenwriter, I think you should try to leverage the fact that you have credits in screenwriting, and you're good at dialogue and story. Don't try to be a game designer off the bat if you aren't one. Just say "let me write the dialogue for this game, because that's where I can add the most value right now."

JS Also, to clarify here, I'm not talking about sending in project pitches via e-mail. Unsolicited stuff like that is a sure-fire way to get yourself prime position in a kill file. Just make contact in that way. If you have an idea you want to get to somebody, talk to them about whom to contact, or to see if they're even interested.

Is it still possible for someone outside of Los Angeles or any of these game producing areas to contact a producer or someone who is creating these works?

BO It's actually a lot easier to approach producers who are doing interactive. They tend to be more wired than film and TV people, which
means you can send them a quick e-mail and actually get a response!

JS And of course, L.A. isn't even the center of interactive production,
which is arguably San Francisco. The great thing about making
games is that it doesn't require the great weather of southern
California, so it's spread out all over the place: Frisco, Chicago,
Austin, D.C.

BO The flip side of that is the talent is also spread out. It's much easier
to find work telecommuting in this field than in many others, in
part because everyone's so comfortable with communicating by
computer.

Are there any particular chat groups which are helpful?

JS On the internet, the Usenet newsgroups rec.games.design and
rec.arts.int-fiction are pretty good areas. You get a wide variety of
people on there, though, so it does take some exercise of the B.S.
detector to weed the wheat from the chaff.

   Compuserve has the Game Developer forum (GO GAMEDEV),
which is very good. Again, a wide variety of people, but they seem a
lot more knowledgeable about things; most of them seem to be
working professionals, and the level of discussion is often very good.

   Secondarily, any of the game newsgroups like rec.game.video.sega
or .nintendo or whatever, any of these forums, they're basically free
market research. You get to listen to all these game players, see
what they love about games, what they hate, and what drives them
nuts. You can really educate yourself in game design by paying
attention; there's a tremendous amount of great feedback—

BO Along with an even more tremendous amount of spam, flame wars,
and idiocy.

JS True enough. But if you have the wherewithal to sift through all
that, you can get a strong sense of what people like in certain kinds
of games. That can be invaluable.

BO By the way, if you're not willing to make the plunge into full-time writing and designing, you might think about hooking up with or starting some sort of design project on your own. Basically you create or join some sort of game in a team environment on a part-time basis. There are rights issues to work out, but it may be a good way to test the waters or even produce a demo you could show when you do make the leap.

What advice would you give those emerging writers who would like to write for interactive.

BO First, do your homework. Play the games. See what works and what doesn't, and what you could have done better.

JS Absolutely. That is job one. Not only will it make you familiar with game conventions, and able to talk with people in the industry and not come off as a wannabe, but it's also a crash course in game design. Unless you're a complete feeb, you'll come away with a growing intuitive sense of what plays and what doesn't.

BO On the dealmaking side, be sure your contract includes a list of deliverables that shows what you need to produce, when it's due, and how much you'll get paid when you turn it in. If rewrites are needed beyond what's included in the deliverables schedule, just make sure there's a provision that lets them assign you rewrites for a certain fee. And don't sign anything that requires you to wash cars on the weekends.

JS Yeah. Was *that* ever a bad deal!

INTERVIEW WITH DAVID HANKIN

David Hankin is an attorney in Los Angeles, California, who is representing many clients working in interactive and the entertainment industry. The following interview presents his experiences working in this emerging area.

When we say "writing for interactive" what areas are we talking about?

Let me preface my remarks by explaining my golden rule of interactive: there are no rules. No product is the same as any other product and no deal is the same as any other deal. This is an underlying theme that I attempt to convey to all of my clients at the outset of any contract negotiation in the interactive arena.

Having expressed the golden rule, your question has several answers, all of which are correct. The writer may operate on several levels, from scripting games to writing text on game packaging. Of course, it should be understood that we are not merely talking about a traditional twitch video game but rather a rich, textured interactive product such as video games with scripted story lines; so-called interactive movies, whether they contain live-action footage or animation; and edutainment products, the goal of which is to educate the user in an entertaining fashion. In addition to what are widely considered consumer CD-ROM products, writers are also participating in the development of location based interactive products such as shopping mall kiosks. The last category may be something as simple as a gas pump which will take a credit card, check the validity of the card, and play a commercial message while a consumer is pumping his or her gas.

In each of these contexts, the writer's job is central in developing an exciting and commercially saleable product. For example, in the edutainment context, the writer must figure out a pleasing way to convey information which might otherwise be difficult to convey. A great example comes to mind–there is a CD-ROM title which features the musical instruments of an orchestra. The program conveys information about the origin of each instrument, the sounds of each instrument, and so on. The writer gave spice to what otherwise might have been dry material by encouraging the user to interact with the product by playing recognizable music pieces and funny musical notes to enhance the written word.

Perhaps the most interesting development in the last year or so is the proliferation of the commercial use of the internet. Advertising has been the hotbed of activity on the World Wide Web—this medium has led to a new specialty, those persons or entities who are able to design and create web sites. Anybody who spends even the slightest amount of time on the Web immediately understands that while some Web sites are media intensive, most are text driven—another opportunity for writers.

What areas are employing, and what is the role of the writer in interactive entertainment?

This is a fluid question in that the identity of employers has increased over time and continues to increase daily. Without question, most writers who are presently employed in the interactive arena are working on games for PCs or Macintosh computers or for dedicated set top video game consoles like the Sony Playstation, Sega Saturn, or Nintendo Ultra 64.

Many different types of employers are engaging writers to assist them in creating interactive products. Software publishers who in the past have principally developed technology driven games and products are now seeking to inject human feeling and emotion into their products. As a result, programmers have been pushed aside in favor of writers who bring to the table a richer, more textured feeling to a given product.

Certainly now that each Hollywood studio has at least one interactive division, writers who in the past were engaged to write for feature films and episodic television are now writing interactive products. The same is true of other creative elements such as directors and producers.

Record companies who have for a long time sat on the sidelines are also becoming more active in the interactive arena–they too are looking to established, as well as new, writers to help them create their products.

As I mentioned earlier, Fortune 500 companies are quickly taking advantage of the use of interactive technologies in a variety of contexts, especially marketing, promotion, and advertising. My favorite service station these days is Union 76. At the pump, I interact with a credit card receptacle which operates the pump. I push a few buttons, pump my gas, and receive a receipt for my purchase. In some stations, I even may watch a short commercial about Union 76 products. This crude application of interactive technology allows me to select premium gasoline, pay with a credit card, confirm that my credit card is valid, see a commercial, and get a receipt. Union Oil or its advertising agency probably employed a writer to write the text of the interface as well as the commercial script.

Another interesting opportunity for writers is working for companies that are operating interactive television test sites. At one time, there were approximately nine test sites nationwide. Initially, the interface designs were conceived by engineers and apparently weren't too user friendly. Later, many of the companies operating the test sites employed writers and designers to create more attractive, user friendly interfaces. The jury is still out on these sites, which means, in all probability, that there will be additional employment opportunities for writers in the future.

How are talent agencies participating in the creation of interactive projects?

As each day passes, I run into another person claiming to be a talent agent in the interactive business. It seems as if there is an endless supply of so-called experts who are willing to take a substantial stake in a project or company in return for their expert advice.

Unfortunately, it really takes away from legitimate agents in the interactive business who do bring a tremendous amount of expertise and contacts to the table. In my mind, International Creative Management (ICM) and William Morris are the two leading agencies in the interactive arena. Both agencies have departments devoted to the new media area. The agents at both agencies are extremely knowledgeable, they understand and can identify good talent (there is a lot of interactive wannabees who have neither the background nor have they even taken the time to learn the slightest bit about the industry), they speak to publishers on a regular basis and understand their needs, and they generally have a sense where the industry has been and where it might be going (because who really knows).

There was a recent announcement that Creative Artists Agency (CAA) opened a new media department. The jury is out on what role, if any, CAA may play in the future. Thus far, CAA has not been as active as ICM or William Morris in the content side of the interactive arena.

There are some smaller agencies that are also dabbling in the interactive arena. There are agents at the Jim Preminger Agency and MontanArtists who represent some high-profile talent.

I was at lunch one day with a programmer client. He had a glazed look in his eyes. He told me that he was reflecting upon how much his life had changed: a few short years prior, he had been writing software applications for financial services companies—now, he was represented by a Hollywood agent.

Agents are increasingly participating in the packaging of talent to create products for software publishers. In addition, agents are assisting their clients in locating and structuring finance and affiliate label deals. They also assist publishers and developers in locating that one missing element to make a project work.

As production budgets for interactive projects increase, agents are steering the agencies' mainstream entertainment clientele into these projects. "A-List" directors, actors, and other elements are now, in large part because of agents, looking into and participating in the creation of interactive projects.

Agencies are also involved in the exploitation of game elements in other media such as television and features. Early attempts at this crossover resulted in box office failures but the success of the *Mortal Kombat* feature film has paved the way for game elements to be repurposed for the big screen or for an episodic television series. I expect agents to play a pivotal role in this area.

Are some of the agencies actually creating or involving themselves not just in interactive products, but in the delivery system?

The most widely know venture is the onslaught of Telco, Inc., which was presumably masterminded by some agents at CAA. Telco, Inc. was a collaborative venture between some serious players in the Telephone and Cable Television industries. As originally conceived, Telco, Inc.'s mission was to determine what would constitute the interactive delivery system of the future. With the recent changes at CAA, it is questionable what role, if any, CAA will have with Telco, Inc. in the future.

ICM represents at least one of the computer subscription services with internet access. For those who ascribe to the view that interactive products will be delivered to the home via the internet or through a computer subscription service, ICM may have sweeping influence over what services are offered, how they are offered, and at what price.

Is the WGA admitting interactive writers?

I am aware of four writers who have been admitted to the WGA on the basis of their interactive work. Many writers who are already guild members are very active in the interactive business. There is no question that the WGA credential is meaningful to software publishers and certainly to studios and production companies when they seek to employ a writer for an interactive project.

The Guild is very active in the interactive arena.* The Guild is present at most of the trade shows (and there are a lot of them), hosts seminars for its members, and has knowledgeable personnel available to respond to member questions about the interactive business.

What problems are writers encountering with interactive writing?

Virtually every creative element involved in the development of an interactive project suffers from the same malady: the lack of vision of the director combined with an ambiguous contract describing the writer's scope of work. This is a recipe for disaster and writer misery.

If the director lacks focus or vision, the project can change many times over the course of its development. Unless the writer's agreement with the developer or publisher clearly spells out what is expected of the writer, the writer may be held hostage by an unscrupulous director and peer pressure from the other elements on the production team. The writer could find that he or she is now performing considerably more work than ever anticipated.

The other problem which writers encounter is that their unfamiliarity with the medium results in a complete underestimation on their part as to the time and energy involved in the development of an interactive project. It simply is not an easy process. So regardless of how well-defined the scope of work is in a writer's agreement, writers oftentimes find themselves in over their heads when it comes

* See note at end of chapter.

down to completing their work. Once a writer goes through the process once, they have a keen understanding of what they are about to get into the next time around.

Another problem that writers must contend with is preventing their ideas or concepts from being stolen. This is a difficult problem to overcome and writers should take great care (and consult a competent attorney) before they share their ideas with others in the interactive business.

What are the problems with interactive writing deals?

Before I make the first telephone call on behalf of a writer client on an interactive deal, I sit down with the writer and explain the state-of-the-art deal, which shifts hourly, and the economics of the interactive business. If I am representing a first time writer, I will also parade out the list of horribles about the development of an interactive project. I want my client to be prepared for the worst and hope that the experience ends up better.

Money is usually the most controversial issue. Hopefully, my client has come to me before he or she has agreed to an eighteen-month exclusive commitment for $20,000 and a back-end bonus of $5,000 after the publisher generates net revenues of $10,000,000.

Relative to features and television, writing for interactive is a poor man's game. The deals are simply incomparable in scope. Typically, I hope to structure deals such that the writer sees most of his or her compensation in the form of a front-end fee with a favorable payment schedule. I prefer royalty structures over bonus structures and insist that if my client is creating characters and environments that he or she participate financially and in the development of sequels, merchandising, and ancillary product. That's the starting point; employers chip away from there.

Credit is also a source of contention. Non-studio publishers are only now beginning to understand Hollywood credits and their significance to a writer. A few years ago, I negotiated a deal with the general counsel of a studio's interactive division who had just left the employ of a software publisher. This attorney was totally unfamiliar with the significance of credit provisions—as a result, I negotiated the full panoply of credits for a virtually unknown writer. This is unlikely to happen again now that software publishers have learned about the significance of credits.

In the interactive arena, unlike in television or in features, writing credits must be negotiated—the WGA has no minimum requirements. As a practical matter, I ask for on-screen, feature style credits in the main titles of the product with favored nations to the other key creative elements. I also seek credit in the product manual, product inserts, and on the product packaging. I also ask for credits on paid advertisement, again tied to the other creative elements involved in the project.

Surprisingly, most software publishers are relatively reasonable about on-screen credits and credits which appear in the product manual and inserts. Paid advertisements are somewhat sticky but as long as they are tied to other creative elements, publishers are more likely to give on this point.

Without question, the most controversial credit tends to be packaging or box credit. Publishers use their marketing department's need for flexibility in the box design to justify no commitments on box credit. Negotiations over box credit can be as spirited as those for compensation.

Note that if the writer is negotiating directly with a developer, the developer may have no control over the accordance of credit. Publishers typically dictate who is accorded credit and in what manner. Obviously, the lesson to be learned is to scope out who has the legal right to call the shots on credit.

Finally, defining the scope of the writer's engagement [translated: how much and what type of work a writer is expected to perform] can be a real nightmare. Oftentimes, the employer has no idea what they want from the writer. In those instances, I work with my client to outline a realistic set of expectations and deliverables over a workable timetable. My goal is to pin down exactly what is expected of the writer before he or she commences her services. Unfortunately, many employers are simply not prepared to make this commitment. Rather than leave the issue open-ended and my client exposed, I attempt to convince the employer to accept a certain set of parameters with the understanding that my client will be flexible in rendering additional services on the project if necessary for additional compensation.

*The Writers Guild of America west ("WGA") has started an Industry Alliance Department in an attempt to understand the role of the writer in the interactive entertainment industry. The Industry Alliance Department has instituted monthly meetings with members of the WGA to discuss the role that writers will play in the interactive entertainment industry. At this point, the WGA has not set minimum rates for members of the WGA who are writing interactive games. However, the WGA has opened the doors to allow membership in the WGA for those writers who are writing in interactive in the following situations: If the employer of the writer will pay the writer's Health and Welfare Benefits (an amount equal to 12.5% of what the writer is being paid for the work), the WGA will allow the writer, if not already a member of the WGA, to become eligible for WGA membership. Units for interactive writing are evaluated on a case-by-case basis. (Note: 24 units are required for WGA membership.)

Although not directly affecting those writers who are writing specifically in interactive, the WGA has established rates of payment for the reuse of WGA literary material and motion picture footage in interactive programs. This establishes payment standards for the use in multimedia material, such as CD-ROM, which combines together sound, image, and text. In the situation in which the game or CD-ROM title included film footage which was based on a script which had been written by a member of the WGA, the writer of the literary material would be paid a specific amount for the use of the material.

As set forth in the WGA's 1995 Agreement with the Alliance of Motion Picture & Television Producers, payment of between 1.2% and 3% is to be made to WGA writers for clips and excerpts from their material used in interactive programs.

Payments will be based on the "applicable gross" of the material, meaning the amount of money that is paid to "exploit" the rights of the work. As stated within the Agreement, "interactive program" includes those "viewed on a TV or computer screen via disc, cartridge, wireless, or wire transmission, and arcade games."

Section 4

RESOURCES AND TOOLS

Glossary of Terms

AGENCY MEETING A gathering in which a potential client of an agency meets with the agents to discuss the agents' plan and goals for creating a career for the potential client.

AGENT Generally an individual who is licensed to obtain work for individuals working in the entertainment industry.

ANNOTATION A comment specifying the source of each script element that is not wholly fictional, including all characters, events, settings, and segments of dialogue. Usually done at the request of a studio.

AUCTION/BIDDING WAR The situation in which a spec script, book, or written material is presented to several studios, all wanting to buy the work. The buying price for the work usually continues to rise until there is only one buyer bidding on the work.

CD-ROM (COMPACT DISK-READ ONLY MEMORY) A compact disk that is used as a digital memory or storage medium (of information, and so forth) for personal computers. CD-ROM is the most popular format on which to create interactive multimedia products due to the increasing sales of CD-ROM players.

CERTIFICATE OF AUTHORSHIP A form signed by the author of a screenplay or other written work that warrants the author's work is original, does not libel another party, does not invade anyone's privacy, and will not cause the buyer of the work to be sued for any legal action.

COMPENSATION/CONSIDERATION With regard to writers, the money paid for writing services or for the sale of a screenplay.

CONTINGENT COMPENSATION A form of compensation received by a writer, after the writing services have been completed, if he is awarded writing credit for the project. The contingent compensation may include a production bonus, net profits, reserved rights, and/or additional payments in the event of a film or television sequel, remake, or spinoff.

COPYRIGHT The body of United States federal laws and international laws that protect original and creative expression that is in a fixed and tangible form.

COVERAGE With regard to a script, the process by which a script is synopsized, reviewed, and evaluated with respect to the story, character development, plot development and so forth, and then rated, with the intention of informing others as to whether or not the script is worthy of further consideration. Coverage is usually done by a "reader."

CREDIT The authorship given to a written work in the entertainment industry. In writing for film, the important credits are "Story by," "Screenplay by," and "Written by." When writing for television, the important credits are "Created by," "Story by," and "Teleplay by."

CREDIT ARBITRATION A process run by the Writers Guild of America in which disputes concerning the award of credit (as in "Story by," "Screenplay by," "Teleplay by," and "Written by") are decided. The method in which these decisions take place has the WGA sending all drafts of the disputed work to three separate individuals; separately and without knowledge of each other, they decide which writer deserves the award of credit. When two of the three individuals agree on the award of credit, the decision is considered final.

DEFERRED COMPENSATION An amount of money to be paid from funds that, for a writer, are generally the net profits. A writer who accepts payment of his services from deferred compensation generally will not see this money.

DEVELOPMENT The process by which a script is altered, changed, modified, and so forth, by a series of collaborative meetings between the writer and/or production executive, studio executive, director, or other individuals who may be attached to the project.

FIRST DRAFT (FIRST DRAFT SCREENPLAY) As set forth in the Writers Guild of America Minimum Basic Agreement, a first complete draft of any script in continuity form, including dialogue.

FREELANCE To work from job to job without a permanent position. A freelance writer is one who is generally selling spec scripts or pitches within the industry.

GENERAL MEETING A "look-see" type of meeting in which a writer meets with a producer, production executive, studio executive, and so forth, as a form of introduction. Generally, in this meeting the producer, production executive, studio executive, and so forth, does not have a specific project in mind for which the writer will be hired.

GREEN LIGHT To give a film project the studio backing and financing to begin principal photography.

GROSS PROFITS (FIRST DOLLAR GROSS) If one is so lucky as to merit this form of participation in a project, the individual will be entitled to a percentage of every dollar of gross receipts.

HIP-POCKETING An agent or agency practice in which an individual(s) is represented by the agent or agency on a single project only, with no agreement that the agency or agent will continue to represent the individual once the project (or interest in the project) has ended.

INFORMATION SUPERHIGHWAY As generally understood, a term that refers to a system of computer and media networks being promoted (and in some cases they are in the process of being created) to provide universal home delivery of all interactive media forms.

LITERARY MANAGER An individual hired by a writer to promote his career, offer advice on the best steps to take to achieve the desired goal, and give guidance on the best people to hire to aid the writer in maximizing his potential.

LONG-FORM TV Basically, movies of the week (MOWs), and miniseries that are aired on free or pay television.

MATERIALS CONTRACT A contract for representation by an agency with regard to the sale of a work that the writer has created on his own, in a situation where the writer was not hired to create the work (in other words, a contract for the sale of a spec work).

MINIMUM BASIC AGREEMENT The fees and basic working conditions for the employment of writers within the entertainment industry as negotiated and set forth by the Writers Guild of America.

MULTIMEDIA The creation of products, mostly software, that may involve the combination of written text, visual imagery, film, and/or music.

NET PROFITS A topic that is regularly and frequently fought over in the entertainment industry. There are two basic categories:

1. Participation based on 100 percent of net profits—generally, the sums remaining after a full recoupment and deduction (which is ongoing) of distribution fees and costs, and after payment of deferments, but with no deduction for other net profit participants.
2. Participation based on a percentage of the "producer's net share"—

the sums remaining after full recoupment, payment of deferments, if any, and thereafter deducting continuing distribution costs and fees, from which another portion (as much as 50 percent) may be retained by the studio or financing entity as compensation for supplying financing and completion advances.

NON-WGA Written work for the entertainment industry that is done for a company which has not signed (or become a signatory) to the Writers Guild of America Minimum Basic Agreement.

OPTION Within the entertainment industry, an agreement by which the optioning party pays a certain amount to the creator of a work, usually a screenplay, to keep the work off the market for a certain amount of time, with the intention that the optioning party will be able to raise the money within the optioning period to actually purchase the work.

PACKAGING The process of putting together on the same project a writer (or screenplay), director, producer, and star talent—all of whom are generally represented by the same agency—and presenting this "bundle" to a studio.

PITCH A meeting in which one party will attempt to interest another party in a particular work or in a version of a particular work by presenting the story of the work in such an exciting manner that the buying party will find great interest in the work and will either buy the work or pay the "pitching" party to write the work. The term is also used to describe the presentation itself.

POLISH As set forth in the Writers Guild of America Minimum Basic Agreement, the writing of changes in dialogue, narration, or action, but not including a rewrite.

PRODUCER (FILM INDUSTRY) Somebody with a script and a telephone who has not written the screenplay but hopes to put together the financing and/or talent necessary to turn the script into a produced work.

PRODUCER (INTERACTIVE) To be determined. At this point it is the individual who puts together the concept, programmer, and/or designer and takes it to a publisher or finds the money so that the work can become a produced title (game, educational work, or program) and be put on the market for sale.

PRODUCER (TELEVISION INDUSTRY) One of, if not the most important role in the creation and production of a television show. Generally, this is a former (or possibly current) writer who has successfully written for a number of years as a staff member on a show and is now responsible for the creative aspects of the show. The executive producer, or the one the show runner, is ultimately responsible for the creative direction of the show.

PRODUCTION BONUS An award of cash given to the writer of a screenplay who receives shared or sole "Screenplay by" or "Written by" credit when the screenplay is turned into a film.

PRODUCTION COMPANY A company that is headed by a producer, director, actor/actress, or writer for the purpose of creating general entertainment products such as motion pictures, television shows, infomercials, commercials, multimedia, and so forth.

PUBLIC DOMAIN The state in which the creator of a work loses the copyright on it through the passage of the copyright period, failure to renew the work, or problems with the original registration of the work with the copyright office.

READER An individual who has the job of providing "coverage" (evaluation and synopsis) of scripts.

READING PERIOD The period after a writer has been hired to write an assignment that a hiring body (such as a producer or studio executive) will review. This body will give suggestions and decide whether to pick up the option to have the writer produce further work. During this period a writer is generally nonexclusive to the production and may do other work but generally must stay available to meet with the producer or other hiring body.

RECOUPMENT The gross funds from a film that are required to pay off negative costs, overhead, ongoing distribution fees, interest, financing and distribution costs, and, in appropriate cases, payment of "gross" participations.

RELEASE FORM A statement signed by an individual that generally frees the creator of the document from any kind of liability.

REWRITE As set forth in the Writers Guild of America Minimum Basic Agreement, this is considered the writing of significant changes in plot, story line, or interrelationship of characters in a screenplay.

RIDER W The provision of the Artists/Managers Basic Agreement of the Writers Guild of America in which the contract between WGA members and signatory agencies has been prenegotiated.

SAMPLE SCRIPT A work that the writer has created on his own initiative and used to attain meetings for the writer in order to expose him to the entertainment industry.

SCALE Writing for payment on the minimum rates set forth in the Writers Guild of America Minimum Basic Agreement. Generally, the basic rate is scale plus 10 percent in order to include the commission that the writer's agent will receive.

SCREENPLAY As set forth in the Writers Guild of America Minimum Basic Agreement, the final script with individual scenes, full dialogue, and camera setups.

SCREEN STORY A credit given to a writer who has written a screenplay based on another writer's work but has used the other writer's work only as a "springboard, a characterization, an incident, or some equally limited contribution, creating a story that is substantially new and different from the other writer's work. The credit "Screen story by" will be given only as a result of credit arbitration by the WGA.

SEPARATION OF RIGHTS Generally, a bundle of rights given to the creator of original, unexploited written material, including, among others, publication, audio, live stage, live dramatic tape, live television, radio, and writer sequels and remakes.

SERVICES CONTRACT A contract that a writer-client signs with an agency for representation in order to receive writing assignments.

SHOW RUNNER The person responsible for hiring all the writers and staff who create a show; generally, the executive producer of a television show.

SPEC (OR SPEC SCRIPT) A work that has been written on the writer's own initiative; that is, the writer was not hired to write it.

STORY As set forth in the Writers Guild of America Minimum Basic Agreement, literary or dramatic material indicating the characterization of the principal characters and containing sequences and action suitable for use in, or representing a substantial contribution to, a final script.

STUDIO The banks of the entertainment industry. The entities within the entertainment industry that have the money to finance and/or distribute the production of an entertainment product, such as a film, television show, or interactive product. If you go to the studio with the correct package (the script, the actors/actresses, the directors), the studio may buy the package for release under its banner. The price for the studio's services will be very high, however, because a completed film generally has to generate four to six times (or more) the cost to complete it before a studio will say that the film was "profitable."

SILLIWOOD The convergence of Silicon Valley and Hollywood, as seen in emerging CD-ROM products such as *Myst* and *Wing Commander.*

SUNDANCE FILM FESTIVAL The most important film event in the United States for the showing of independent films and the discovery of emerging talent.

TALENT AGENCY A group of agents who are (usually) licensed to find work for individuals working in the entertainment industry.

TELEPLAY As set forth in the Writers Guild of America Minimum Basic Agreement, in television, the final script with individual scenes and full dialogue or monologue (including whatever narration is required).

THE TRADES The newspapers that report the daily or weekly entertainment news of the entertainment industry; these usually denote *The Hollywood Reporter, Daily Variety,* and *Weekly Variety.*

TREATMENT As set forth in the Writers Guild of America Minimum Basic Agreement, an adaptation of a story, book, play, or other literary, dramatic, or musical material for motion picture purposes in a form suitable for use as the basis of a screenplay. "Original treatment" is defined as an original story written for motion picture purposes in a form suitable for use as the basis of a screenplay within the Minimum Basic Agreement.

VIRTUAL REALITY A program that creates a simulated existence that allows the participant (wearing a headset and gloves) to experience this existence as if part of it.

WGAEAST The Writers Guild of America in the East that represents writers living east of the Mississippi who work in film, television, or radio; it also represents fiction writers.

WGAWEST The Writers Guild of America in the West that represents writers living west of the Mississippi (don't ask me why) working in television, radio, and film.

WRITING PERIOD The time during which a writer is to complete his work. During this time the writer's services are generally exclusive to the production that has hired him.

WRITTEN BY The credit given when one or several writers have created both the story and the screenplay, and there is no source material (the work is based on the original ideas of the writers). The credit is also given in television if the writer has created both the story and the teleplay.

WORLD WIDE WEB A growing part of the Internet that offers users instant and easy access to a broad range of information and graphics that are available on so-called Web pages. The Web gets its name from the concept of an endlessly connected series of electronic strands. Each strand is linked to another, allowing users to move through the Web without having to know where they are or how they got there.

Competitions and Fellowships

The following is a list of competitions for screenplays, with brief information on them. When writing to inquire about contest details, it is necessary to include a stamped self-addressed envelope (SASE) in every case.

In each listing, basic details such as application dates, entry fees, and restrictions on who may enter have been noted. Specific fees and dates change, however, and readers should request this information in writing.

Some awards have monetary prizes, but you should keep in mind that the size of the financial reward does not necessarily reflect the value of the contest to the aspiring screenwriter's future career.

A useful resource for competition information is: *The Writers Aide Screenplay Competition Guide*. This book tracks screenplay competitions and includes entry forms for many of them. Its current cost is $24.90. Write to or phone:

Writers Aide Publishing
1685 So. Colorado Boulevard, #237Q
Denver, CO 80222
(303) 430-4839

Carl Sautter Memorial Scriptwriting Competition for Film and Television

For Film and TV. Winners are guaranteed to be read by producers in the industry. There is an entry fee, and entrants must be members of the Scriptwriters Network.

For information write to:

Scriptwriters Network
11684 Ventura Boulevard, Box 508
Studio City, CA 91604

Chanticleer Award

This is a not-for-profit program. Applicants enter screenplays for the award, and the winning script is made into a film. There is an entry fee. Entries are usually due around May or June.

The Discovery Program

1680 N. Vine Street, Suite 1212
Hollywood, CA 90028
(213) 462-4705

Christopher Columbus Discovery Program

Entries are accepted year-round. There is a discovery of the month and of the year, which runs from December 1 to December 1. Scripts may be optioned for sums ranging up to $10,000. There is an entry fee.

Christopher Columbus Discovery Awards
433 N. Camden Drive, Suite 600
Beverly Hills, CA 90210
(310) 288-1988

Disney Fellowship

This program offers selected writers a one-year fellowship at the studio. Fellows are paid $30,000 during the fellowship, and there is a possibility of a second year as a fellow at a higher payment. Writers with a WGA-recognized credit are excluded. There is a minority focus.

Applications are generally due in March/April.

Disney Fellowship Program Administrator
The Walt Disney Studios
500 S. Buena Vista Street
Burbank, CA 91521-0880
(818) 560-6894

The Guy Alexander Hanks and Marvin Miller Screenwriting Program

A fifteen-week workshop to help experienced African-American screenwriters complete a film or television script. Established by Bill and Camille Cosby, and held at the University of Southern California. Free. Send an SASE to:

The Guy Alexander Hanks and Marvin Miller Screenwriting Program
USC School of Cinema-Television
Lucas Building, Room 400
University Park
Los Angeles, CA 90089-2211

Houston International Film and Video Festival and Charleston Film Festival

Both of these have a screenwriting competition run by the same organization. Houston entries are due around March; Charleston entries are due around September. These have several genre categories for screenplays plus one overall grand prize. There is an entry fee and an additional fee to receive evaluations. For information:

Attention: Entry Director
Worldfest Houston
P.O. Box 56566
Houston, TX 77256
(713) 965-9955

Independent Feature Project

The IFP has an annual Beigel Screenplay Award competition which is held in conjunction with its annual screenplay conference "From Script to Screen." An award for most promising screenplay comes with a cash prize of $5,000. The deadline for submitting a screenplay is generally early April. To be eligible for the award, entrants must be a member of the IFP or WGAeast. For details, call (212) 465-8200, ext. 221.

Nate Monaster Award

Up to four winners. Prize money variable plus an internship on a television program in Los Angeles. The competition is for television scripts: half-hour comedy, one-hour drama, or a television movie. Restricted to undergraduate or graduate students of accredited film schools, through which applications should be made.

Nevada State Contest

Entries in late April. Entry fee (a higher fee is charged to out-of-state applicants). Scripts must be 60 percent filmable in Nevada.

Nevada Motion Picture Division
555 East Washington Avenue, #5400
Las Vegas, NV 89101
(702) 486-2700

New Harmony Project

Winners enter a script laboratory. Plays are also eligible. Applications are due in early January.

The New Harmony Project
613 N. East Street
Indianapolis, IN 46202
(317) 464-9405

New Professional Theater Screenwriting and Playwriting Festival

Screenplays or plays are eligible, and the winning entry receives a professional reading. Entries are generally due between April and June.

New Professional Theater
Sheila K. Davis
443 W. 50th Street
New York, NY 10019
(212) 484-9811

Don and Gee Nicholl Academy Fellowships

Administered by the Academy of Motion Picture Arts and Sciences. Awarded by an elimination process, and the five finalists receive $25,000. No one who has earned money by screen or television writing or from the sale of an option may enter unless the sale was for less than $1,000. Entries are due in May.

Academy Foundation
Nicholl Fellowship in Screenwriting
8949 Wilshire Boulevard
Beverly Hills, CA 90211
(310) 247-3000

Set In Philadelphia

Story must be set in Greater Philadelphia area. There is an entry fee. Apply in the fall to:

Set In Philadelphia/PFWC
International House
3701 Chestnut Street
Philadelphia, PA 19104
(215) 895-6593

Sundance Institute

The prestigious Sundance Institute founded by Robert Redford offers a program in which script writers get to develop their screenplays in special workshops. Two workshops are held each year, one in January and one in June. There is an entry fee. Sen an SASE for information to:

Sundance Institute
225 Santa Monica Boulevard, 8th Floor
Santa Monica, CA 90401
(310) 394-4662

UCLA Extension Diane Thomas Awards

These awards, presented by the UCLA Extension Writers program and Amblin Entertainment, offer a small financial award but valuable publicity. First place receives $500; second, $350; and third, $150. Entrants must have taken units in the UCLA Extension writing program.

Writers Program
UCLA Extension
10995 Le Conte Avenue, Room 440
Los Angeles, CA 90024-2883
(310) 825-9418

Universal Studios Chesterfield Writers Project

This program offers selected writers a ten-month workshop program in Los Angeles that is based on the studio lot. Those selected also receive a stipend of $20,000 to cover their living expenses during the time in the program. There is an entry fee. Original written materials other than screenplays are acceptable as submissions. Applications are due around May.

The Chesterfield Film Company
Writer's Film Project
Universal Studios
100 Universal City Plaza, Bungalow 447
Universal City, CA 91608
(818) 777-0998

Virginia State Governor's Screenwriting Competition

This competition is held every two years. The applicant must be a Virginia resident and the script must have 75% Virginia locations. Entries are accepted between May and July.

Virginia Film Office
Attention: Governor's Screenwriting Competition
P.O. Box 798
Richmond, VA 23206-0798
(804) 371-8204

Wisconsin Screenwriters Forum Contest

Each entry gets feedback. There is an entry fee. The deadline is in October.

Wisconsin Screenwriter's Forum Contest
c/o Mark Borchardt
5747 North 82 Court

Milwaukee, WI 53218
(414) 464-4350

DGA/WGA Women Filmmakers program

Run by the Writers Guild and Directors Guild, this program is aimed at developing opportunities for women in the film industry and providing them with a forum as well as exposure. Women who are members of either guild are eligible for the program.

Writers Guild of Americawest
7000 West 3rd Street
West Hollywood, CA 90048

Writers Digest Writing Competition

Details from:

Writer's Digest Writing Competition
1507 Dana Avenue
Cincinnati, OH 45207
(513) 531-2222

Writers Workshop

This program was formerly run by the AFI but is now independent. Entries are accepted year round and writers receive critiques and script development. Some screenplays are staged for industry audiences and help is also given in getting selected screenplays to producers. There is an entry fee.

Writers Workshop
PO Box 69799
Los Angeles, CA 90069
(213) 933-9232

Writers Workshop Minority Screenwriters Contest

This program is also run by the Writers Workshop, but entries in it are restricted to members of ethnic minorities and are accepted between September and December. There are five Awards of $500 and a ceremony is held. Otherwise the entrants receive the same treatment as in the program above. Applications should be addressed as above but marked:

ATTN: Minority Screenwriters Contest.

Writers Guild List of Agencies

The following is a partial list of the agencies that have agreed to abide by Rider W of the Writers Guild of America. Most of the agencies listed here are located in either Los Angeles, California, or New York, New York. The actual list compiled by the WGA contains more than 240 agencies around the country. This list can be obtained by writing the WGAwest, 7000 West 3rd Street, West Hollywood, California 90048, enclosing a check for $2.00 and a self-addressed stamped envelope. In addition, if you are interested in a directory of agents and managers throughout the country that is not limited to those that have agreed to abide by Rider W of the Writers Guild of America (which also lists the name of individual agents within the agencies), I recommend *The Hollywood Agents and Managers Directory,* published by The Hollywood Creative Directory, 3000 Olympic Boulevard, Suite 2413, Santa Monica, California 90404; telephone: (310) 315-4815; fax: (310) 315-4816.

The Agency
1800 Avenue of the Stars, #400
Los Angeles, CA 90067
(310) 551-3000

Agency for the Performing Arts
9000 Sunset Boulevard, #1200
Los Angeles, CA 90069
(310) 273-0744

Agency for the Performing Arts
888 Seventh Avenue
New York, NY 10106
(212) 582-1500

The Artists Agency
10000 Santa Monica Boulevard, #305
Los Angeles, CA 90069
(310) 277-7779

Artists First, Inc.
450 S. Wetherly Drive
Beverly Hills, CA 90211
(310) 229-0211; (310) 552-1100

The Artists Group Ltd.
1930 Century Park West, Suite 403
Los Angeles, CA 90067
(310) 552-1100

J. Michael Bloom & Assoc.
9255 Sunset Boulevard, 8th Floor
Los Angeles, CA 90069
(310) 275-6800

Broder/Kurland/Webb/Uffner
9242 Beverly Boulevard, #200
Beverly Hills, CA 90210
(310) 281-3400

Don Buchwald & Assoc., Inc.
10 East 44th Street
New York, NY 10017
(212) 867-1070

Don Buchwald & Assoc., Inc.
9229 Sunset Boulevard
West Hollywood, CA 90069
(310) 278-3600

Creative Artists Agency
9830 Wilshire Boulevard
Beverly Hills, CA 90212

endeavor
350 S. Beverly Drive, Suite 300
Beverly Hills, CA 90212

Favored Artists Agency
122 S. Robertson Boulevard, Suite 202
Los Angeles, CA 90048

The Gage Group, Inc.
9255 Sunset Boulevard
Los Angeles, CA 90069

Gersh Agency, Inc.
232 North Canon Drive, Suite 201
Beverly Hills, CA 90201

Gersh Agency, Inc.
130 West 42nd Street
New York, NY 10036

The Susan Gurman Agency
865 West End Avenue, #4B
New York, NY 10025

Innovative Artists
1999 Avenue of the Stars, Suite 2850
Los Angeles, CA 90067

International Creative Management
8942 Wilshire Boulevard
Beverly Hills, CA 90211

International Creative Management
40 West 57th Street
New York, NY 10019

Patricia Karlan Agency
3575 Cahenga Boulevard West, Suite 201
Los Angeles, CA 90068

Paul Kohner Inc.
9300 Wilshire Boulevard
Suite 555
Beverly Hills, CA 90212

L.A. Premiere Artists Agency
8899 Beverly Boulevard, Suite 102
Los Angeles, CA 90048

Major Clients Agency
345 North Maple Drive, Suite 395
Beverly Hills, CA 90210

Elaine Markson Literary Agency
44 Greenwich Avenue
New York, NY 10011

William Morris Agency
151 El Camino Drive
Beverly Hills, CA 90212

William Morris Agency
1350 Avenue of the Americas
New York, NY 10019

Paradigm
10100 Santa Monica Boulevard, Suite 2500
Los Angeles, CA 90067

Pleshette & Green Agency
2700 N. Beachwood Drive
Hollywood, CA 90068

Preferred Artists
16633 Ventura Boulevard, Suite 1421
Encino, CA 91436

Premiere Artists Agency
1611 S. Robertson Boulevard
Los Angeles, CA 90035

Renaissance Agency
8523 Sunset Boulevard
Los Angeles, CA 90069

Richland/Wunch/Hohman
9220 Sunset Boulevard
Suite 311
Los Angeles, CA 90069

The Marion Rosenberg Office
8428 Melrose Place, Suite B
Los Angeles, CA 90069

Sanford-Skouras-Gross & Associates
1015 Gayley Avenue, Suite 300
Los Angeles, CA 90024

The Irv Schechter Company
9300 Wilshire Boulevard
Suite 400
Beverly Hills, CA 90212

Shapiro-Lichtman, Inc.
8827 Beverly Boulevard
Los Angeles, CA 90048

Susan Smith & Associates
121 N. San Vicente Boulevard
Beverly Hills, CA 90211

The Stone Manners Agency
8091 Selma Avenue
Los Angeles, CA 90046

H. M. Swanson Agency, Inc.
8523 Sunset Boulevard
Los Angeles, CA 90069

Thal Literary Management
1680 North Vine Street
Los Angeles, CA 90028

United Talent Agency
9560 Wilshire Boulevard, 5th Floor
Beverly Hills, CA 90212

The Marion Wright Agency
4317 Bluebell Avenue
Studio City, CA 91436

Writers & Artists Agency
924 Westwood Boulevard, Suite 900
Los Angeles, CA 90024

Writers & Artists Agency
19 West 44th Street, Suite 1000
New York, NY 10036

Legal Organizations for Writers

The following organizations provide legal information, access to attorneys, and seminars concerning the arts and the law to artists and writers for free or reduced cost.

Atlanta Lawyers for the Arts
152 Nassau Street
Atlanta, GA 30303
(404) 688-5500

Buffalo Management Assistance Program for
Cultural Organizations & Artists of Buffalo & Erie County
700 Main Street
New York, NY 14202
(716) 856-7520

California Lawyers for the Arts
1549 11th Street, Suite 200
Santa Monica, CA 90401
(310) 395-8893

California Lawyers for the Arts
Fort Mason Center, Building C
Room 255
San Francisco, CA 94123
(415) 775-7200

California Lawyers for the Arts
247 4th Street, Suite 110
Oakland, CA 94607
(510) 444-6351

Colorado Lawyers for the Arts
200 Grant Street, Suite 303 E.
Denver, CO
(303) 722-7994

Lawyers for the Creative Arts
213 West Institute Place, Suite 411
Chicago, IL 60610
(312) 944-2787

Texas Accountants & Lawyers for the Arts
1540 Sul Ross
Houston, TX 77006
(713) 526-4876

St. Louis Volunteer Lawyers for the Arts
3540 Washington
St. Louis, MO 63103
(314) 652-2410

Volunteer Lawyers for the Arts
1285 Avenue of the Americas
New York, NY 10019
(212) 977-9270

Washington Area Lawyers for the Arts
Stables Arts Center
410 8th Street, Northwest
Washington, D.C. 20004
(202) 393-2826

Internships

Internships can be a valuable means of learning about the film and television business. They offer the opportunity to see how material is treated by production companies, but more important, they help interns make and establish the contacts and relationships that are all-important in the entertainment industry.

The following list of film and television studios and production companies is not exhaustive but suggests the range and types of companies that occasionally offer internships. Every company has different policies and needs for interns. What follows are some guidelines for writers applying for internships.

Most internships are unpaid. In the case of major film studios or television networks, the internship programs may be run as separate summer programs. Almost all internship positions are aimed at students and offer college credit. Many production companies also offer their internships exclusively to students on a "for credit" basis.

In the case of major studios and networks, those seeking internships are normally expected to apply through the Human Resources Department of the organization. When doing so, it is very important to state the department of the company in which your internship interest lies because these are large organizations offering internships in many different areas, some of which will be of little use or interest to would-be writers (for example, corporate, financial, and legal divisions).

For the writer, internships in the creative and development areas of film and television production are the most valuable. Here you will not only observe how films and television programs are made at the story level but will also make contact with the kinds of people who will be most able to assist you with your writing career.

In the case of television companies, the departments of interest are divided up very specifically in terms of television genres. For example, separate development units are devoted to movies of the week, comedy series, drama series, daytime or mini-series, to name the major areas. An internship will be most useful in the area that suits your own writing goal.

In film studios, the departmental area generically known as "Development" is where writers want to find internships. It should be noted that many production companies that have deals with studios do not take interns directly but seek them through the studio Human Resources Department. These are not listed here.

Duties required of interns vary widely. As a general rule, interns are usually required to do a range of clerical tasks and to write coverage on scripts that have been received at the company.

In the case of large studios and networks, inquiries should be addressed to the Human Resources Department, and your cover letter should clearly indicate that your interest is in the development area. In the case of smaller production companies, the most appropriate person to approach is the Director of Development. In all cases you should include your résumé.

Studios

ABC Entertainment
2040 Avenue of the Stars
Los Angeles, CA 90067-4785

CBS Entertainment
7800 Beverly Boulevard
Los Angeles, CA 90036-2105

Metro Goldwyn Mayer
2500 Broadway Street
Santa Monica, CA 90404

NBC Entertainment
3000 W. Alameda Boulevard
Burbank, CA 91523-0001

New Line Productions
116 N. Robertson, #200
Los Angeles, CA 90048

Paramount Studios
5555 Melrose Avenue
Los Angeles, CA 90038-3197

Showtime Networks Inc.
10 Universal City Plaza, 31st Floor
Universal City, CA 91608-1002

Sony Pictures Entertainment
(includes Columbia, Tristar)

10202 West Washington Boulevard
Culver City, CA 90232-3195

Turner Broadcasting Systems
1888 Century Park East, Suite 416
Los Angeles, CA 90067

USA Network
1230 Avenue of the Americas
New York, NY 10020

Universal
100 Universal City Plaza
Universal City, CA 91608-1002

Walt Disney Pictures
(includes Hollywood and Touchstone Pictures)
500 S. Buena Vista
Burbank CA 91521-0001

Warner Bros. Studios
4000 Warner Boulevard
Burbank, CA 91522-0001

Production Companies

This is a nonexhaustive list of production companies that have indicated they take interns from time to time. The best approach is to send a résumé to the company concerned.

Adam Productions
4000 Warner Boulevard,
Prod. Bldg. 2, #1106
Los Angeles, CA 91522

All Girl Productions
c/o Walt Disney Pictures
500 S. Buena Vista Street
Burbank, CA 91521-0001

Amen Ra Films
c/o Twentieth Century-Fox
10201 W. Pico Boulevard,
Bldg. 77, #2
Los Angeles, CA 90035

Atlas Entertainment
(formerly Steel Pictures)
9169 Sunset Boulevard
Los Angeles, CA 90069

Baywatch Production Company
5433 Beethoven Street
Los Angeles, CA 90066

Beacon Pictures
1041 N. Formosa Avenue
Los Angeles, CA 90046-6798

Blue Tulip Productions
c/o 20th Century-Fox Film Corp.
10201 W. Pico Boulevard
Los Angeles, CA 90035

Brillstein-Grey Ent.
9150 Wilshire Boulevard, Suite 350
Beverly Hills, CA 90212

Cinergi Pictures Entertainment Inc.
2308 Broadway
Santa Monica, CA 90404-2916

Concorde/New Horizons Corp.
11600 San Vicente Boulevard
Los Angeles, CA 90049

Davis Entertainment Co.
2121 Avenue of the Stars
Los Angeles, CA 90067

Daybreak Prods.
c/o Universal Studios
100 Universal Plaza, Bung. 64/124
Universal City, CA 91608

Donner/Shuler-Donner Prods.
c/o Warner Bros. Pictures
4000 Warner Boulevard
Bldgs. 102 & 103, #4
Burbank, CA 91522-0001

Douglas/Reuther Productions
5555 Melrose Avenue, Lewis Bldg.
Los Angeles CA 90038

Egg Pictures
7920 Sunset Boulevard, Suite 200
Los Angeles, CA 90046

Esparza-Katz Prods.
8899 Beverly Boulevard, Suite 812
Los Angeles, CA 90048

The Robert Evans Co.
c/o Paramount Studios
5555 Melrose Avenue, Lubitsch #117
Los Angeles, CA 90038-3197

Wendy Finerman Prods.
c/o Sony Studios
10202 W. Washington Boulevard, TriStar #222
Culver City, CA 90232-3195

40 Acres & A Mule Filmworks
124 Dekalb Avenue
Brooklyn, NY 11217

Samuel Goldwyn Co.
10203 Santa Monica Boulevard
Los Angeles, CA 90067

The Haft-Nasatir Co.
1440 S. Sepulveda Boulevard, Suite 225
Los Angeles, CA 90025

The Haft-Nasatir Co.
625 Madison Avenue, 11th Floor
New York, NY 10022

Hanna-Barbera, Inc.
3400 Cahuenga Boulevard
Hollywood, CA 90068-1376

Interscope Communications Inc.
10900 Wilshire Boulevard, Suite 1400
Los Angeles, CA 90024

Ixtlan
210 Santa Monica Boulevard, Suite 610
Santa Monica, CA 90401

Jersey Films
c/o Columbia Pictures
10202 W. Washington Boulevard, Capra #112
Culver City, CA 90232

Mark Johnson Productions
c/o Paramount Studios
5555 Melrose Avenue, Bob Hope Bldg. #206
Los Angeles, CA 90038

Kennedy-Marshall Company
c/o Raleigh Studios
650 N. Bronson Avenue, Clinton Bldg.
Hollywood, CA 90004

Arnold Kopelson Prods.
6100 Wilshire Boulevard, Suite 1500
Los Angeles, CA 90048

The Ladd Company
c/o Paramount Studios
5555 Melrose Avenue, Chevalier 117
Los Angeles, CA 90038

Lightstorm Entertainment
919 Santa Monica Boulevard
Santa Monica, CA 90401

The Ministry of Film Inc.
9220 Sunset Boulevard, Suite 224
Los Angeles, CA 90069

Miramax Films
c/o Tribeca Film Center
375 Greenwich Street
New York, NY 10013-2338

Miramax Films
7920 Sunset Boulevard, Suite 230
Los Angeles, CA 90046

The Mount/Kramer Company
715 N. Crescent Heights Boulevard
Hollywood, CA 90046

Northern Lights Ent.
100 Universal City Plaza, Bldg. 489
Universal City, CA 91608

Lynda Obst Prods.
c/o Twentieth Century-Fox
10201 W. Pico Boulevard, Bldg. 43
Los Angeles, CA 90035

Outlaw Prods.
827 N. Hilldale Avenue
West Hollywood, CA 90069

Pacific Western Productions
c/o Paramount
5555 Melrose Avenue
Los Angeles, CA 90038

Peters Entertainment
4000 Warner Boulevard, Bldg. 15
Burbank CA 91522

Picturemaker Prods.
2821 Main Street
Santa Monica, CA 90405

The Frederick S. Pierce Co.
5670 Wilshire Boulevard, Suite 1350
Los Angeles, CA 90036

Propaganda Films
940 N. Mansfield Avenue
Los Angeles, CA 90038–3197

Radiant Productions
c/o Tristar Pictures
10202 W. Washington Boulevard, Tristar #220
Culver City, CA 90232

Scott Rudin Prods.
c/o Paramount Pictures
5555 Melrose Avenue
Los Angeles, CA 90038-3197

Sandollar Prods.
c/o Walt Disney Studios
500 S. Buena Vista
Burbank, CA 91521-7259

Sanford/Pillsbury Prods.
1459 Sixth Street
Santa Monica, CA 90401

Paul Schiff Prods.
c/o Twentieth Century-Fox
10201 W. Pico Boulevard, Bldg. 215
Los Angeles, CA 90035

Schindler-Swerdlow Prods.
110 W. 57th Street, Suite 401
New York, NY 10019

Silver Pictures
4000 Warner Boulevard, Bldg. 90
Burbank, CA 91522-0001

Spelling Entertainment
5700 Wilshire Boulevard, 5th Floor
Los Angeles, CA 90036-3696

Spring Creek Prods.
c/o Warner Bros. Pictures
4000 Warner Boulevard, Producers 7, #8
Burbank, CA 91522-0001

Sundance Institute
225 Santa Monica Boulevard, 8th Floor
Santa Monica, CA 90401

The Steve Tisch Co.
3815 Hughes Avenue
Culver City, CA 90232-2715

Todman-Simon Prods.
4000 Warner Boulevard
Prod. Bldg. 2, #1202
Burbank, CA 91522

Tribeca Productions
375 Greenwich Street
New York, NY 10013

Trilogy Entertainment Group
c/o Metro-Goldwyn-Mayer
2401 Colorado Avenue, Suite 100
Santa Monica, CA 90404-3061

Jerry Weintraub Prods.
c/o Warner Bros.
4000 Warner Boulevard, Bung. 1
Burbank, CA 91522-0001

Whitewater Films
2232 Cotner Avenue
Los Angeles, CA 90064

Witt-Thomas Films
400 Warner Boulevard
Prod. Bldg. 3, #2
Burbank, CA 91522

Working Title Films
9247 Alden Drive
Beverly Hills, CA 90210

Yorktown Prods. Inc
3000 W. Olympic Boulevard
Bldg. 4, #1314
Santa Monica, CA 90404

Internships with the Academy of Television Arts & Sciences

The Academy of Television Arts & Sciences offers a variety of internships that seek to provide **qualified full-time college and university undergraduate and graduate students** with in-depth exposure to professional television production facilities, techniques, and practices. Generally, students must be in school when applying for the internship.

All Academy internships are located in the Los Angeles area. The Academy of Television Arts & Sciences offers a small (and I mean *small*) stipend to each intern accepted in the program.

Interns are responsible for their own housing, food, and transportation arrangements, and all expenses. In addition, interns must have a car for transportation in Los Angeles. All positions are full-time.

There is an application process for the internships, and the final date to apply is approximatley March 31. Each applicant may apply for only one internship. Most internships begin in late June or early July and end eight weeks after the start date. For futher information contact the Director of Educational Programs, Academy of Television Arts & Sciences, 5220 Lankershim Boulevard, North Hollywood, California 91601-3109; (818) 754-2830. (In 1995, the Academy of Arts & Sciences offered twenty-four internships.)

Index